SPIDER-MAN

VS. SANDMAN AND VENOM

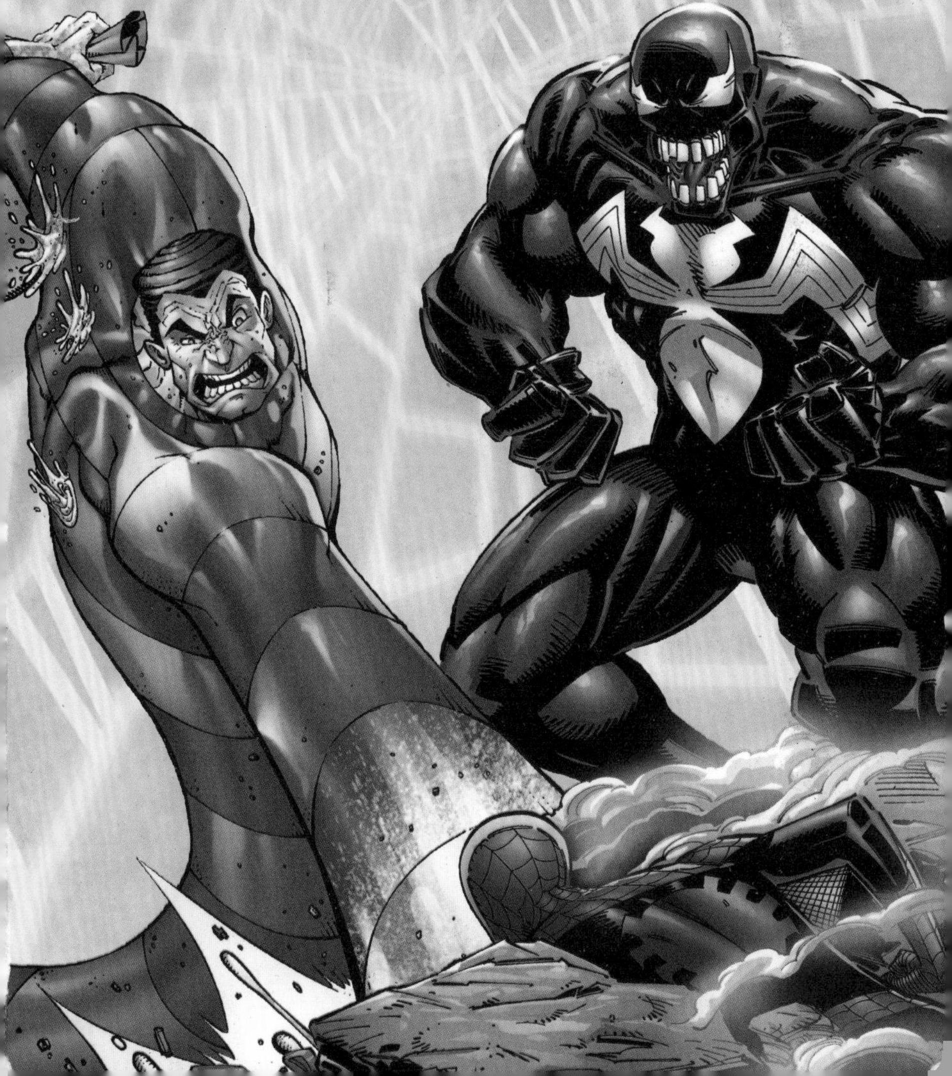

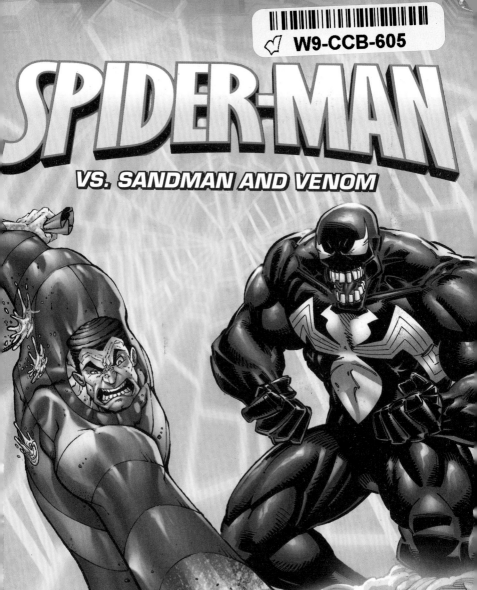

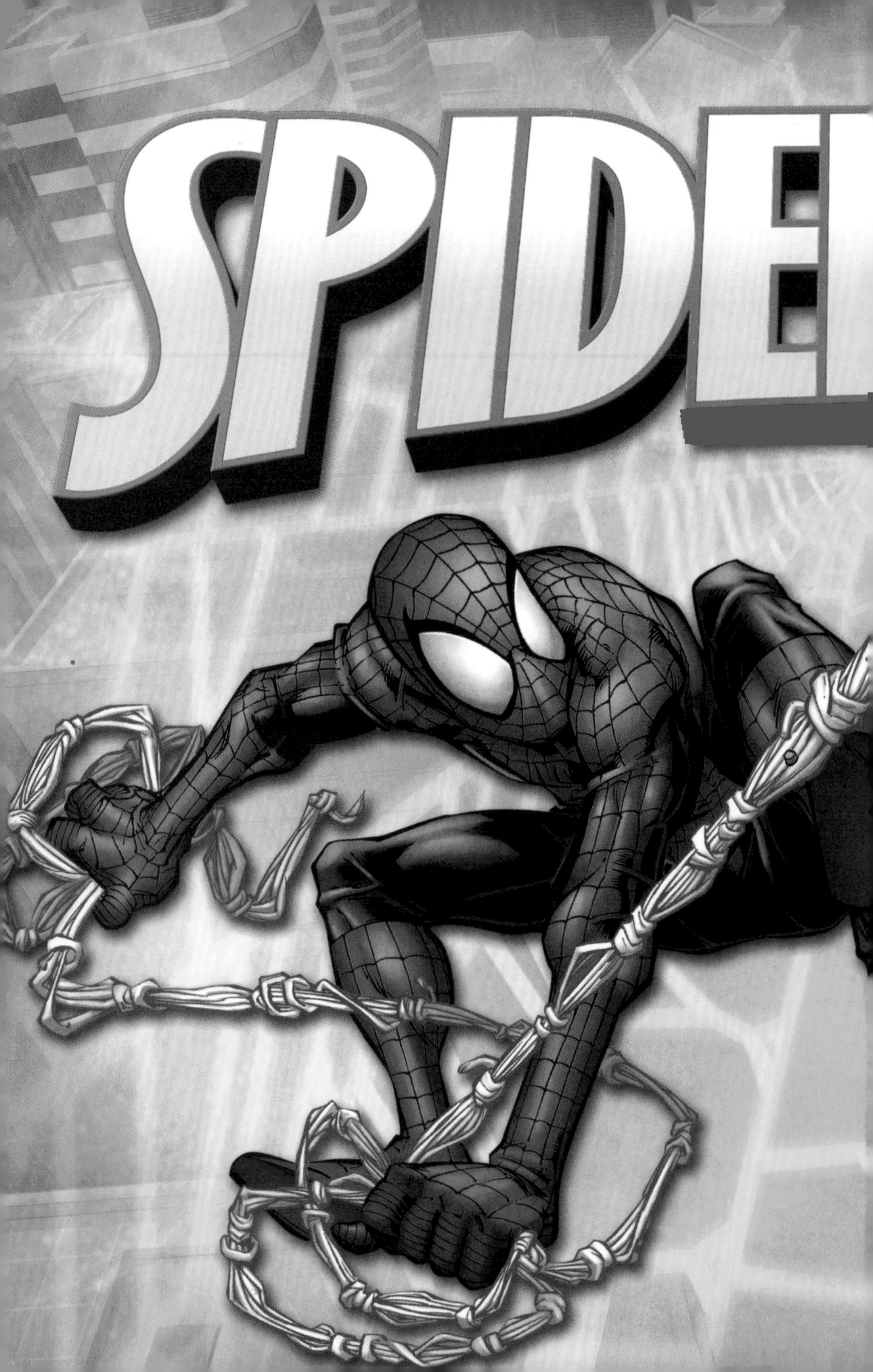
SPIDE

R-MAN

VS. SANDMAN AND VENOM

Writers: **Fred Van Lente & Marc Sumerak**

Artists: **Cory Hamscher & Gurihiru**

Colorists: **Guru eFX & Gurihiru**

Letterer: **Dave Sharpe**

Cover Artists: **Patrick Scherberger, Cory Hamscher, Guru eFX & Gurihiru**

Editors: **Mark Paniccia & Nathan Cosby**

Collection Editor: **Cory Levine**

Assistant Editor: **Michael Short**

Associate Editors: **Jennifer Grünwald & Mark D. Beazley**

Senior Editor, Special Projects: **Jeff Youngquist**

Senior Vice President of Sales: **David Gabriel**

Production: **Jerron Quality Color & Jerry Kalinowski**

Vice President of Creative: **Tom Marvelli**

Editor in Chief: **Joe Quesada**

Publisher: **Dan Buckley**

SCHOLASTIC SPIDER-MAN VS. SANDMAN AND VENOM. Contains material originally published in magazine form as MARVEL ADVENTURES SPIDER-MAN #23-24 and SPIDER-MAN AND POWER PACK #1-2. First printing 2007. ISBN# 978-0-7851-2874-8. Published by MARVEL PUBLISHING, INC., a subsidiary of MARVEL ENTERTAINMENT, INC. OFFICE OF PUBLICATION: 417 5th Avenue, New York, NY 10016. Copyright © 2006 and 2007 Marvel Characters, Inc. All rights reserved. $6.99 per copy in the U.S. and $11.25 in Canada (GST #R127032852); Canadian Agreement #40668537. All characters featured in this issue and the distinctive names and likenesses thereof, and all related indicia are trademarks of Marvel Characters, Inc. No similarity between any of the names, characters, persons, and/or institutions in this magazine with those of any living or dead person or institution is intended, and any such similarity which may exist is purely coincidental. Printed in Canada. ALAN FINE, CEO Marvel Toys & Publishing Divisions and CMO Marvel Entertainment, Inc.; DAVID GABRIEL, Senior VP of Publishing Sales & Circulation; DAVID BOGART, VP of Business Affairs & Editorial Operations; MICHAEL PASCIULLO, VP Merchandising & Communications; JIM BOYLE, VP of Publishing Operations; DAN CARR, Executive Director of Publishing Technology; JUSTIN F. GABRIE, Managing Editor; SUSAN CRESPI, Production Manager; STAN LEE, Chairman Emeritus. For information regarding advertising in Marvel Comics or on Marvel.com, please contact Joe Maimone, Advertising Director, at jmaimone@marvel.com or 212-576-8534.

10 9 8 7 6 5 4 3 2 1

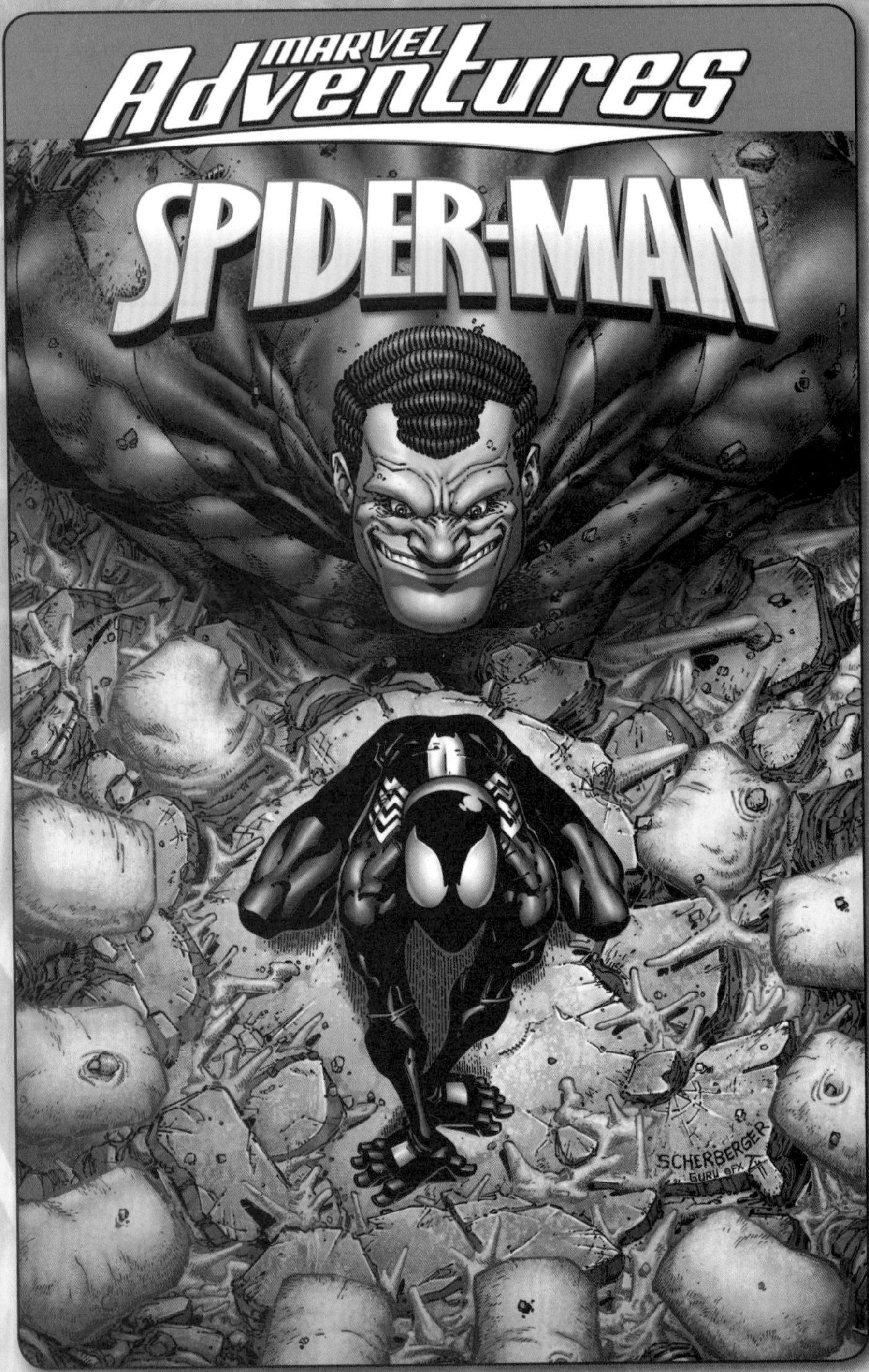
MARVEL Adventures
SPIDER-MAN
SCHERBERGER
GURU eFX

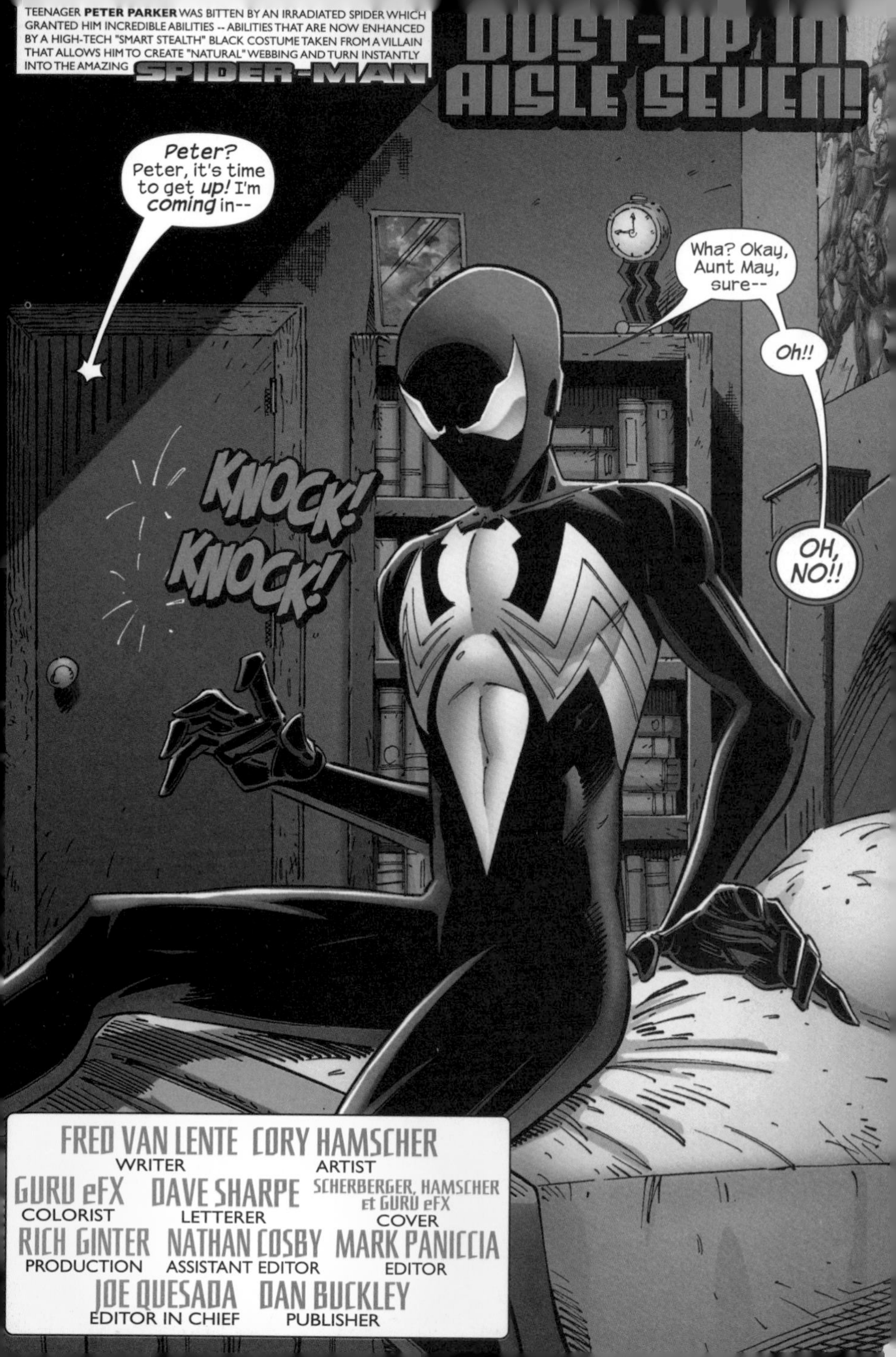
TEENAGER PETER PARKER WAS BITTEN BY AN IRRADIATED SPIDER WHICH GRANTED HIM INCREDIBLE ABILITIES -- ABILITIES THAT ARE NOW ENHANCED BY A HIGH-TECH "SMART STEALTH" BLACK COSTUME TAKEN FROM A VILLAIN THAT ALLOWS HIM TO CREATE "NATURAL" WEBBING AND TURN INSTANTLY INTO THE AMAZING SPIDER-MAN
DUST-UP IN AISLE SEVEN!
Peter? Peter, it's time to get up! I'm coming in--
KNOCK! KNOCK!
Wha? Okay, Aunt May, sure--
Oh!!
OH, NO!!
FRED VAN LENTE WRITER
CORY HAMSCHER ARTIST
GURU eFX COLORIST
DAVE SHARPE LETTERER
SCHERBERGER, HAMSCHER et GURU eFX COVER
RICH GINTER PRODUCTION
NATHAN COSBY ASSISTANT EDITOR
MARK PANICCIA EDITOR
JOE QUESADA EDITOR IN CHIEF
DAN BUCKLEY PUBLISHER

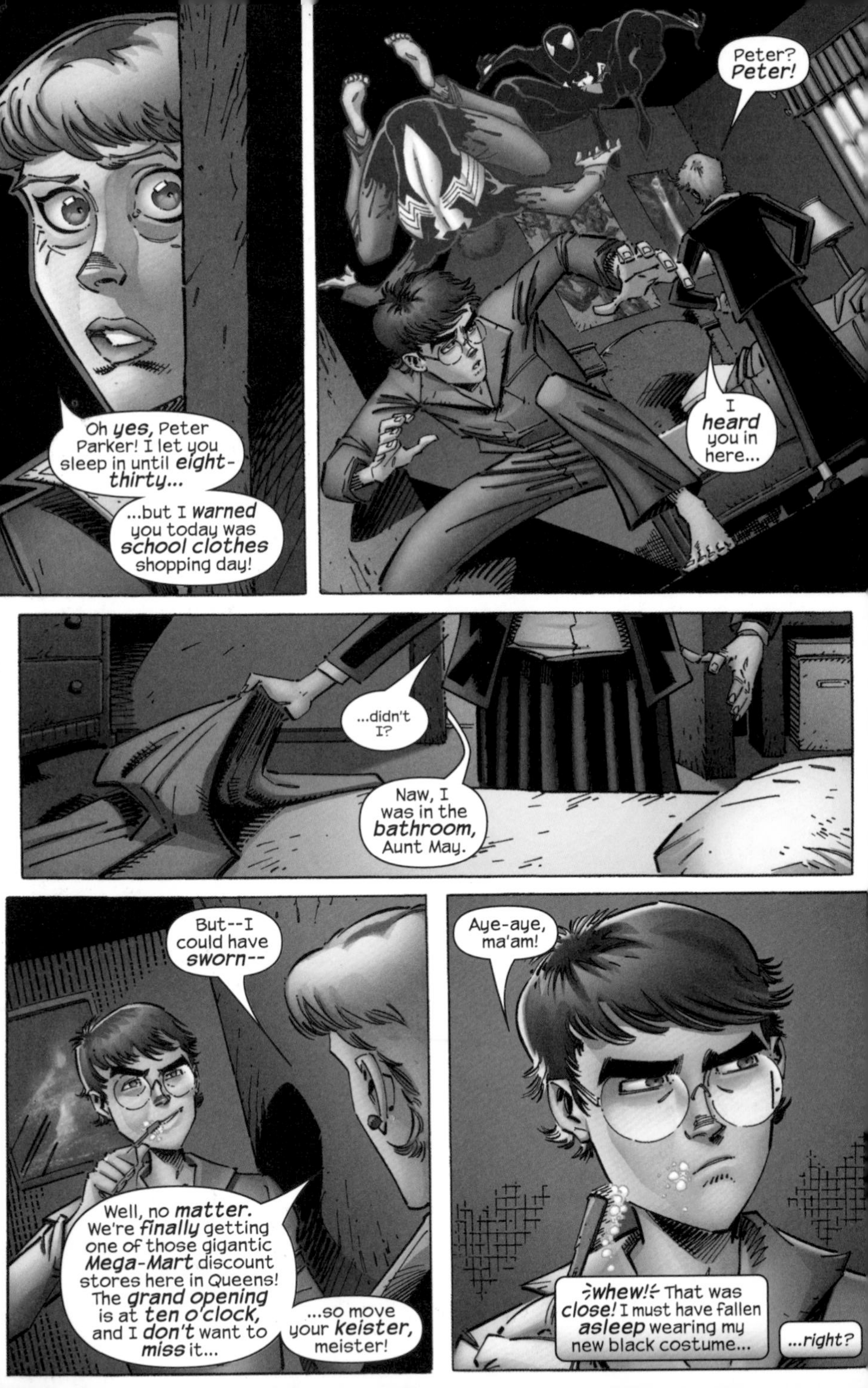
Oh **yes,** Peter Parker! I let you sleep in until **eight-thirty...**
...but I **warned** you today was **school clothes** shopping day!
Peter? **Peter!**
I **heard** you in here...
...didn't I?
Naw, I was in the **bathroom,** Aunt May.
But--I could have **sworn--**
Well, no **matter.** We're **finally** getting one of those gigantic **Mega-Mart** discount stores here in Queens! The **grand opening** is at **ten o'clock,** and I **don't** want to **miss** it...
...so move your **keister,** meister!
Aye-aye, ma'am!
whew! That was **close!** I must have fallen **asleep** wearing my new black costume...
...right?

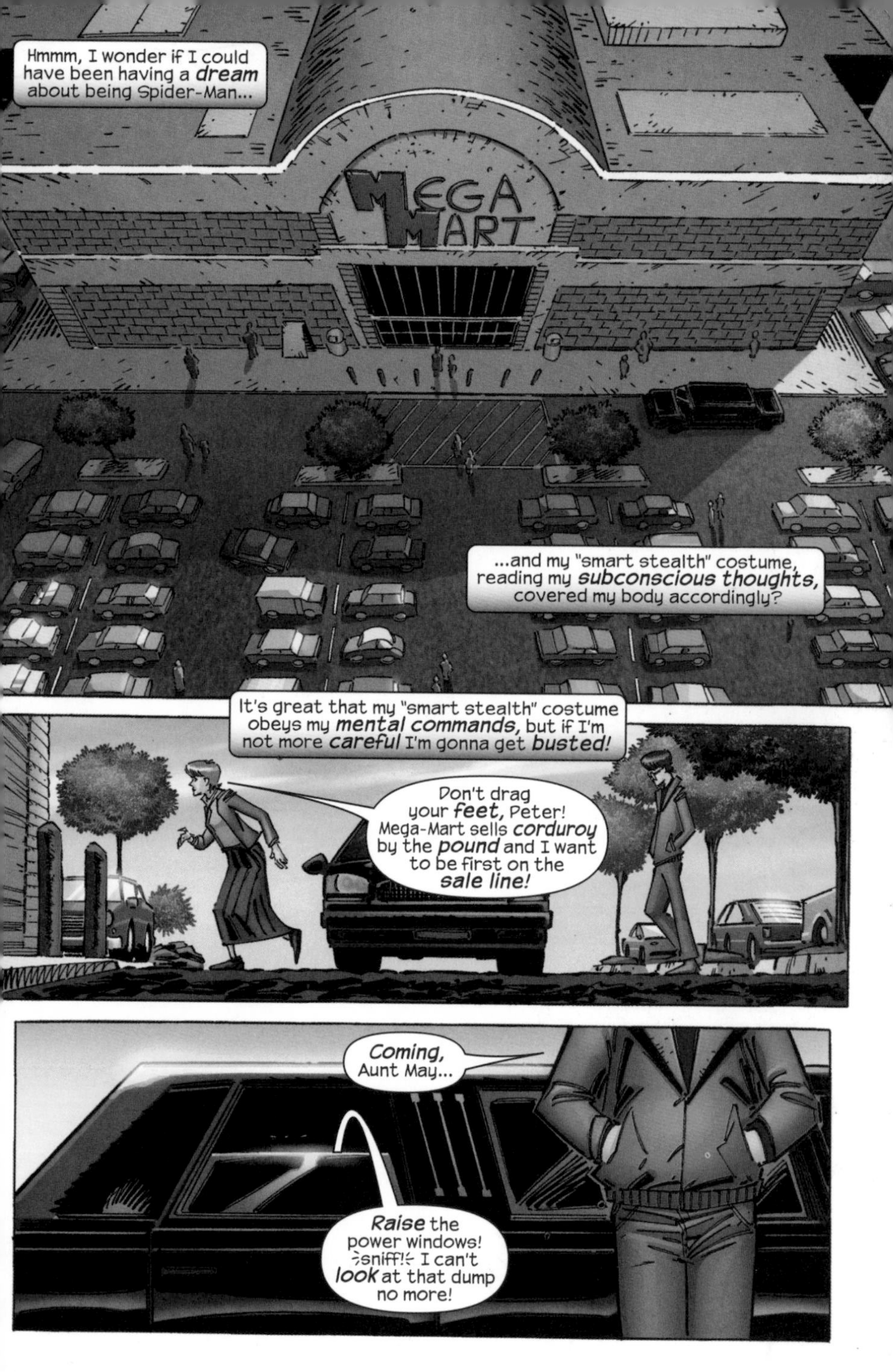
Hmmm, I wonder if I could have been having a *dream* about being Spider-Man...
MEGA MART
...and my "smart stealth" costume, reading my *subconscious thoughts,* covered my body accordingly?
It's great that my "smart stealth" costume obeys my *mental commands,* but if I'm not more *careful* I'm gonna get *busted!*
Don't drag your *feet,* Peter! Mega-Mart sells *corduroy* by the *pound* and I want to be first on the *sale line!*
Coming, Aunt May...
Raise the power windows! ⁝sniff!⁝ I can't *look* at that dump no more!

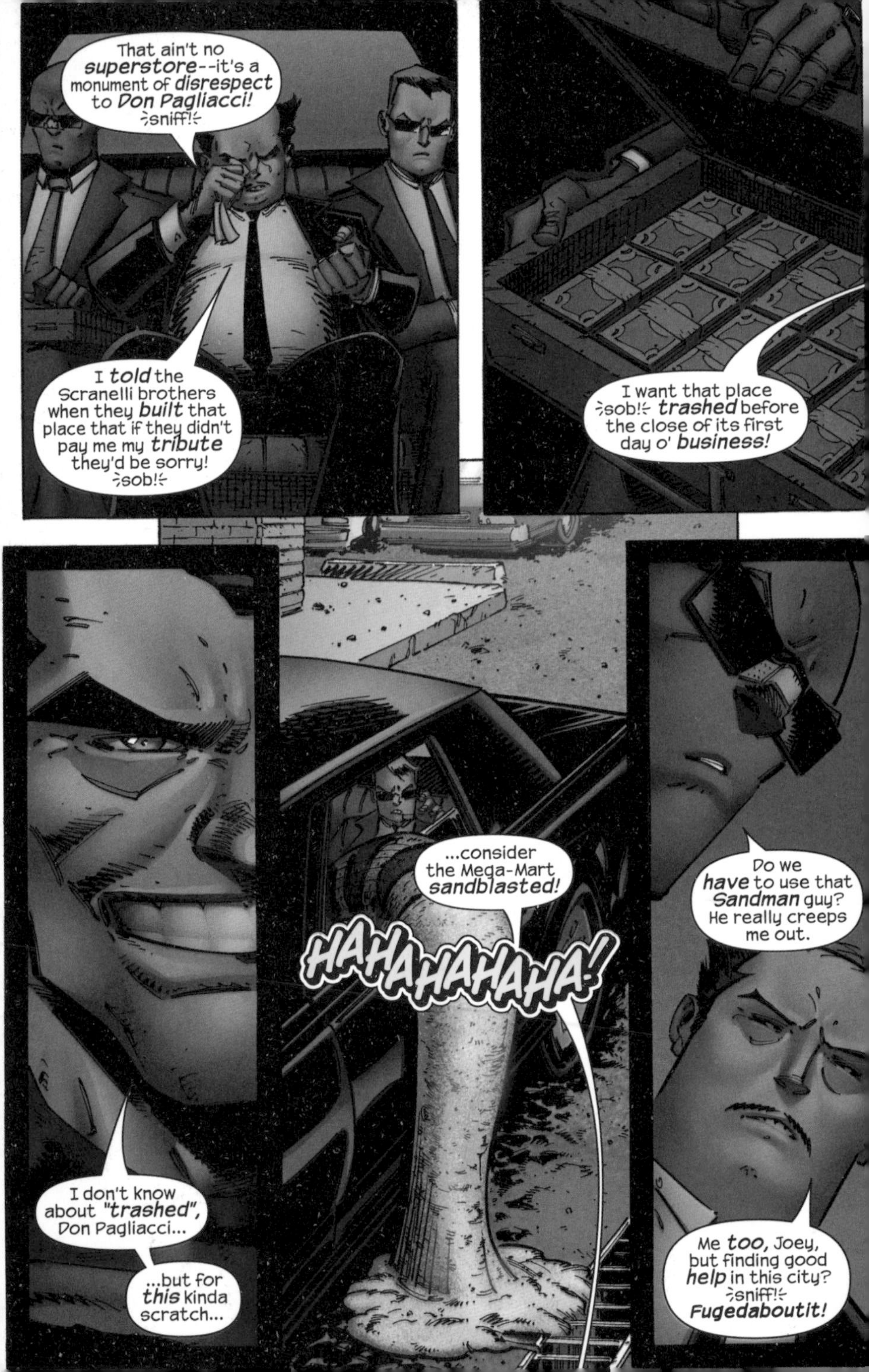
That ain't no ***superstore***--it's a monument of ***disrespect*** to ***Don Pagliacci!*** ⁒sniff!⁒
I ***told*** the Scranelli brothers when they ***built*** that place that if they didn't pay me my ***tribute*** they'd be sorry! ⁒sob!⁒
I want that place ⁒sob!⁒ ***trashed*** before the close of its first day o' ***business!***
I don't know about ***"trashed"***, Don Pagliacci...
...but for ***this*** kinda scratch...
...consider the Mega-Mart ***sandblasted!***
HAHAHAHAHAHA!
Do we ***have*** to use that ***Sandman*** guy? He really creeps me out.
Me ***too***, Joey, but finding good ***help*** in this city? ⁒sniff!⁒ ***Fugedaboutit!***

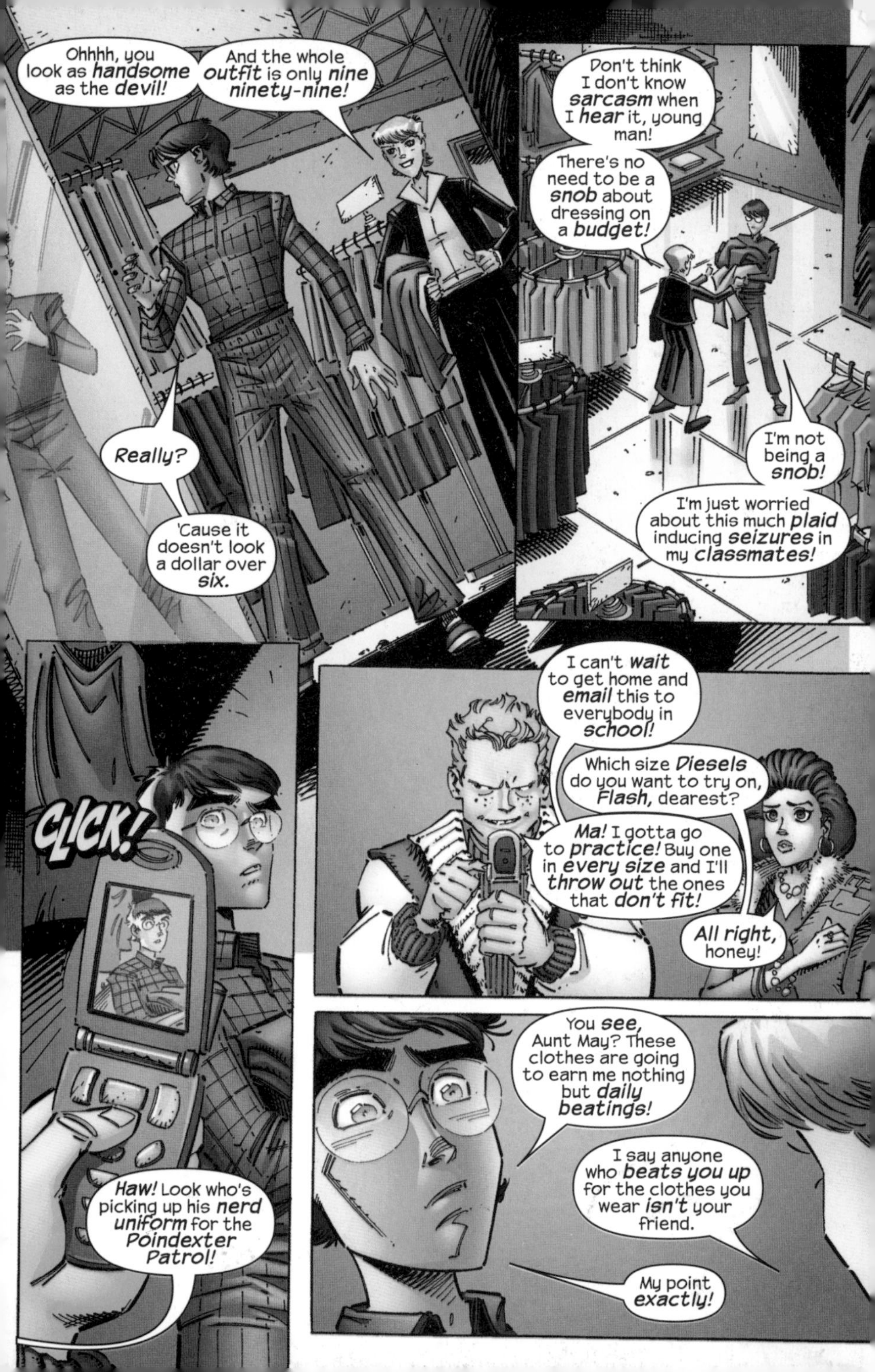

Ohhhh, you look as handsome as the devil!
And the whole outfit is only nine ninety-nine!
Really?
'Cause it doesn't look a dollar over six.
Don't think I don't know sarcasm when I hear it, young man!
There's no need to be a snob about dressing on a budget!
I'm not being a snob!
I'm just worried about this much plaid inducing seizures in my classmates!
CLICK!
Haw! Look who's picking up his nerd uniform for the Poindexter Patrol!
I can't wait to get home and email this to everybody in school!
Which size Diesels do you want to try on, Flash, dearest?
Ma! I gotta go to practice! Buy one in every size and I'll throw out the ones that don't fit!
All right, honey!
You see, Aunt May? These clothes are going to earn me nothing but daily beatings!
I say anyone who beats you up for the clothes you wear isn't your friend.
My point exactly!

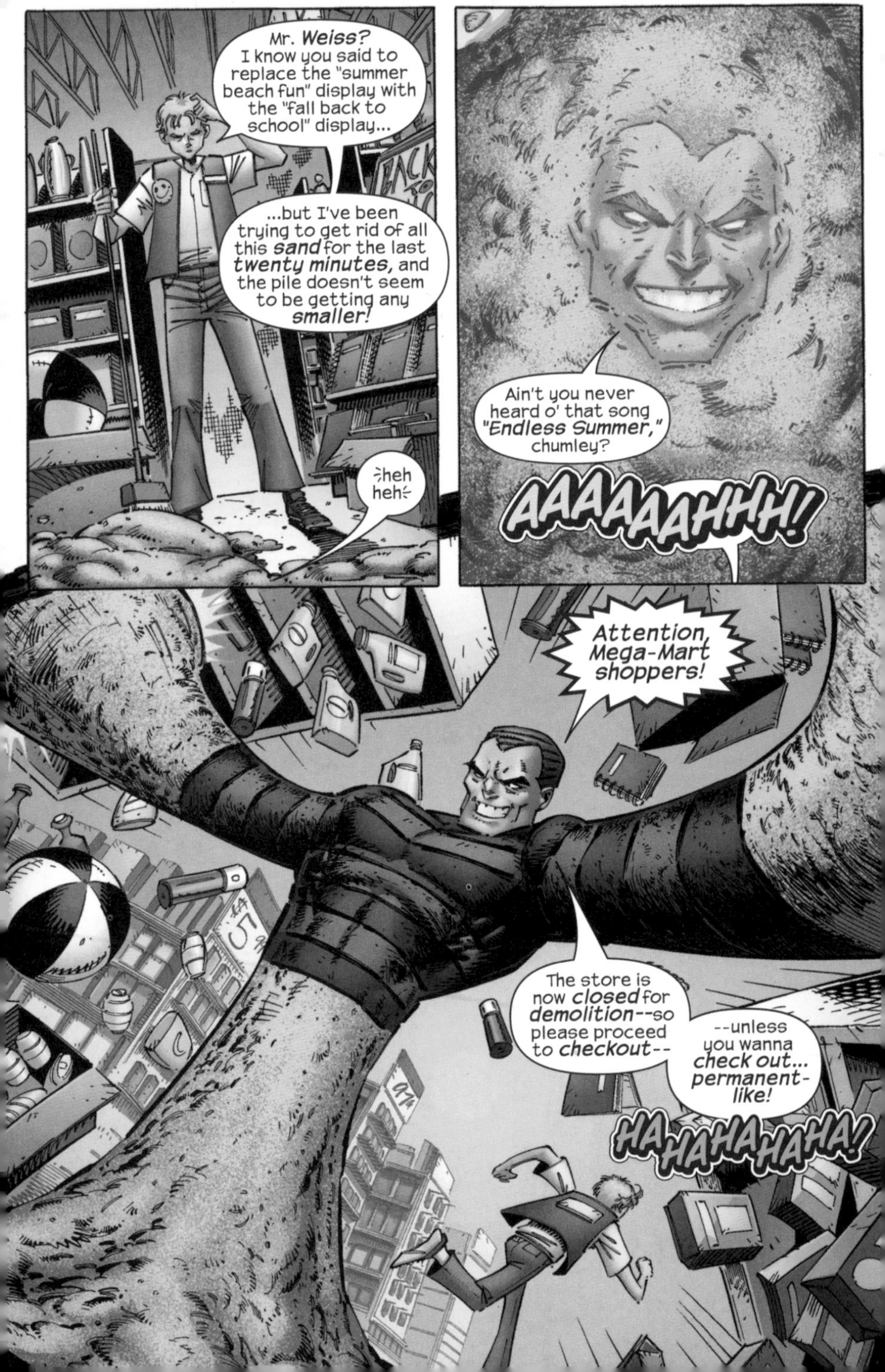
Mr. Weiss? I know you said to replace the "summer beach fun" display with the "fall back to school" display...
...but I've been trying to get rid of all this sand for the last twenty minutes, and the pile doesn't seem to be getting any smaller!
heh heh
Ain't you never heard o' that song "Endless Summer," chumley?
AAAAAAHHH!
Attention, Mega-Mart shoppers!
The store is now closed for demolition--so please proceed to checkout--
--unless you wanna check out... permanent-like!
HAHAHAHAHA!

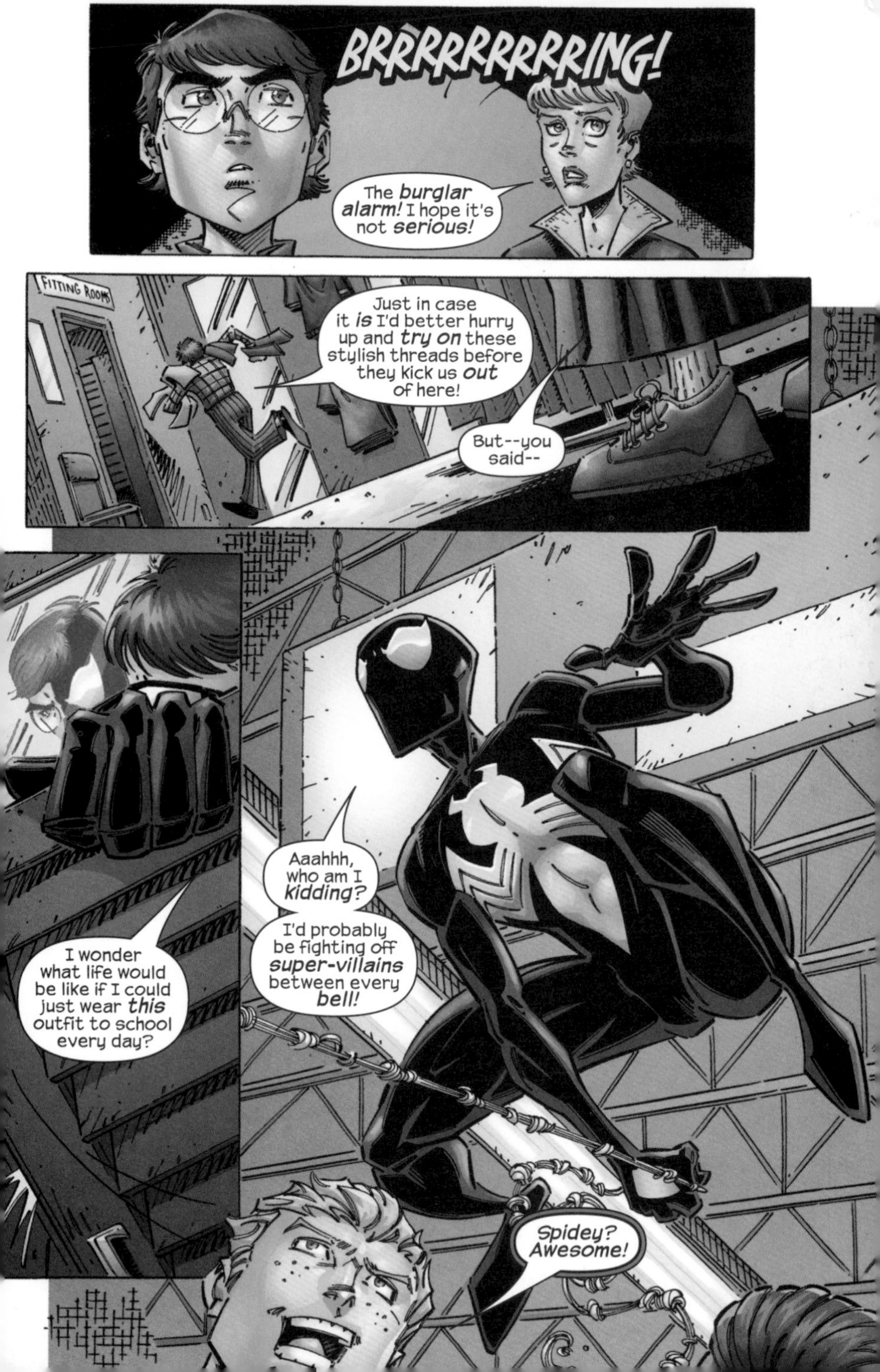
BRRRRRRRRRING!
The burglar alarm! I hope it's not serious!
FITTING ROOMS
Just in case it is I'd better hurry up and try on these stylish threads before they kick us out of here!
But--you said--
I wonder what life would be like if I could just wear this outfit to school every day?
Aaahhh, who am I kidding?
I'd probably be fighting off super-villains between every bell!
Spidey? Awesome!

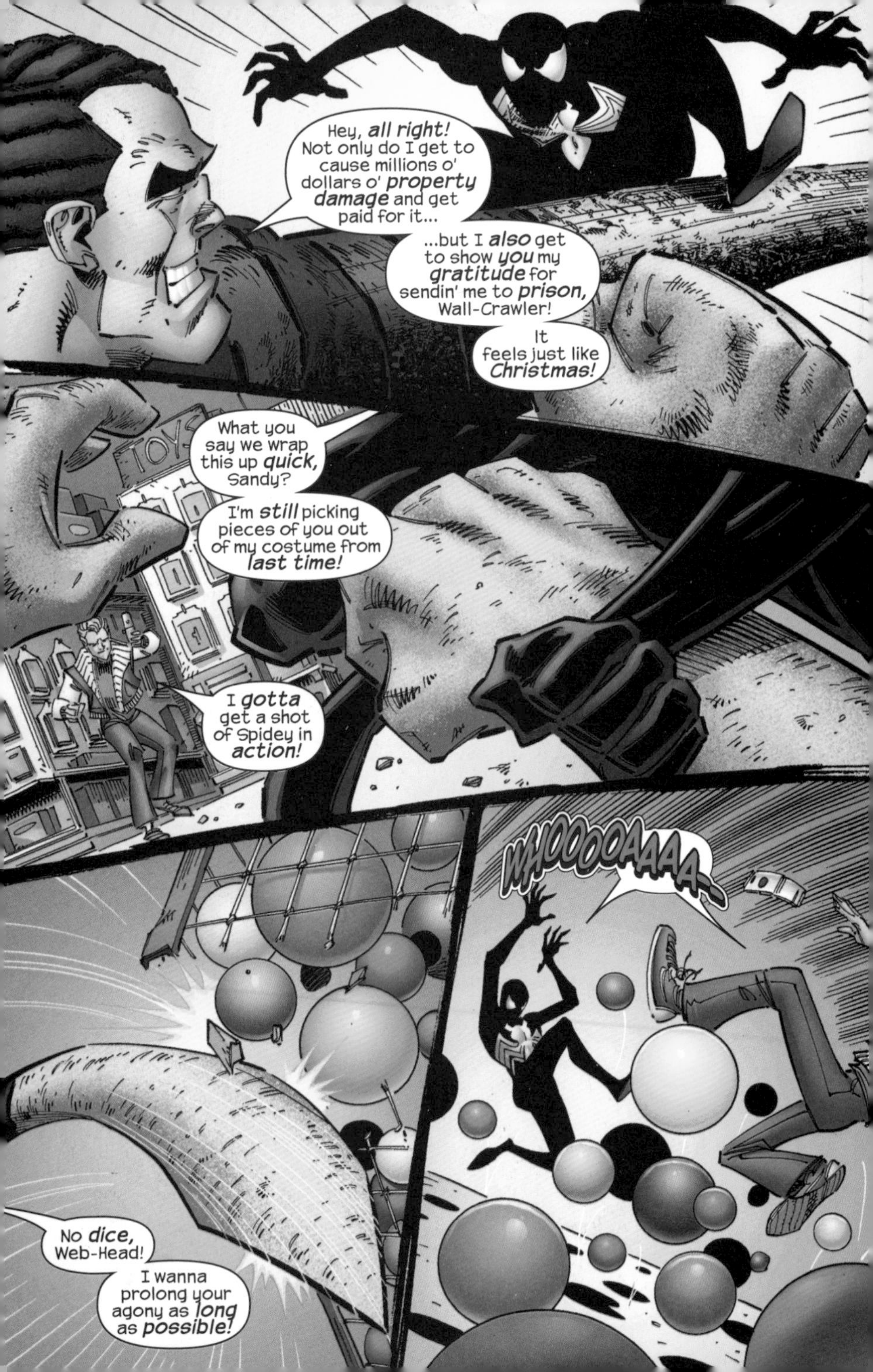
Hey, all right! Not only do I get to cause millions o' dollars o' property damage and get paid for it...
...but I also get to show you my gratitude for sendin' me to prison, Wall-Crawler!
It feels just like Christmas!
TOYS
What you say we wrap this up quick, Sandy?
I'm still picking pieces of you out of my costume from last time!
I gotta get a shot of Spidey in action!
WHOOOOAAAA--
No dice, Web-Head!
I wanna prolong your agony as long as possible!

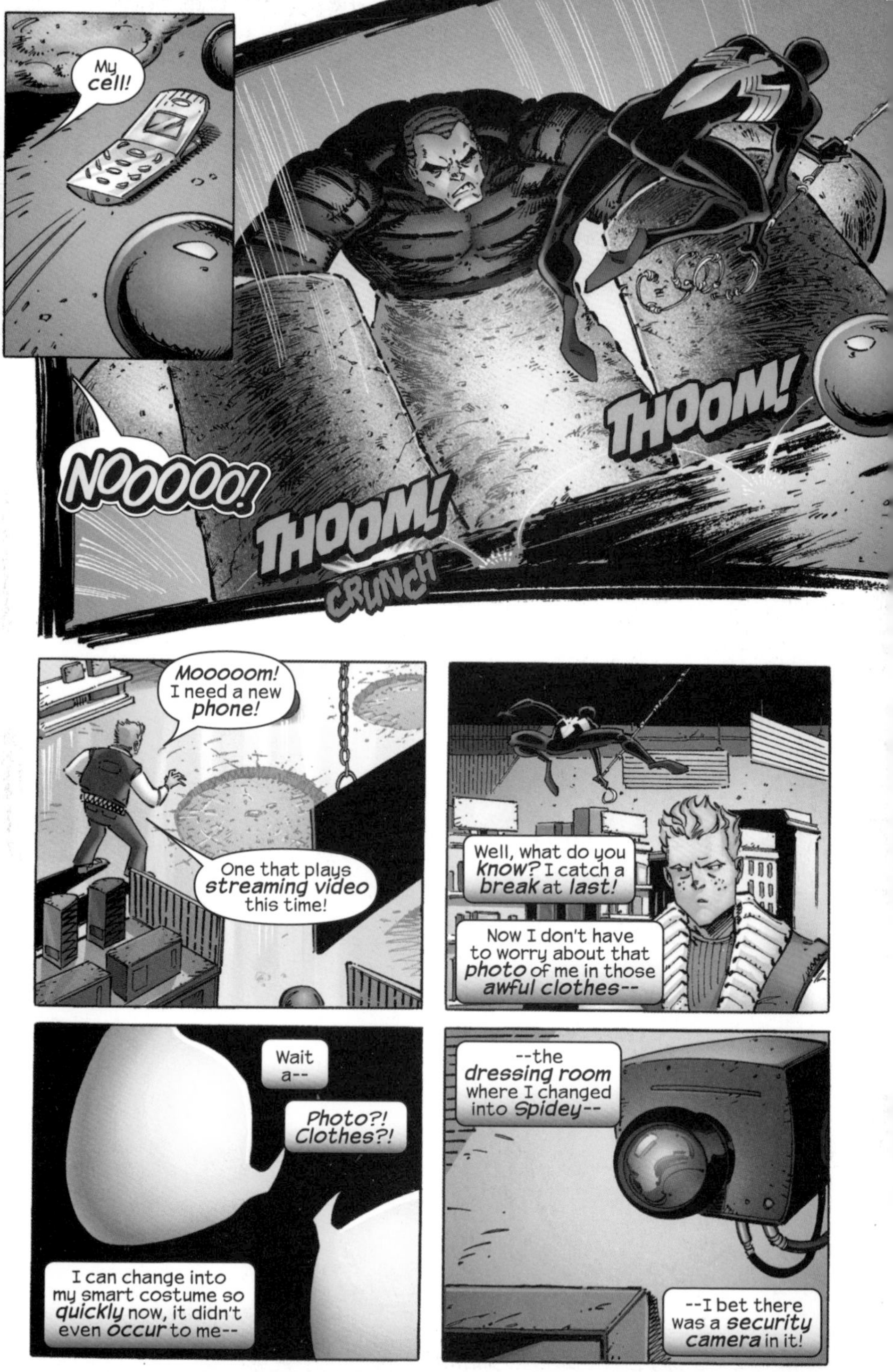
My cell!
NOOOOO!
THOOM!
THOOM!
CRUNCH
Moooooom! I need a new phone!
One that plays streaming video this time!
Well, what do you know? I catch a break at last!
Now I don't have to worry about that photo of me in those awful clothes--
--the dressing room where I changed into Spidey--
--I bet there was a security camera in it!
Wait a--
Photo?! Clothes?!
I can change into my smart costume so quickly now, it didn't even occur to me--

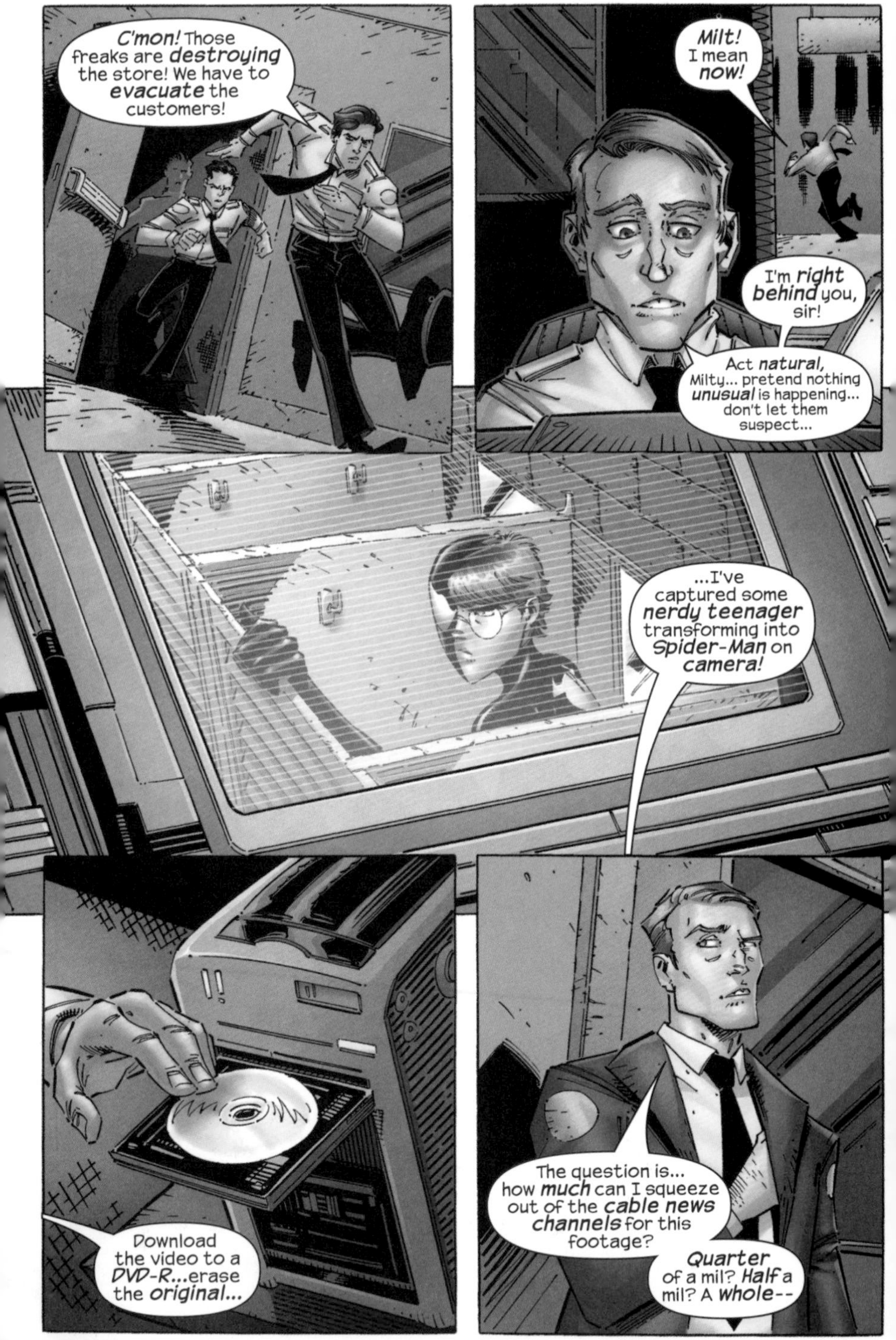
C'mon! Those freaks are destroying the store! We have to evacuate the customers!
Milt! I mean now!
I'm right behind you, sir!
Act natural, Milty... pretend nothing unusual is happening... don't let them suspect...
...I've captured some nerdy teenager transforming into Spider-Man on camera!
Download the video to a DVD-R...erase the original...
The question is... how much can I squeeze out of the cable news channels for this footage?
Quarter of a mil? Half a mil? A whole--

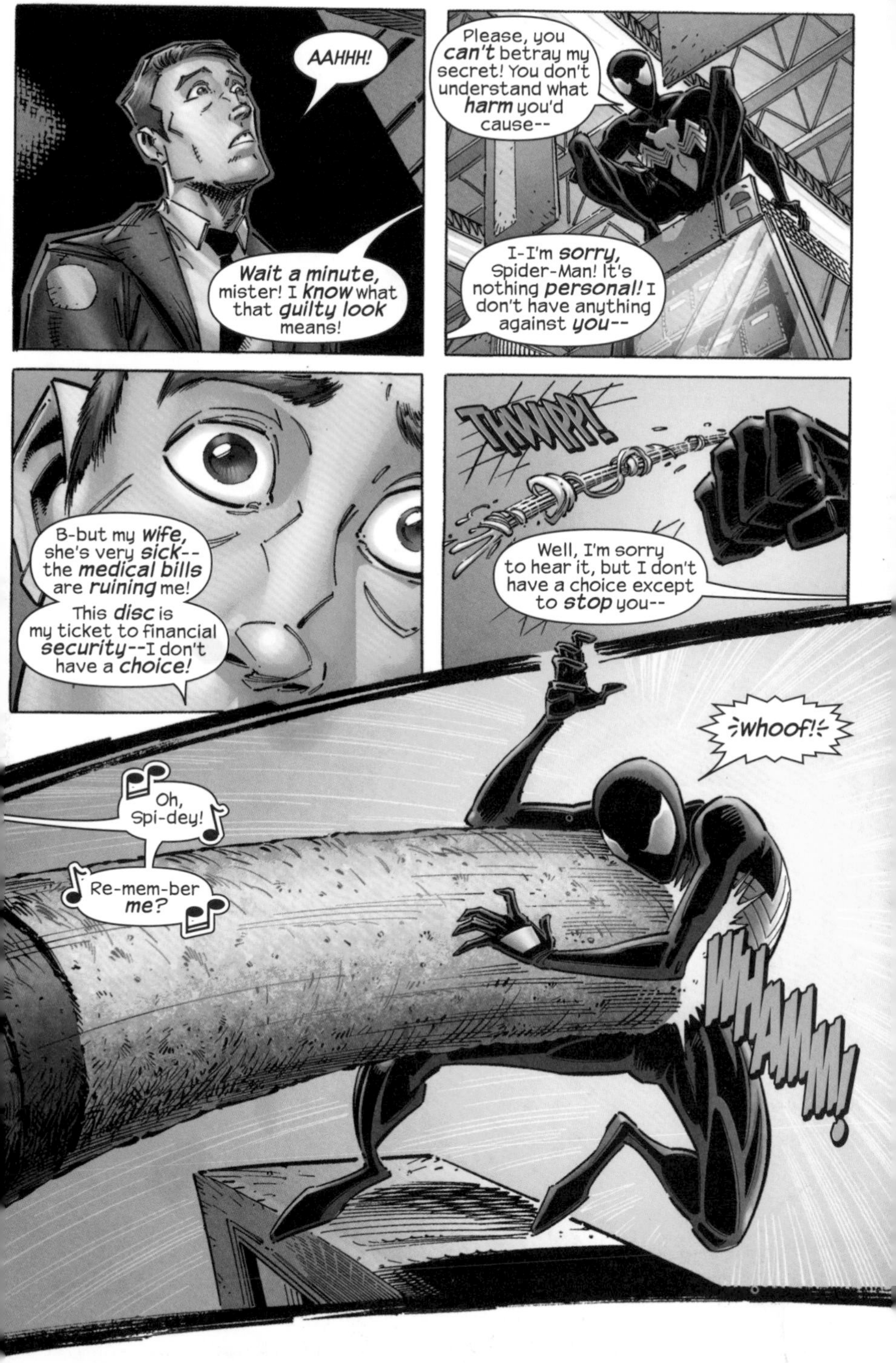
AAHHH!
Wait a minute, mister! I know what that guilty look means!
Please, you can't betray my secret! You don't understand what harm you'd cause--
I-I'm sorry, Spider-Man! It's nothing personal! I don't have anything against you--
B-but my wife, she's very sick--the medical bills are ruining me!
This disc is my ticket to financial security--I don't have a choice!
THWIPP!
Well, I'm sorry to hear it, but I don't have a choice except to stop you--
whoof!
Oh, Spi-dey!
Re-mem-ber me?
WHAMM!

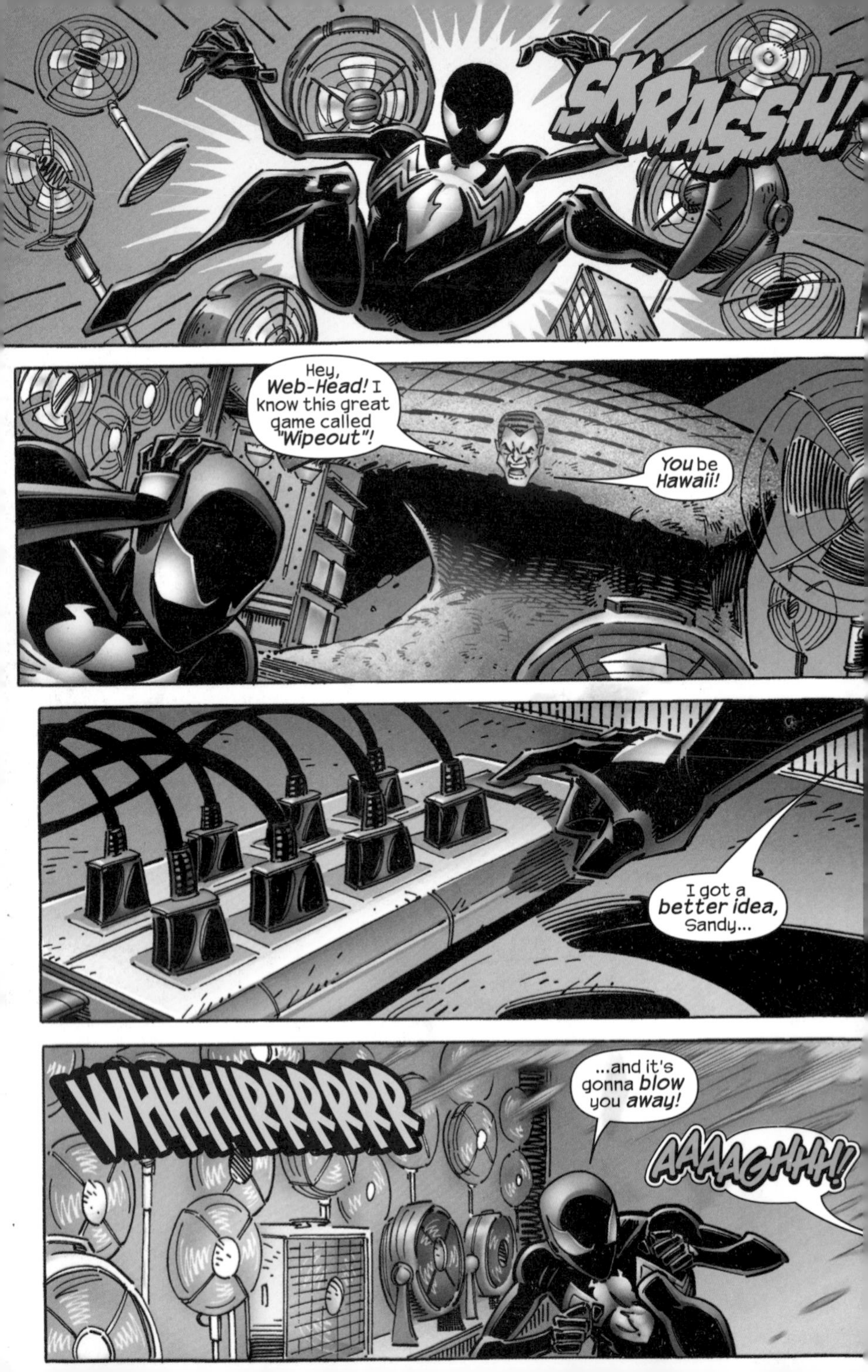
SKRASSH!
Hey, Web-Head! I know this great game called "Wipeout"!
You be Hawaii!
I got a better idea, Sandy...
WHHHIRRRRRR
...and it's gonna blow you away!
AAAAGHHH!

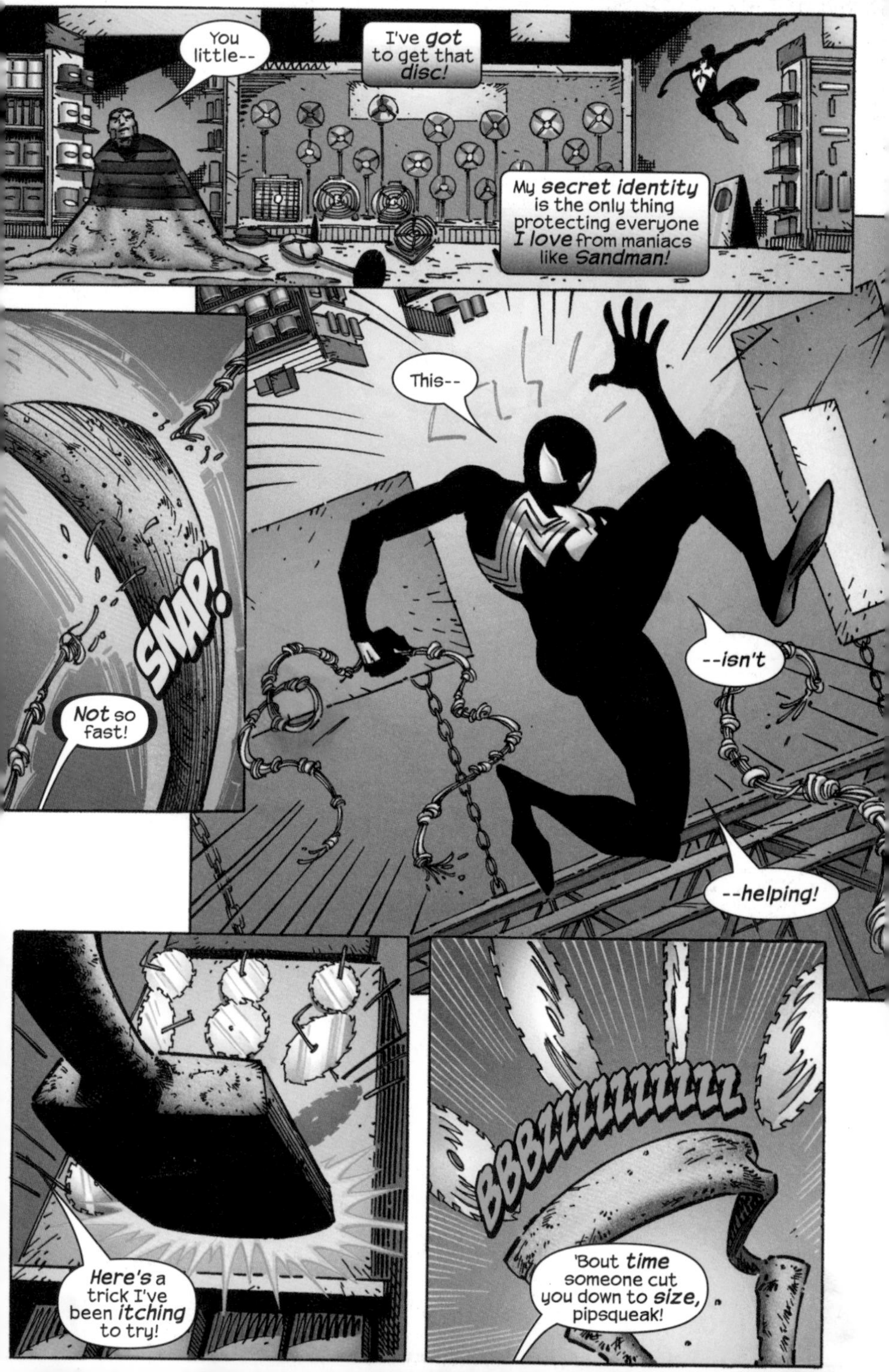

You little--
I've got to get that disc!
My secret identity is the only thing protecting everyone I love from maniacs like Sandman!
SNAP!
Not so fast!
This--
--isn't
--helping!
Here's a trick I've been itching to try!
BBBZZZZZZZZZZ
'Bout time someone cut you down to size, pipsqueak!

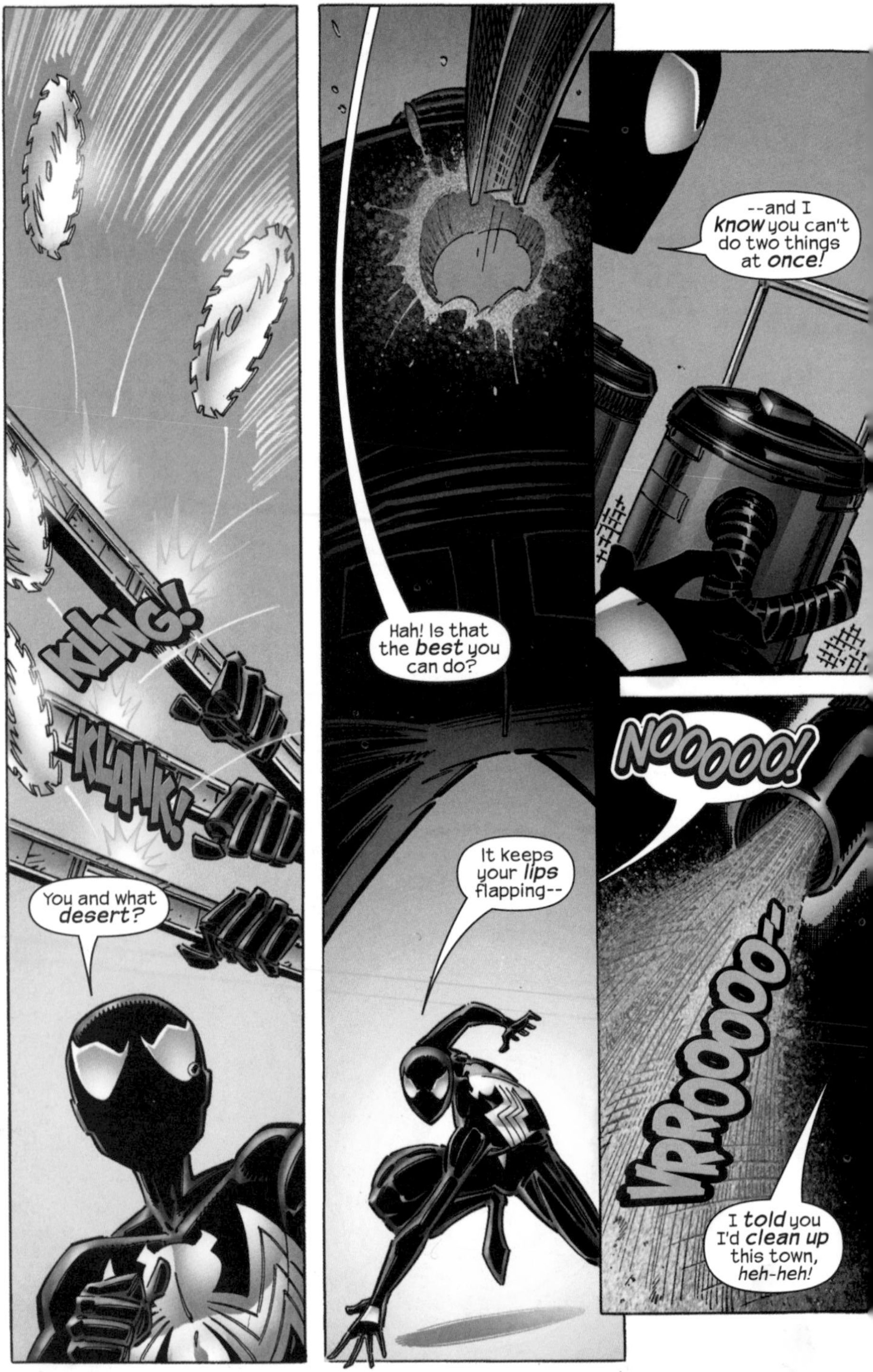

KLING!
KLANK!
You and what desert?
Hah! Is that the best you can do?
It keeps your lips flapping--
--and I know you can't do two things at once!
NOOOOOO!
VRROOOOOO--
I told you I'd clean up this town, heh-heh!

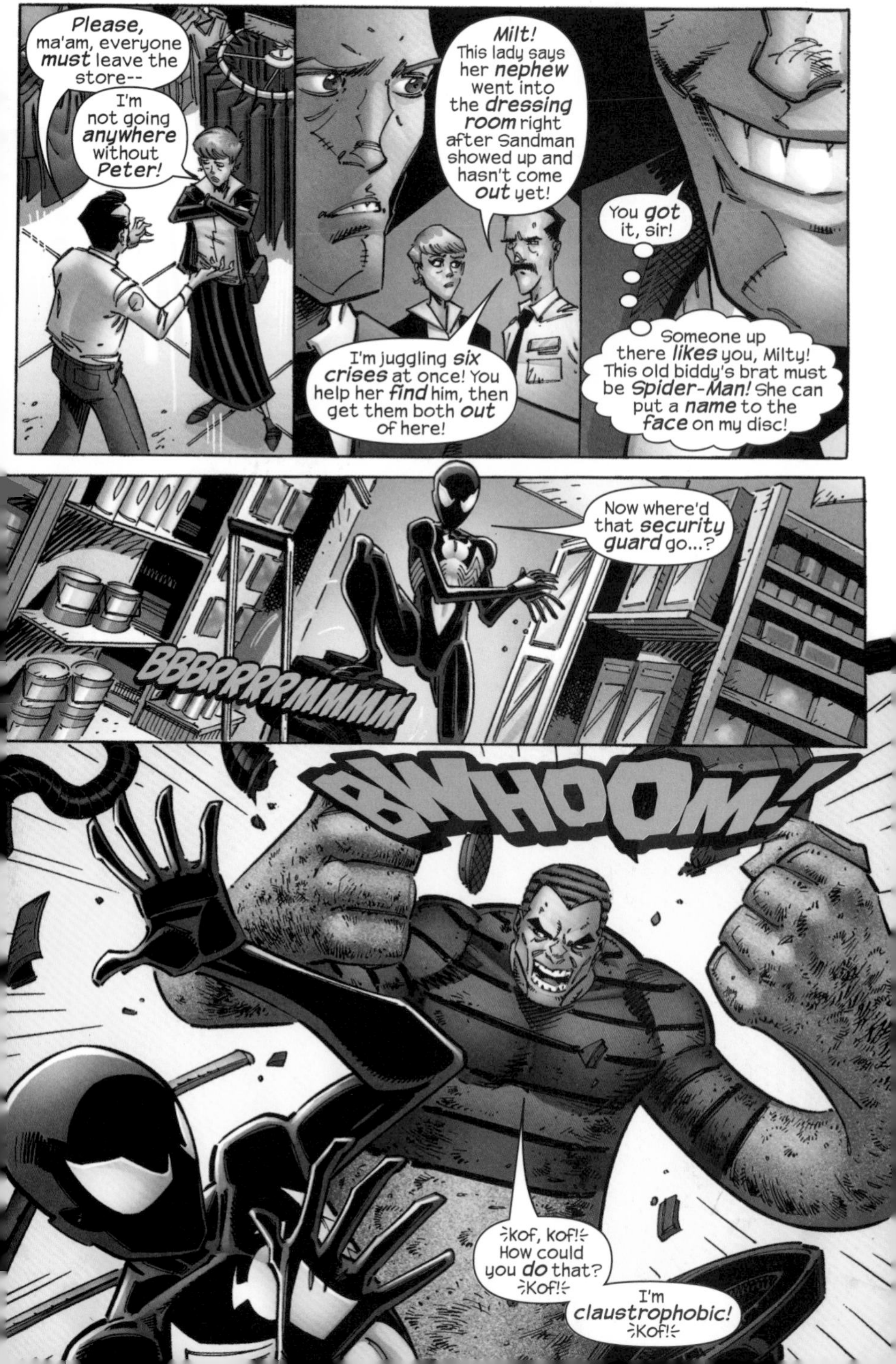
Please, ma'am, everyone must leave the store--
I'm not going anywhere without Peter!
Milt! This lady says her nephew went into the dressing room right after Sandman showed up and hasn't come out yet!
I'm juggling six crises at once! You help her find him, then get them both out of here!
You got it, sir!
Someone up there likes you, Milty! This old biddy's brat must be Spider-Man! She can put a name to the face on my disc!
Now where'd that security guard go...?
BBBRRRRRMMMMM
BWHOOM!
Kof, kof! How could you do that? Kof!
I'm claustrophobic! Kof!

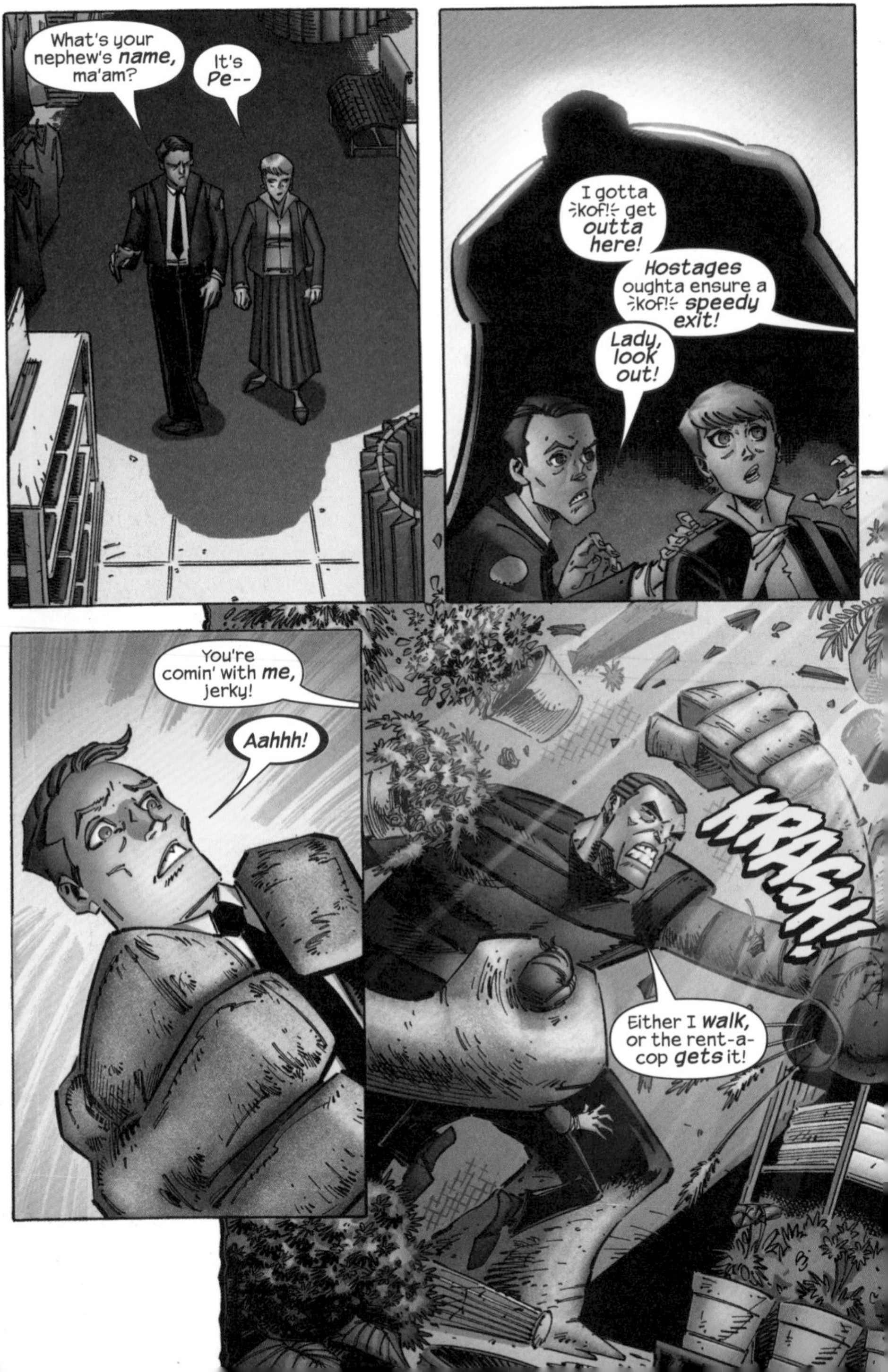
What's your nephew's name, ma'am?
It's Pe--
I gotta ¡kof!¡ get outta here!
Hostages oughta ensure a ¡kof!¡ speedy exit!
Lady, look out!
You're comin' with me, jerky!
Aahhh!
KRASH!
Either I walk, or the rent-a-cop gets it!

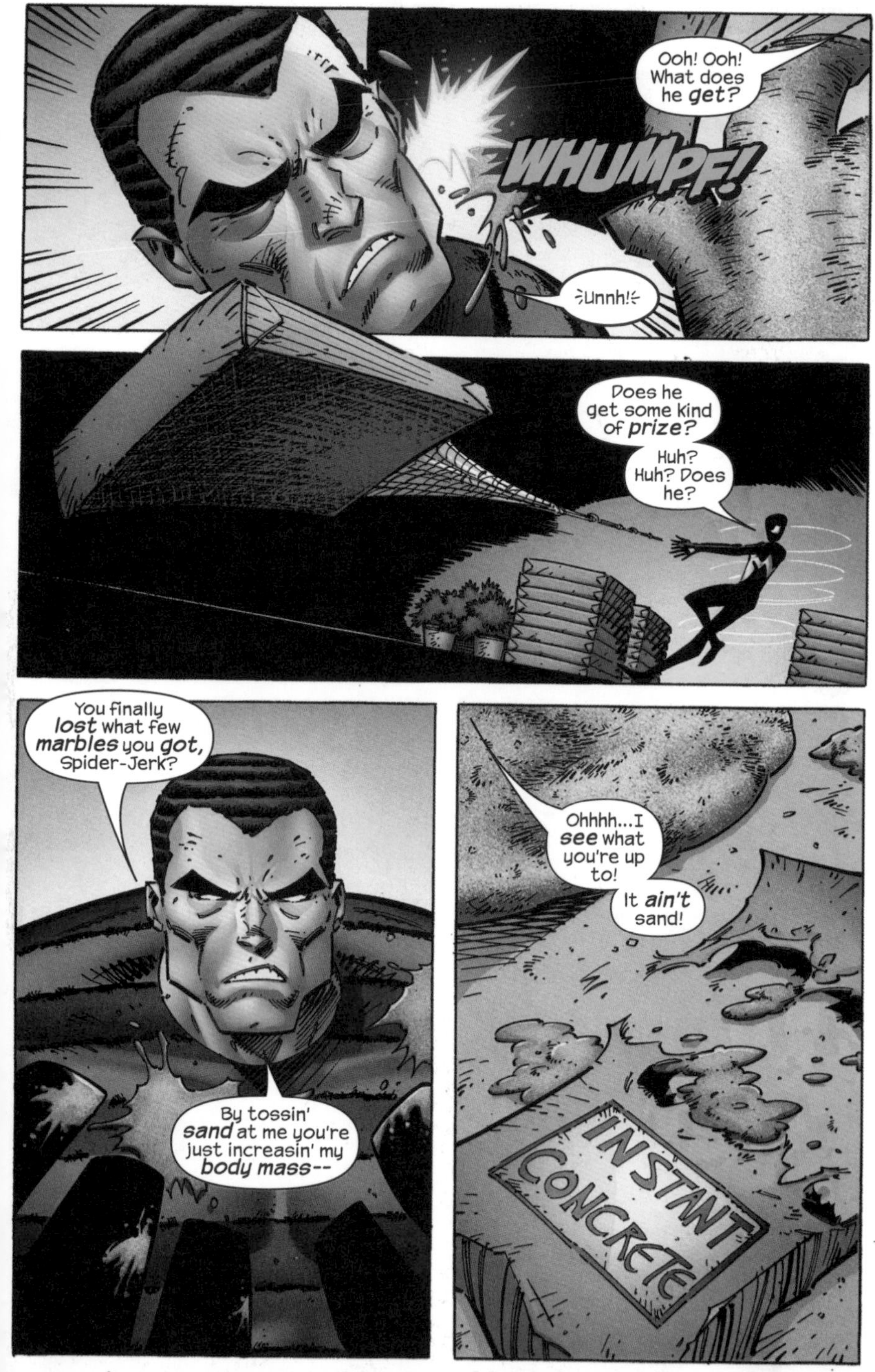
Ooh! Ooh! What does he get?
WHUMPF!
Unnh!
Does he get some kind of prize?
Huh? Huh? Does he?
You finally lost what few marbles you got, Spider-Jerk?
By tossin' sand at me you're just increasin' my body mass--
Ohhhh...I see what you're up to!
It ain't sand!
INSTANT CONCRETE

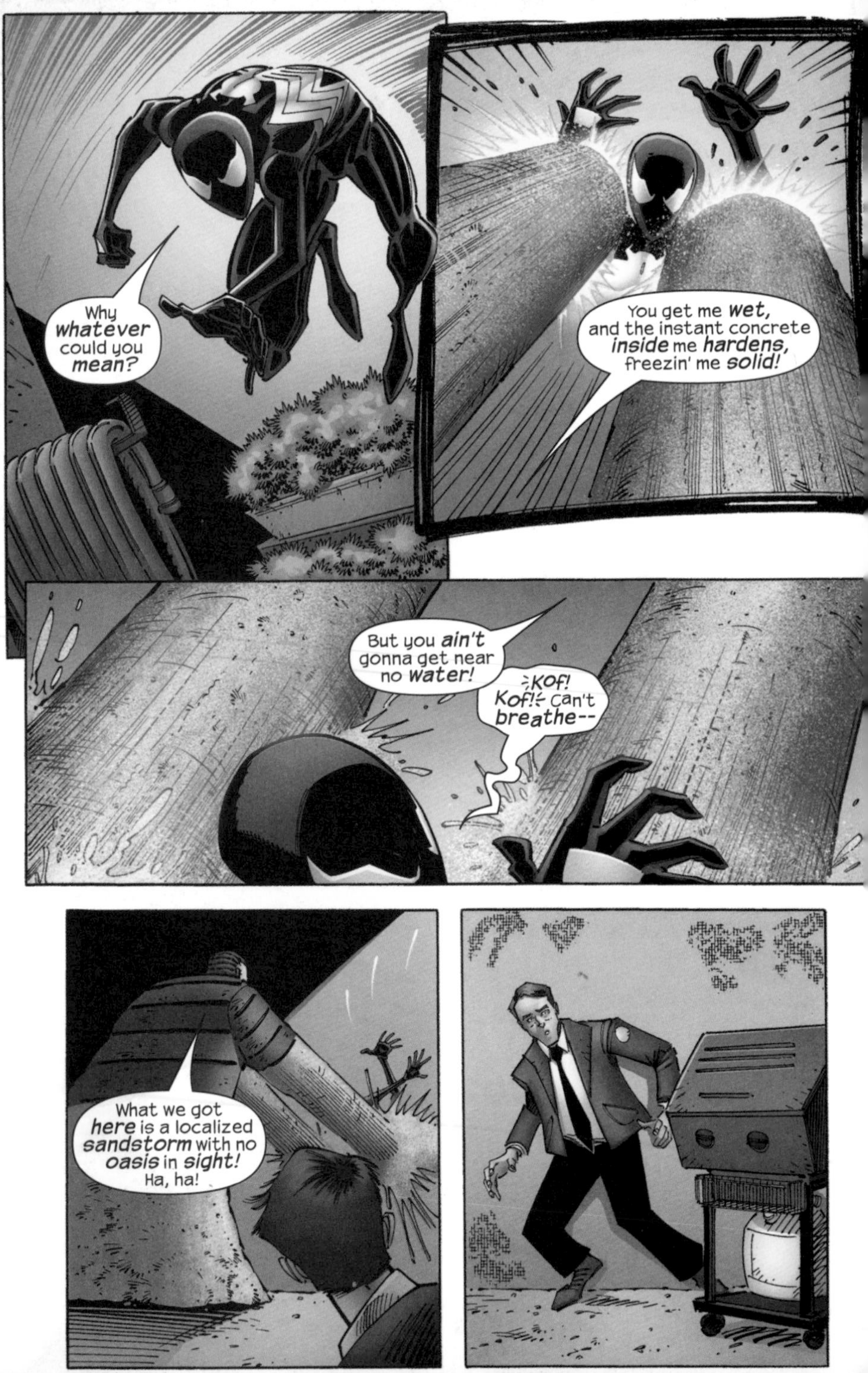
Why whatever could you mean?
You get me wet, and the instant concrete inside me hardens, freezin' me solid!
But you ain't gonna get near no water!
Kof! Kof! Can't breathe--
What we got here is a localized sandstorm with no oasis in sight! Ha, ha!

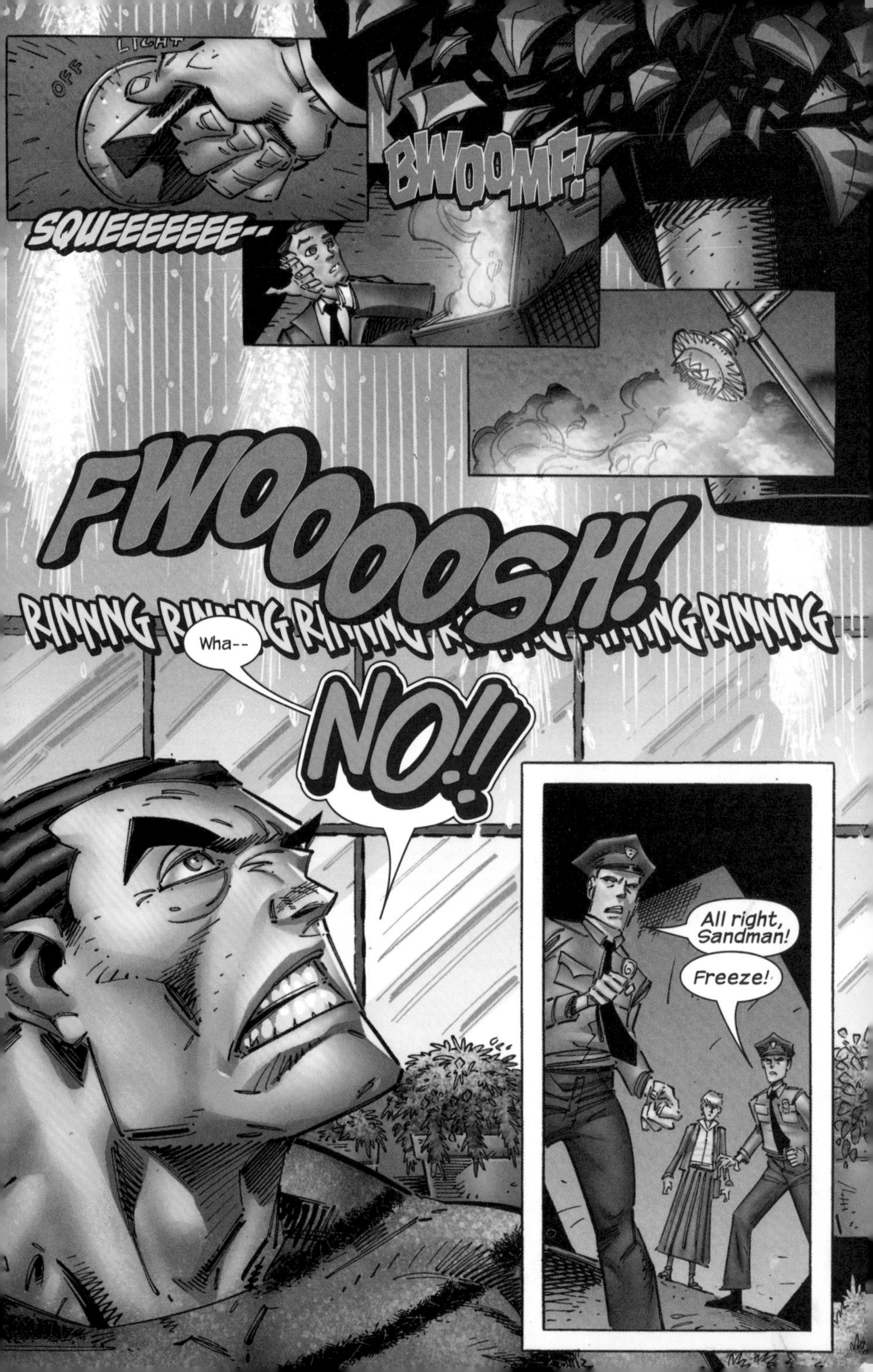
LIGHT
OFF
SQUEEEEEEEE--
BWOOMF!
FWOOOOSH!
RINNNG RINNNG
Wha--
NO!!
All right, Sandman!
Freeze!

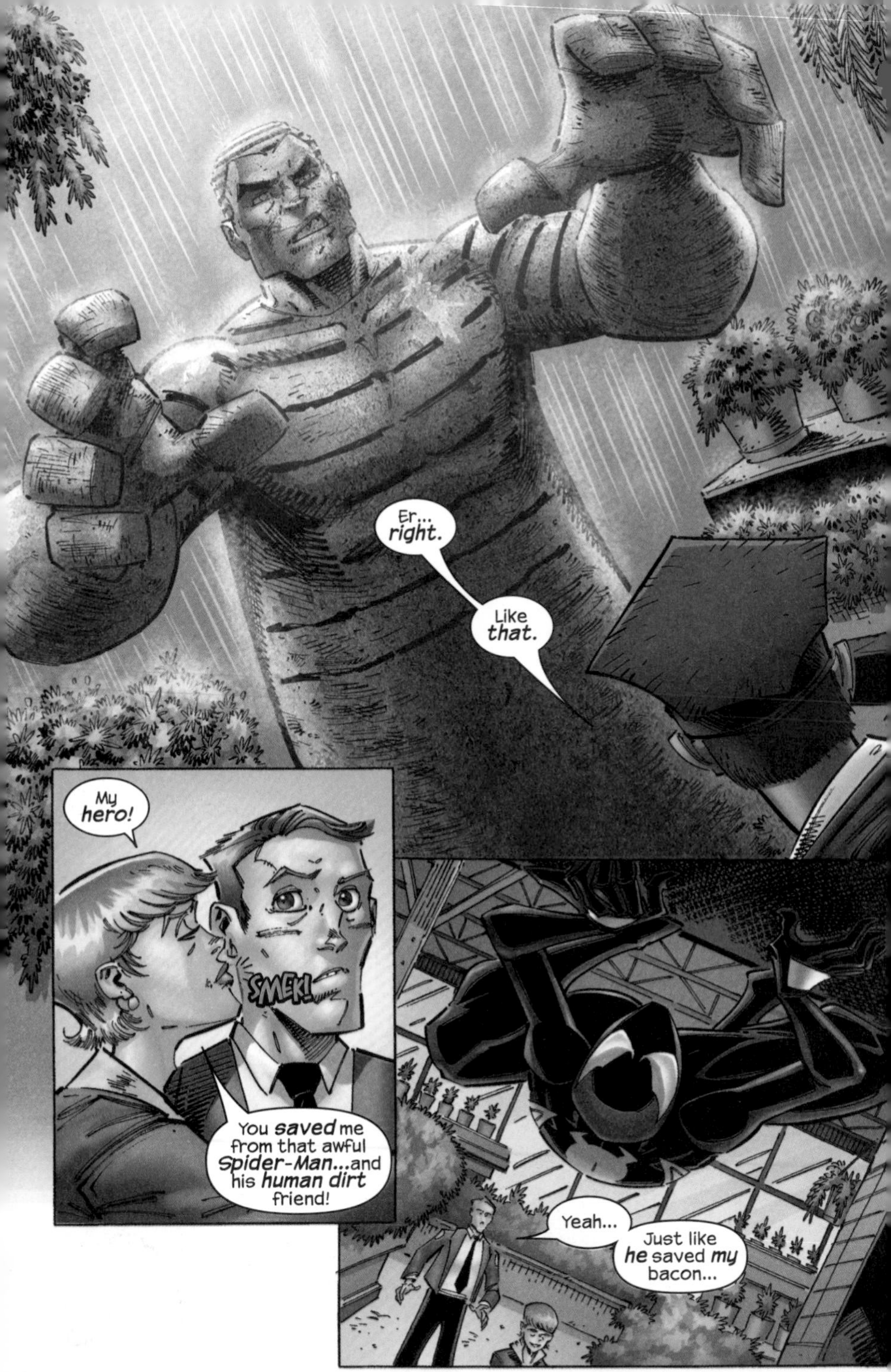
Er... *right.*
Like *that.*
My *hero!*
SMEK!
You *saved* me from that awful *Spider-Man*...and his *human dirt* friend!
Yeah...
Just like *he* saved *my* bacon...

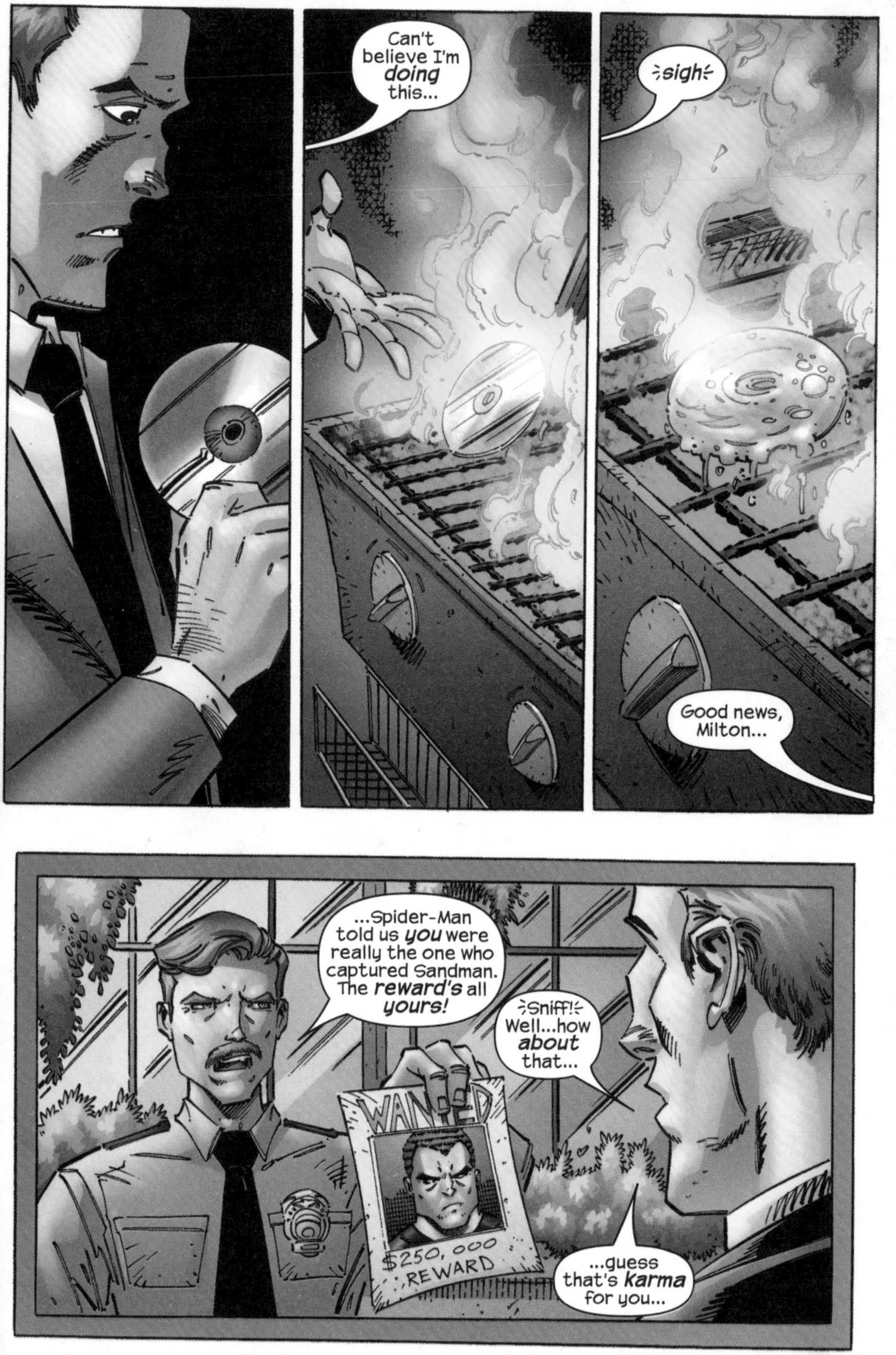
Can't believe I'm *doing* this...
sigh
Good news, Milton...
...Spider-Man told us *you* were really the one who captured Sandman. The *reward's* all *yours!*
WANTED
$250,000 REWARD
Sniff! Well...how *about* that...
...guess that's *karma* for you...

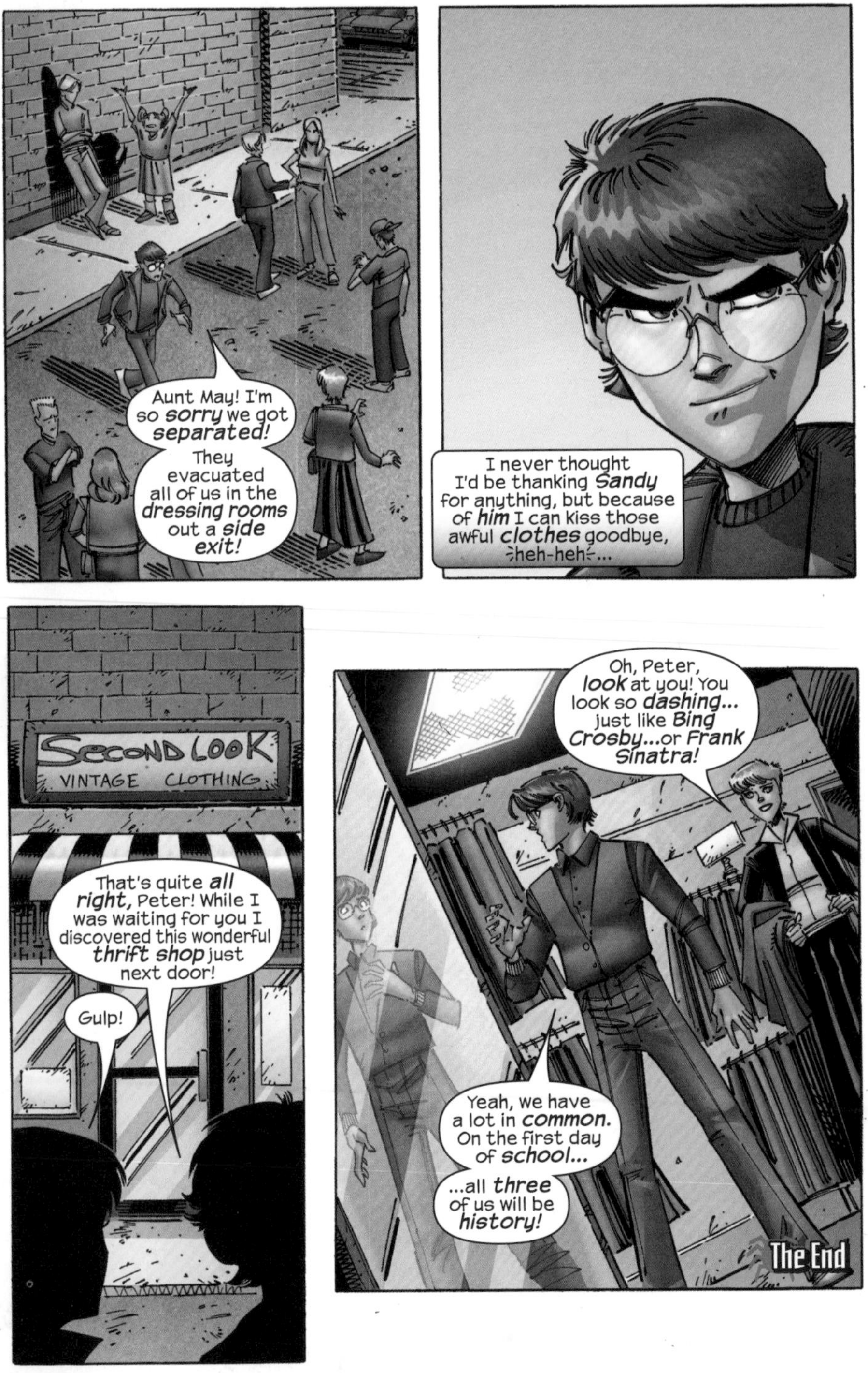
Aunt May! I'm so *sorry* we got *separated!*
They evacuated all of us in the *dressing rooms* out a *side exit!*
I never thought I'd be thanking *Sandy* for anything, but because of *him* I can kiss those awful *clothes* goodbye, heh-heh...
SECOND LOOK VINTAGE CLOTHING
That's quite *all right,* Peter! While I was waiting for you I discovered this wonderful *thrift shop* just next door!
Gulp!
Oh, Peter, *look* at you! You look so *dashing...* just like *Bing Crosby...*or *Frank Sinatra!*
Yeah, we have a lot in *common.* On the first day of *school...*
...all *three* of us will be *history!*
The End

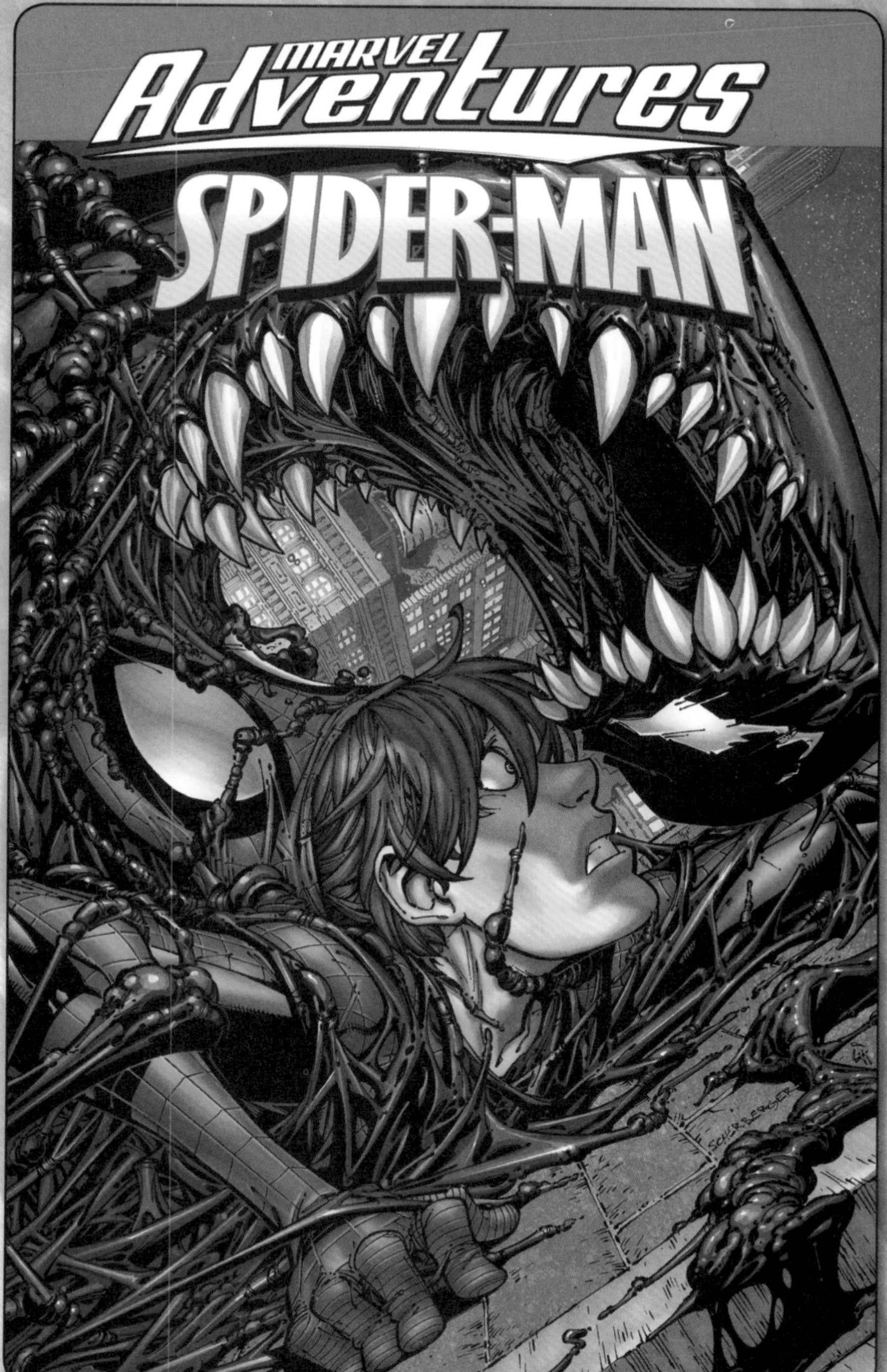
MARVEL Adventures
SPIDER-MAN
SCHERBERGER

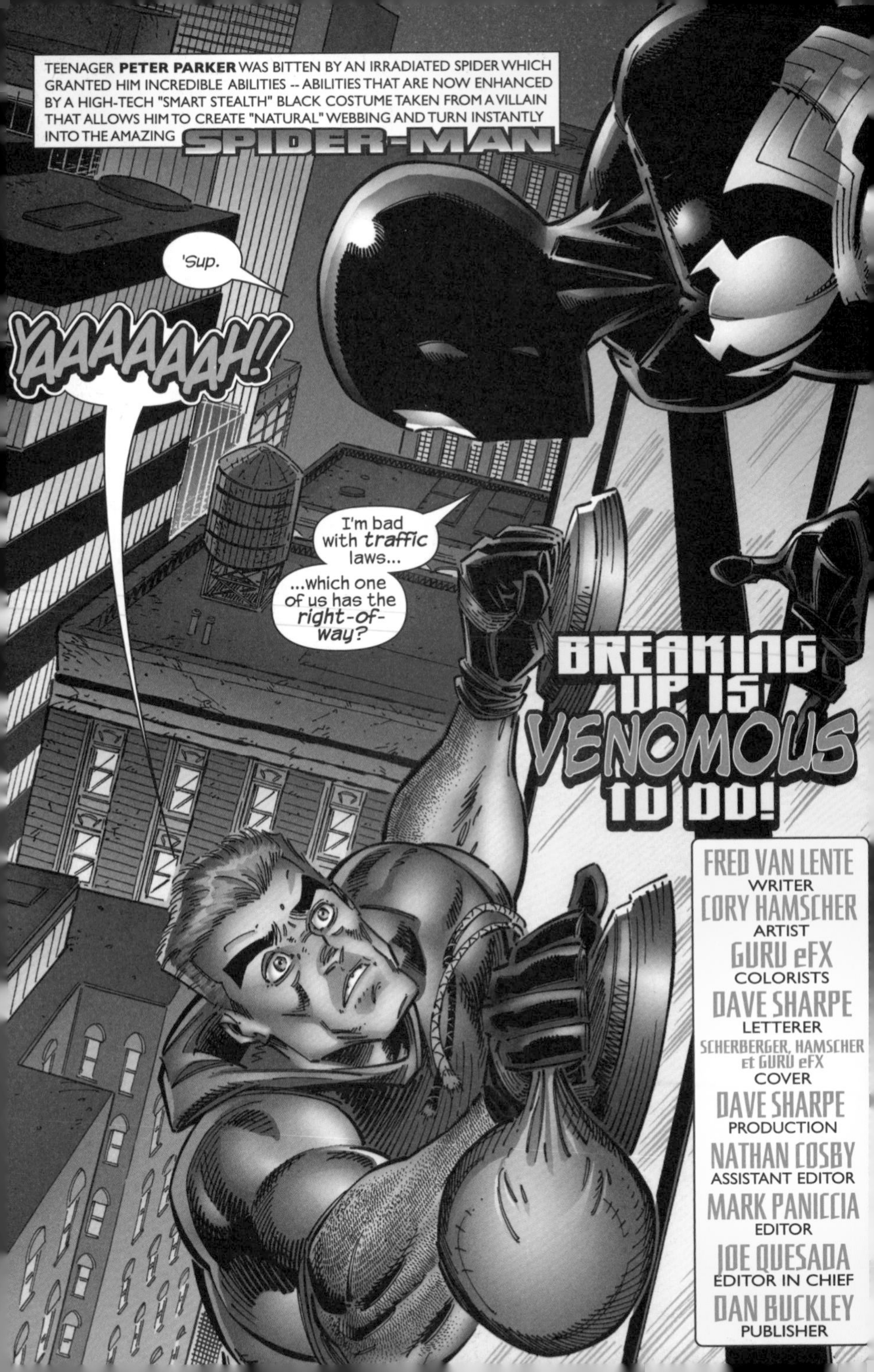

TEENAGER **PETER PARKER** WAS BITTEN BY AN IRRADIATED SPIDER WHICH GRANTED HIM INCREDIBLE ABILITIES -- ABILITIES THAT ARE NOW ENHANCED BY A HIGH-TECH "SMART STEALTH" BLACK COSTUME TAKEN FROM A VILLAIN THAT ALLOWS HIM TO CREATE "NATURAL" WEBBING AND TURN INSTANTLY INTO THE AMAZING SPIDER-MAN
'Sup.
YAAAAAAH!
I'm bad with *traffic* laws...
...which one of us has the *right-of-way?*
BREAKING UP IS VENOMOUS TO DO!
FRED VAN LENTE
WRITER
CORY HAMSCHER
ARTIST
GURU eFX
COLORISTS
DAVE SHARPE
LETTERER
SCHERBERGER, HAMSCHER et GURU eFX
COVER
DAVE SHARPE
PRODUCTION
NATHAN COSBY
ASSISTANT EDITOR
MARK PANICCIA
EDITOR
JOE QUESADA
EDITOR IN CHIEF
DAN BUCKLEY
PUBLISHER

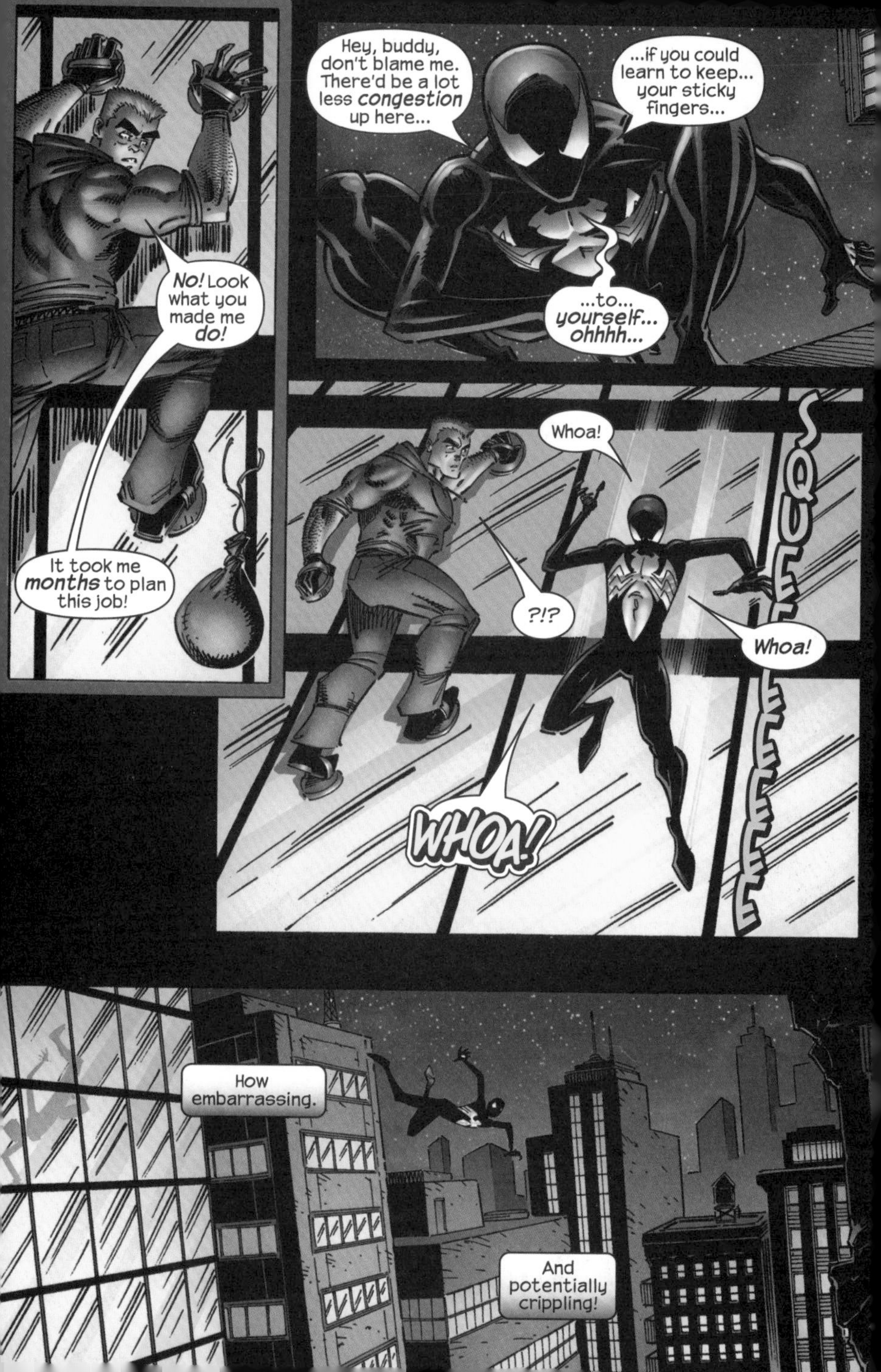
No! Look what you made me do!
It took me months to plan this job!
Hey, buddy, don't blame me. There'd be a lot less congestion up here...
...if you could learn to keep... your sticky fingers...
...to... yourself... ohhhh...
Whoa!
?!?
Whoa!
WHOA!
How embarrassing.
And potentially crippling!

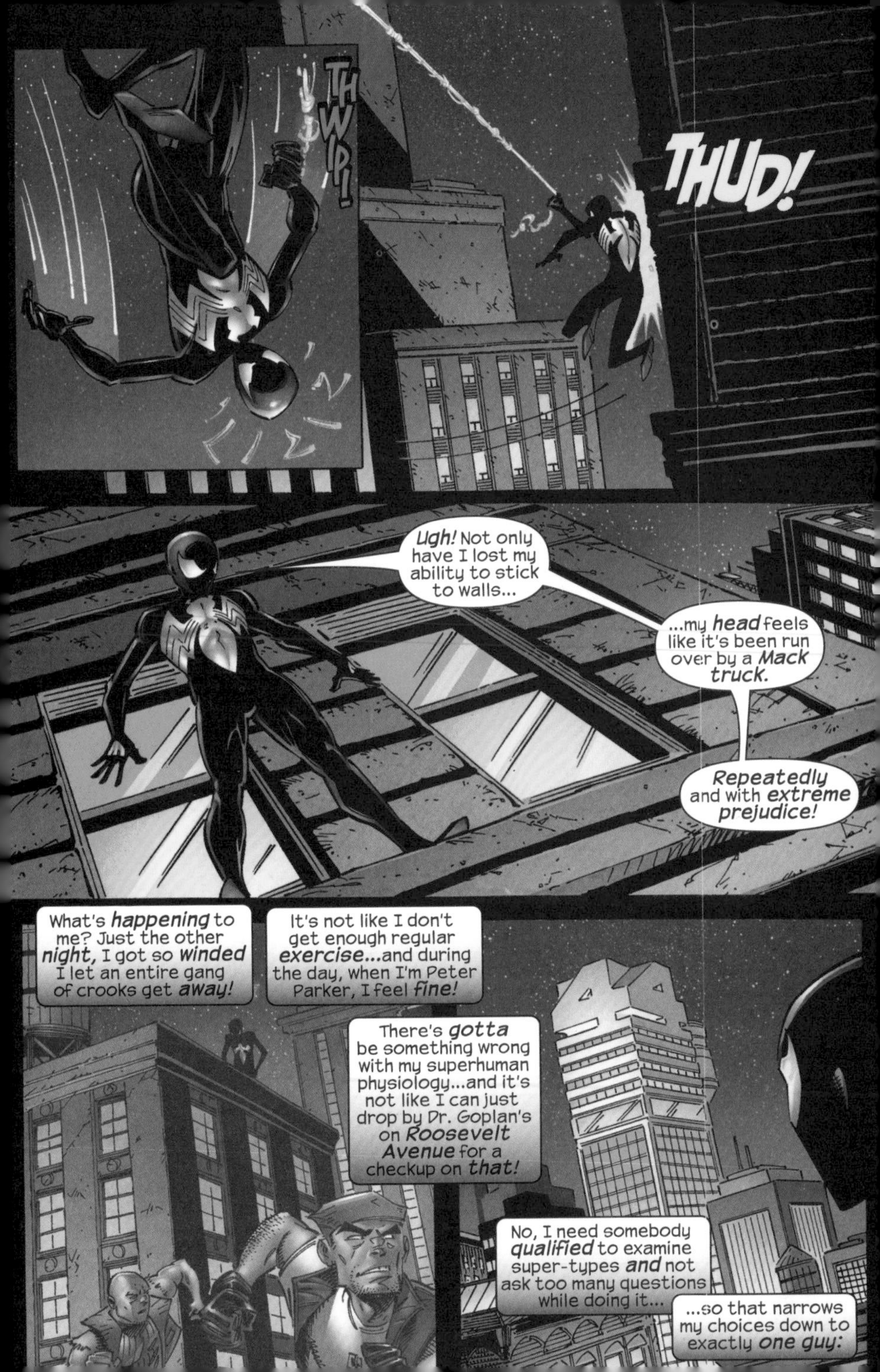
THWIP!
THUD!
Ugh! Not only have I lost my ability to stick to walls...
...my head feels like it's been run over by a Mack truck.
Repeatedly and with extreme prejudice!
What's happening to me? Just the other night, I got so winded I let an entire gang of crooks get away!
It's not like I don't get enough regular exercise...and during the day, when I'm Peter Parker, I feel fine!
There's gotta be something wrong with my superhuman physiology...and it's not like I can just drop by Dr. Goplan's on Roosevelt Avenue for a checkup on that!
No, I need somebody qualified to examine super-types and not ask too many questions while doing it...
...so that narrows my choices down to exactly one guy:

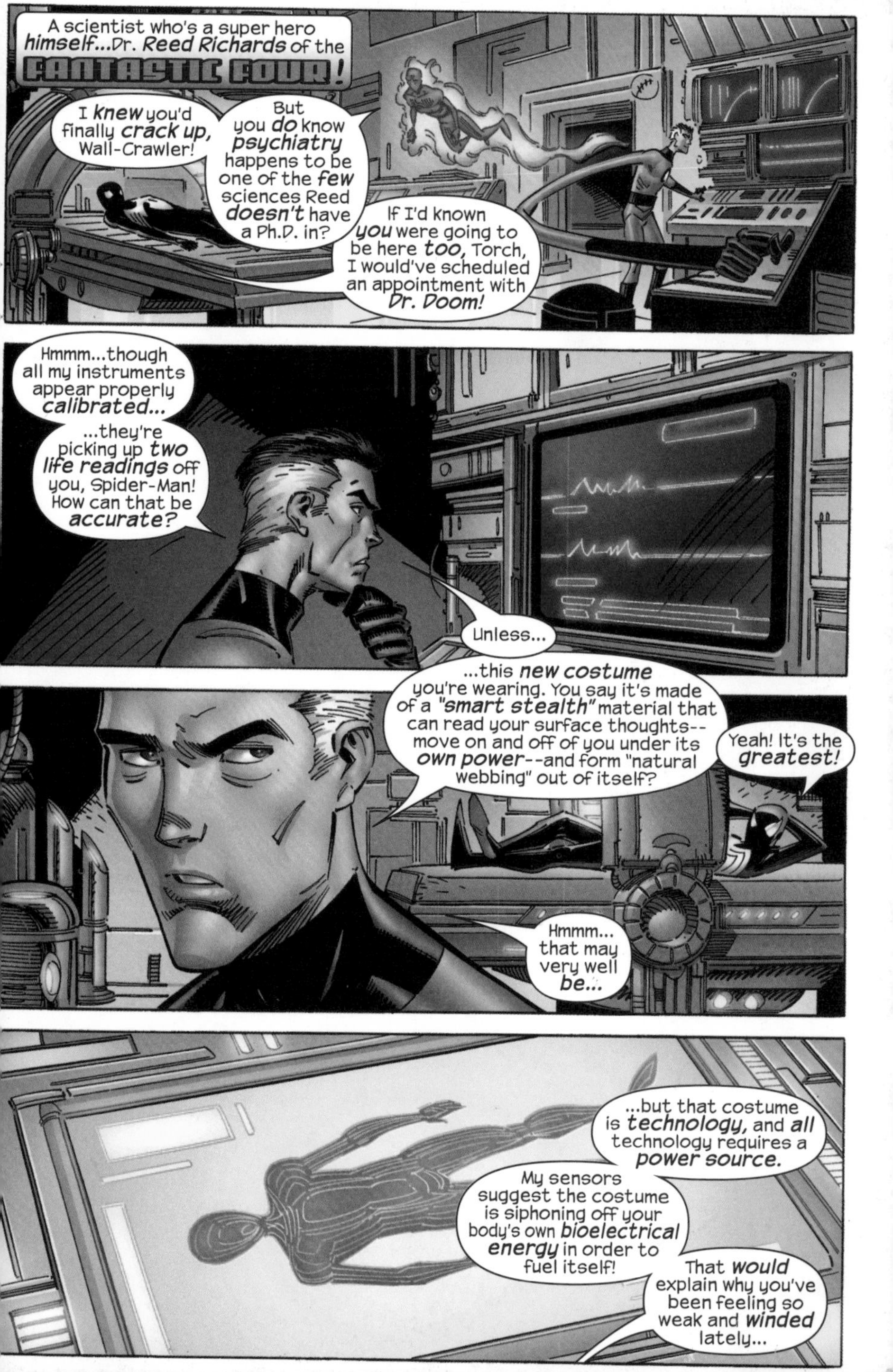
A scientist who's a super hero himself...Dr. Reed Richards of the FANTASTIC FOUR!
I knew you'd finally crack up, Wall-Crawler!
But you do know psychiatry happens to be one of the few sciences Reed doesn't have a Ph.D. in?
If I'd known you were going to be here too, Torch, I would've scheduled an appointment with Dr. Doom!
Hmmm...though all my instruments appear properly calibrated...
...they're picking up two life readings off you, Spider-Man! How can that be accurate?
Unless...
...this new costume you're wearing. You say it's made of a "smart stealth" material that can read your surface thoughts--move on and off of you under its own power--and form "natural webbing" out of itself?
Yeah! It's the greatest!
Hmmm... that may very well be...
...but that costume is technology, and all technology requires a power source.
My sensors suggest the costume is siphoning off your body's own bioelectrical energy in order to fuel itself!
That would explain why you've been feeling so weak and winded lately...

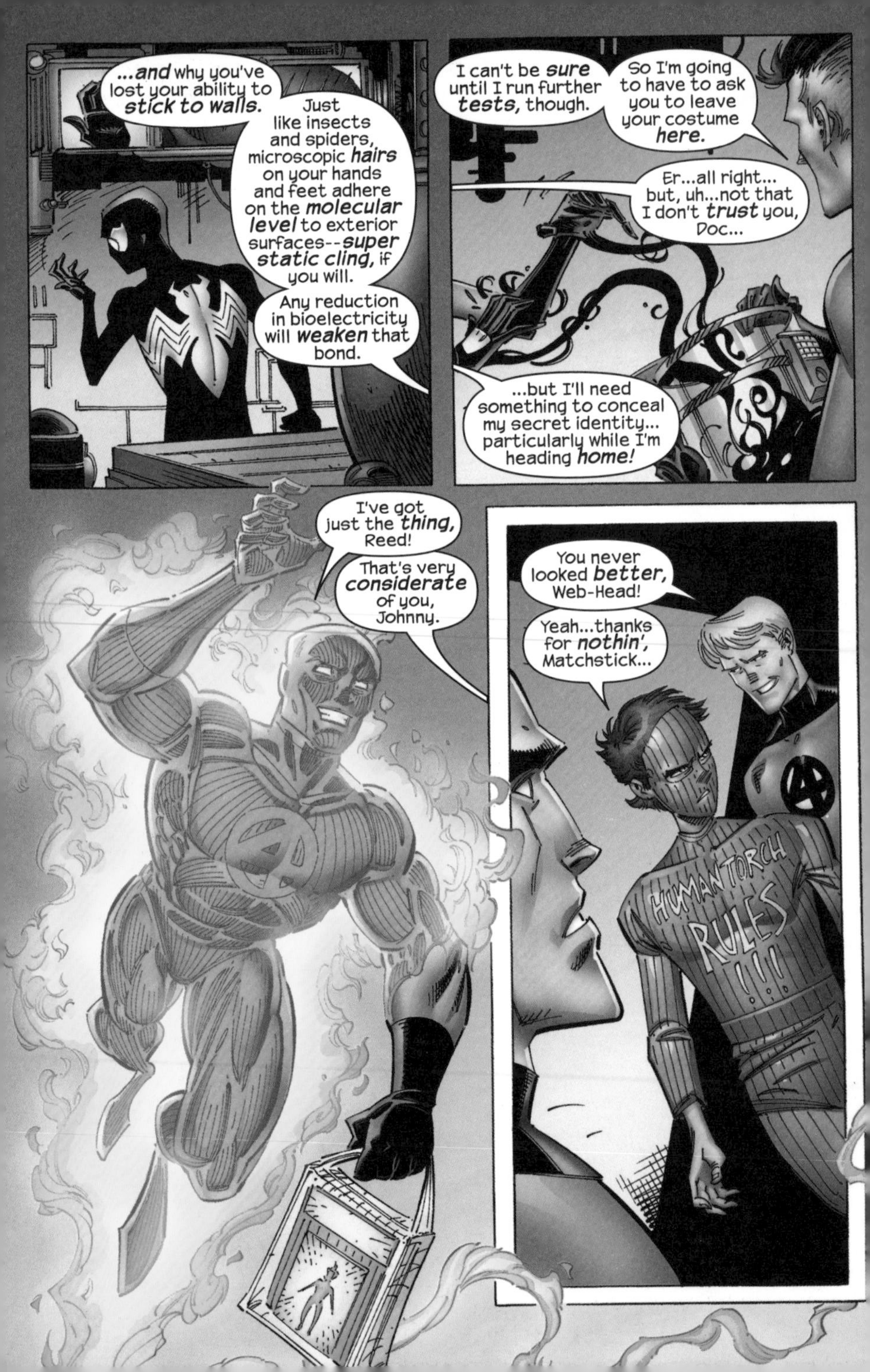
...and why you've lost your ability to stick to walls.
Just like insects and spiders, microscopic hairs on your hands and feet adhere on the molecular level to exterior surfaces--super static cling, if you will.
Any reduction in bioelectricity will weaken that bond.
I can't be sure until I run further tests, though.
So I'm going to have to ask you to leave your costume here.
Er...all right... but, uh...not that I don't trust you, Doc...
...but I'll need something to conceal my secret identity... particularly while I'm heading home!
I've got just the thing, Reed!
That's very considerate of you, Johnny.
You never looked better, Web-Head!
Yeah...thanks for nothin', Matchstick...
HUMAN TORCH RULES !!!

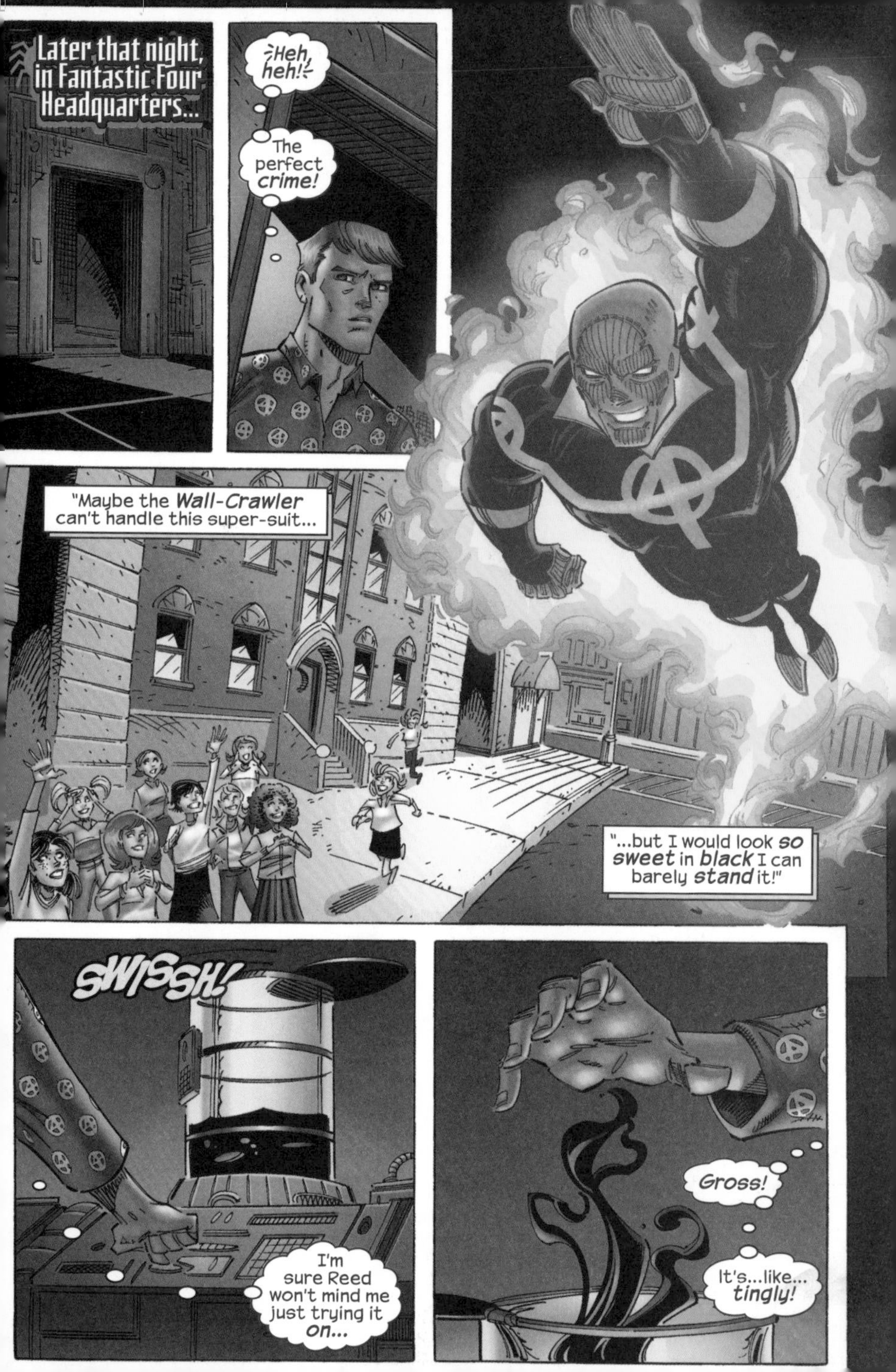
Later that night, in Fantastic Four Headquarters...
Heh, heh!
The perfect crime!
"Maybe the Wall-Crawler can't handle this super-suit...
"...but I would look so sweet in black I can barely stand it!"
SWISSH!
I'm sure Reed won't mind me just trying it on...
Gross!
It's...like... tingly!

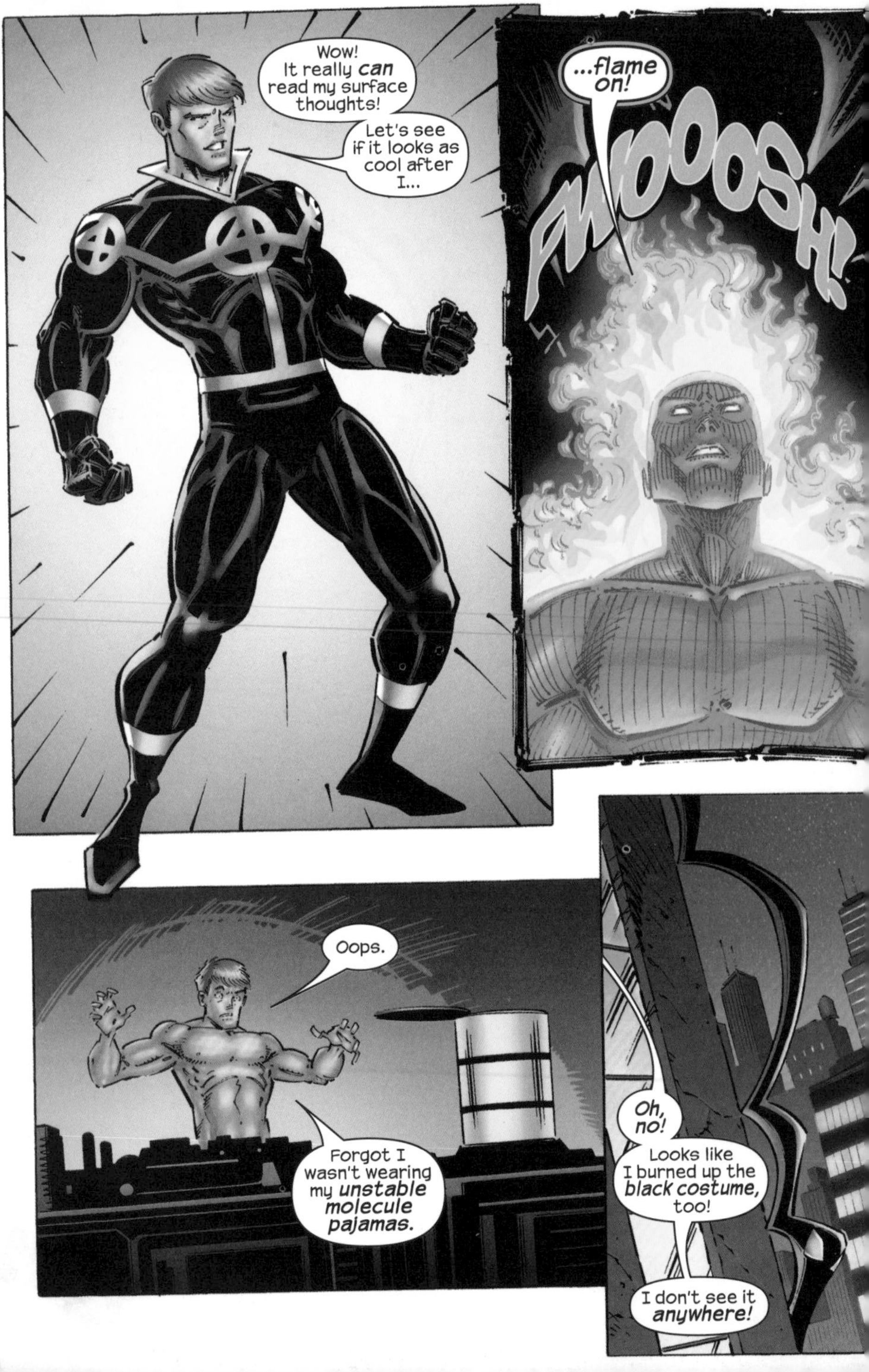

Wow! It really *can* read my surface thoughts!
Let's see if it looks as cool after I...
...*flame on!*
FWOOOSH!
Oops.
Forgot I wasn't wearing my ***unstable molecule pajamas.***
Oh, no!
Looks like I burned up the *black costume,* too!
I don't see it ***anywhere!***

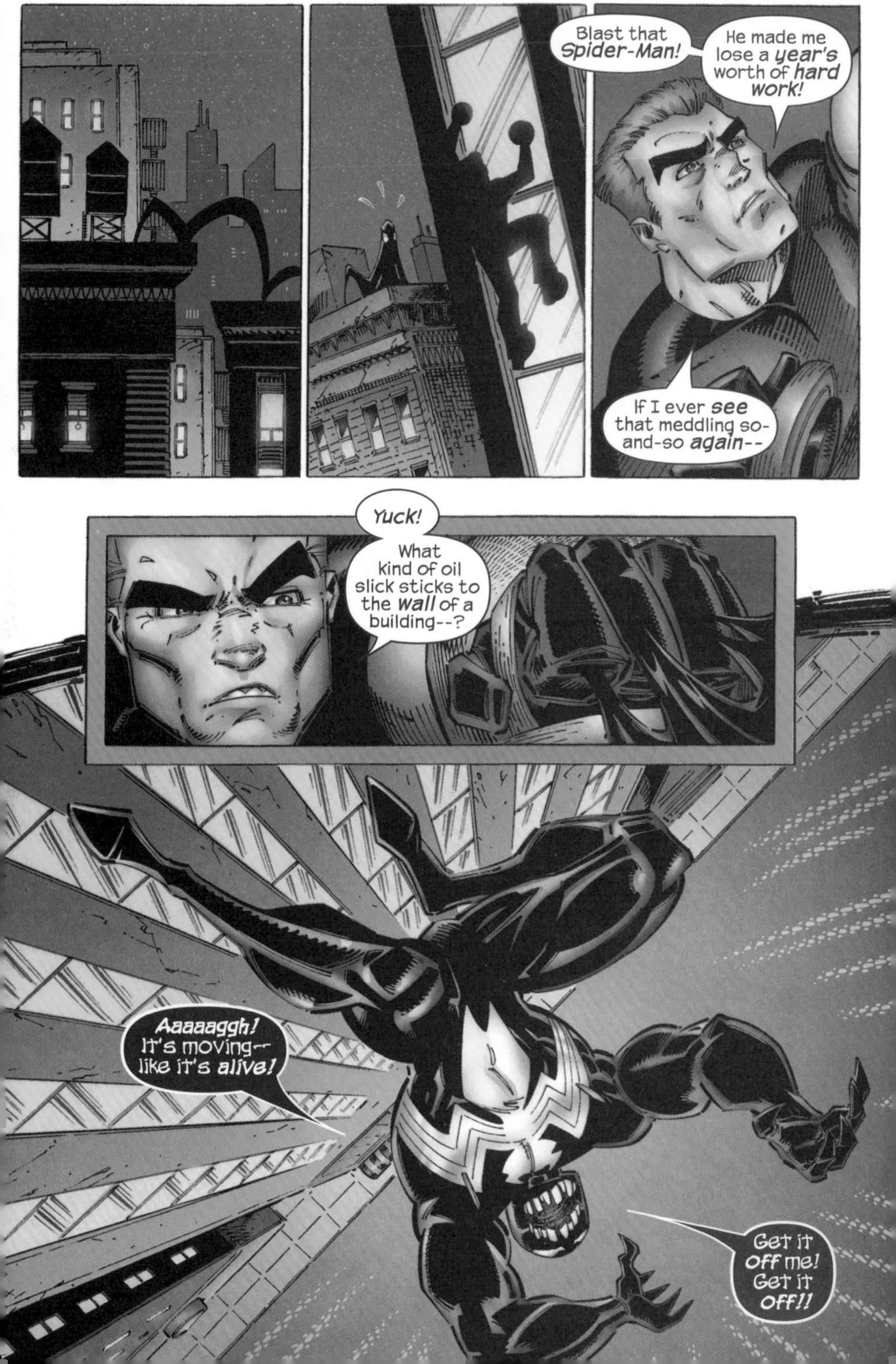

Blast that Spider-Man!
He made me lose a year's worth of hard work!
If I ever see that meddling so-and-so again--
Yuck!
What kind of oil slick sticks to the wall of a building--?
Aaaaaggh! It's moving--like it's alive!
Get it off me! Get it off!!

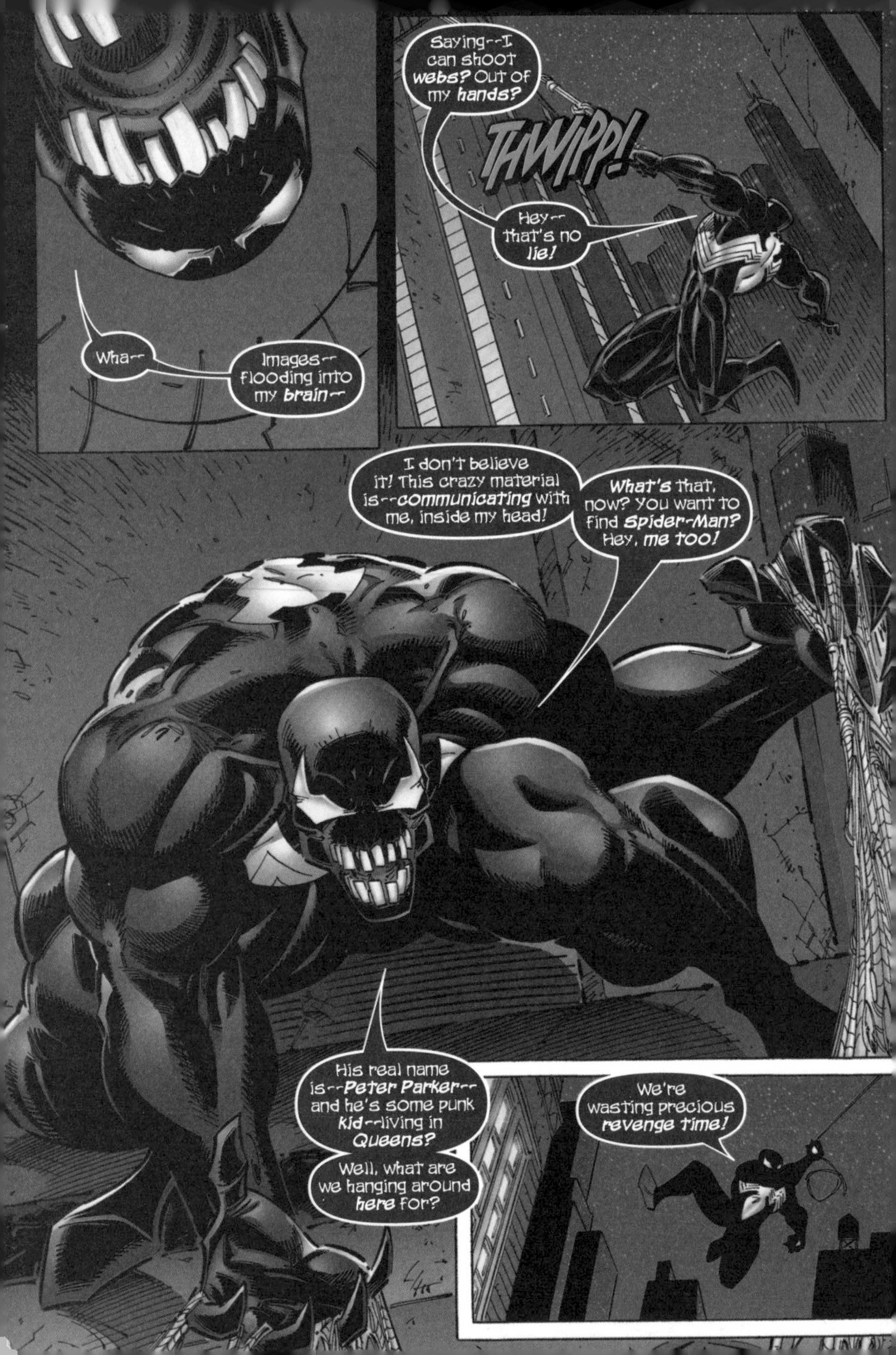
Wha--
Images--flooding into my brain--
Saying--I can shoot webs? Out of my hands?
THWIPP!
Hey--that's no lie!
I don't believe it! This crazy material is--communicating with me, inside my head!
What's that, now? You want to find Spider-Man? Hey, me too!
His real name is--Peter Parker--and he's some punk kid--living in Queens?
Well, what are we hanging around here for?
We're wasting precious revenge time!

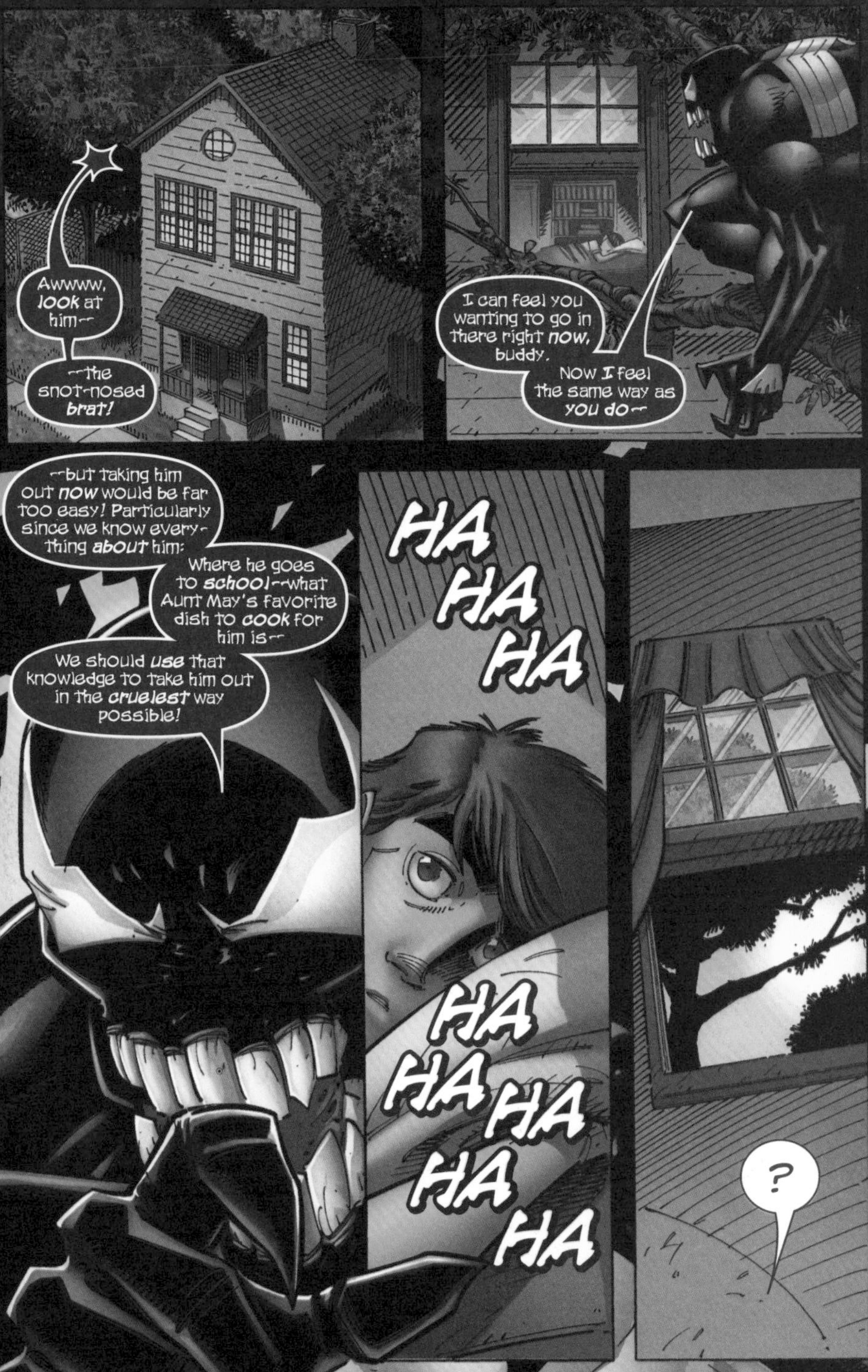

Awwww, *look* at him--
--the snot-nosed *brat!*
I can feel you wanting to go in there right *now,* buddy.
Now *I* feel the same way as *you do*--
--but taking him out *now* would be far too easy! Particularly since we know every-thing *about* him:
Where he goes to *school*--what Aunt May's favorite dish to *cook* for him is--
We should *use* that knowledge to take him out in the *cruelest* way possible!
HA HA HA
HA HA HA HA HA
?

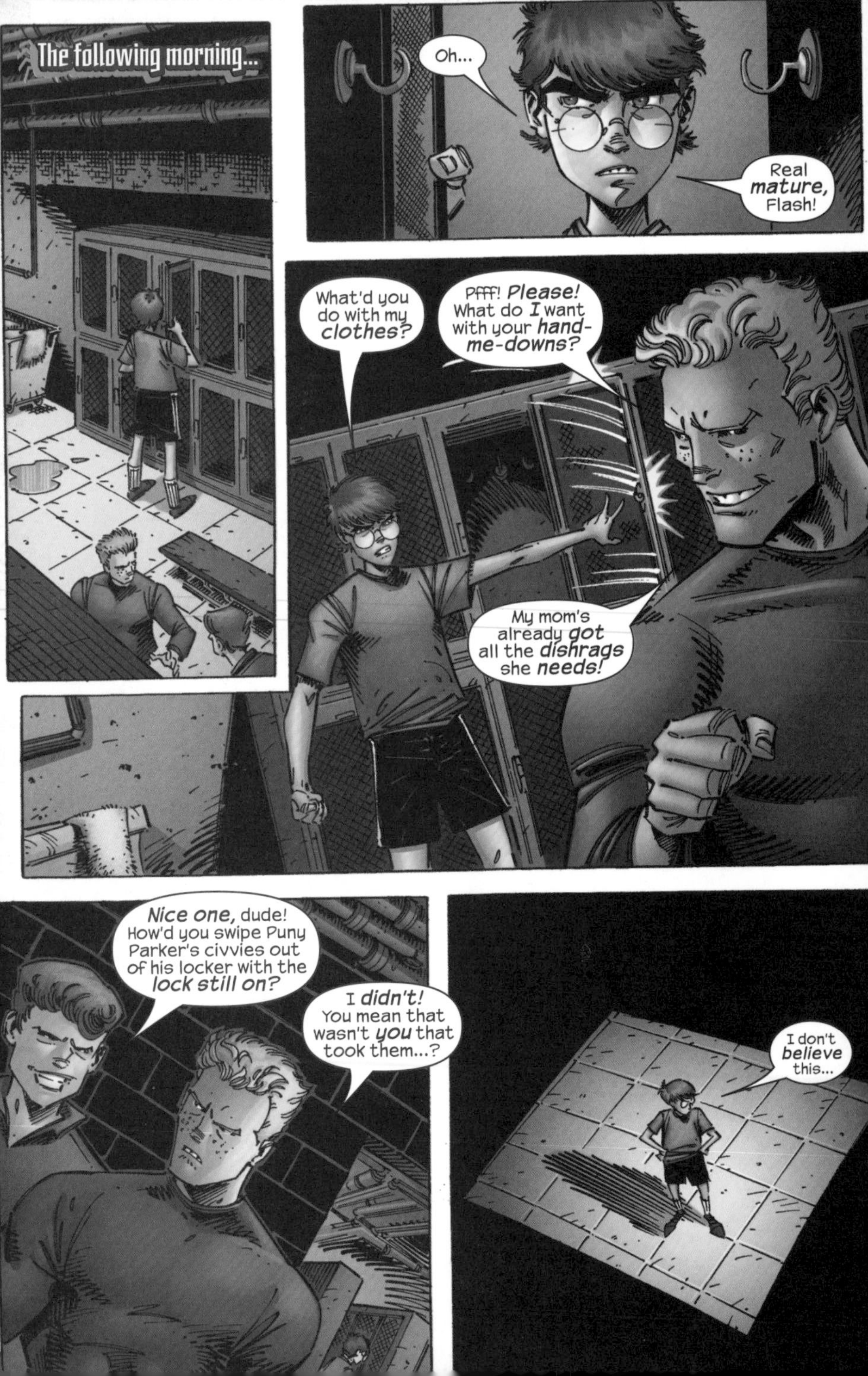
The following morning...
Oh...
Real *mature,* Flash!
What'd you do with my *clothes?*
Pfff! *Please!* What do *I* want with your *hand-me-downs?*
My mom's already *got* all the *dishrags* she *needs!*
Nice one, dude! How'd you swipe Puny Parker's civvies out of his locker with the *lock still on?*
I *didn't!* You mean that wasn't *you* that took them...?
I don't *believe* this...

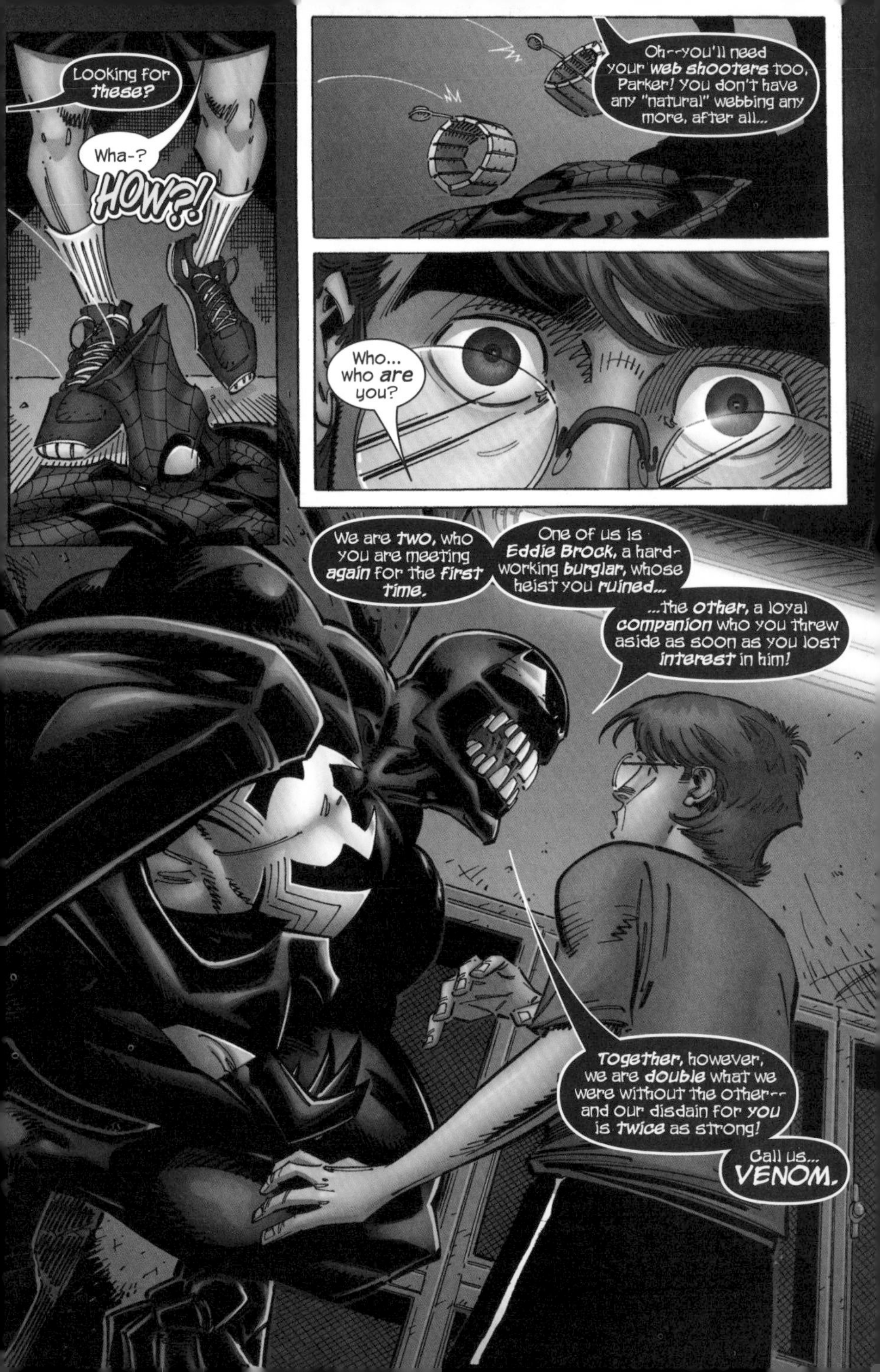

Looking for *these?*
Wha-?
HOW?!
Oh--you'll need your ***web shooters*** too, Parker! You don't have any "natural" webbing any more, after all...
Who... who ***are*** you?
We are ***two,*** who you are meeting ***again*** for the ***first time.***
One of us is **Eddie Brock,** a hard-working **burglar,** whose heist you ***ruined...***
...the ***other,*** a loyal **companion** who you threw aside as soon as you lost ***interest*** in him!
Together, however, we are ***double*** what we were without the other--and our disdain for ***you*** is ***twice*** as strong!
Call us... **VENOM.**

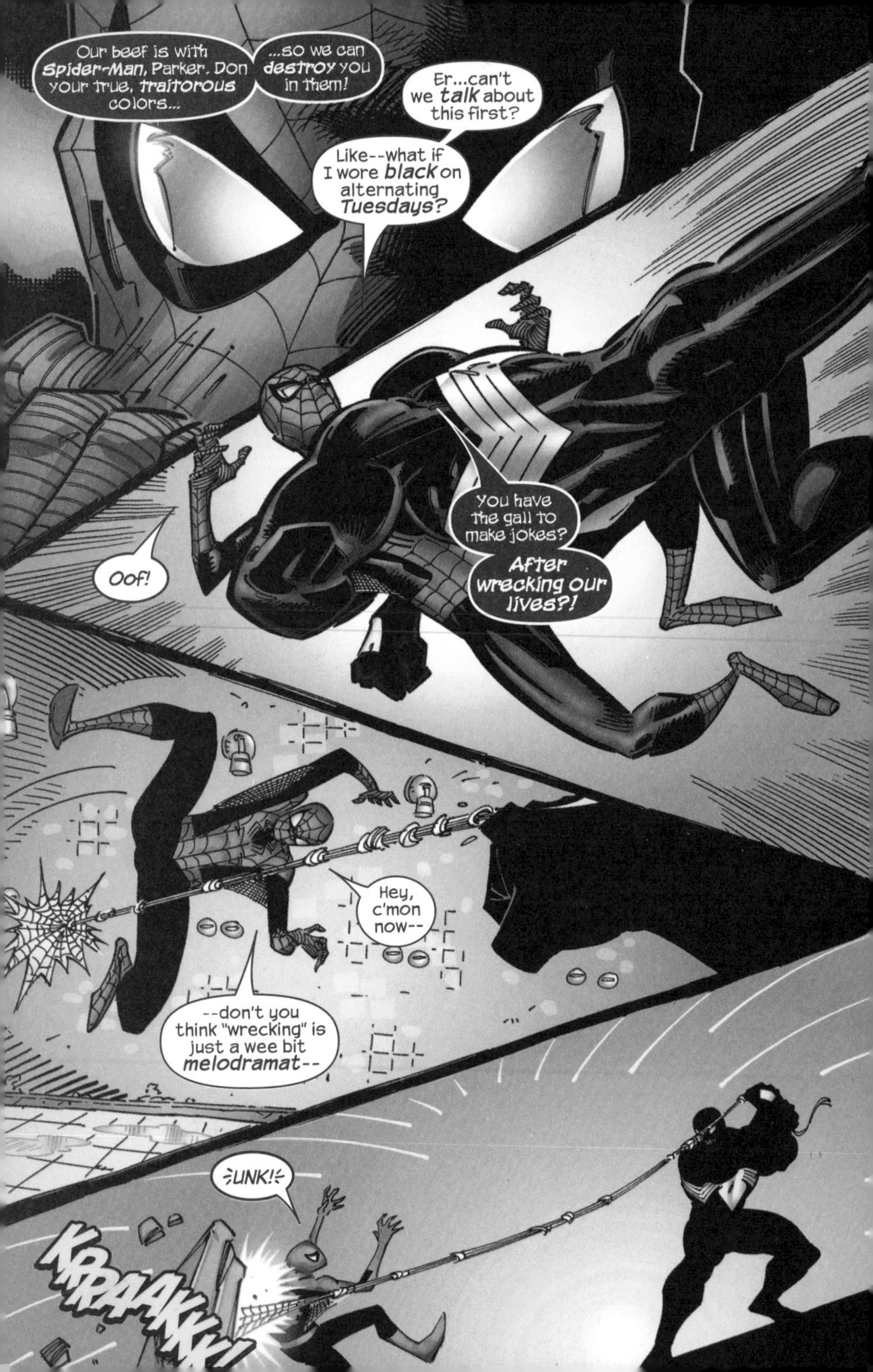
Our beef is with Spider-Man, Parker. Don your true, traitorous colors...
...so we can destroy you in them!
Er...can't we talk about this first?
Like--what if I wore black on alternating Tuesdays?
Oof!
You have the gall to make jokes?
After wrecking our lives?!
Hey, c'mon now--
--don't you think "wrecking" is just a wee bit melodramat--
UNK!
KRRAAKK!

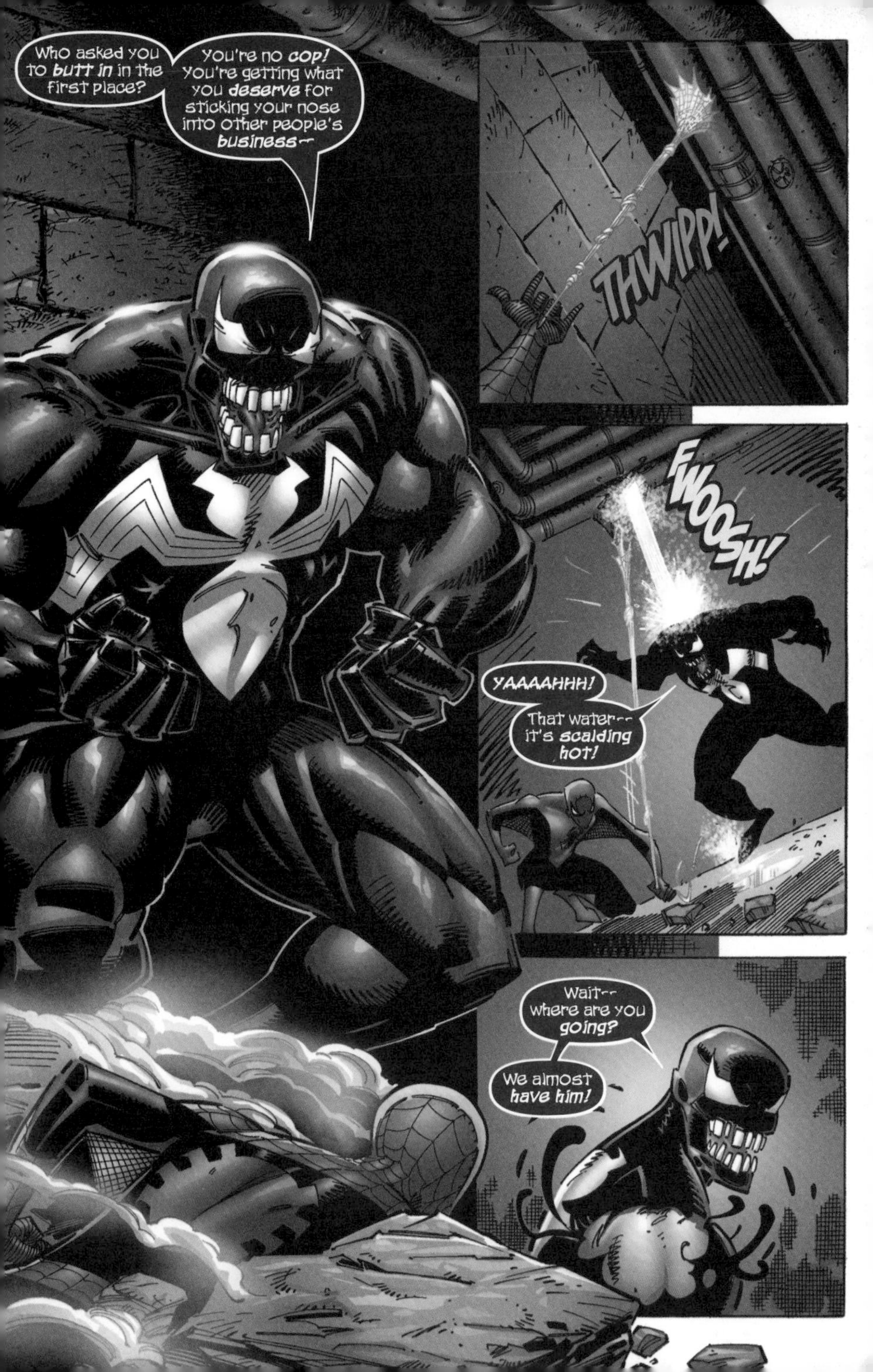

Who asked you to **butt in** in the first place?
You're no **cop!** You're getting what you **deserve** for sticking your nose into other people's **business**--
THWIPP!
FWOOSH!
YAAAAHHH!
That water-- it's **scalding hot!**
Wait-- where are you **going?**
We almost **have him!**

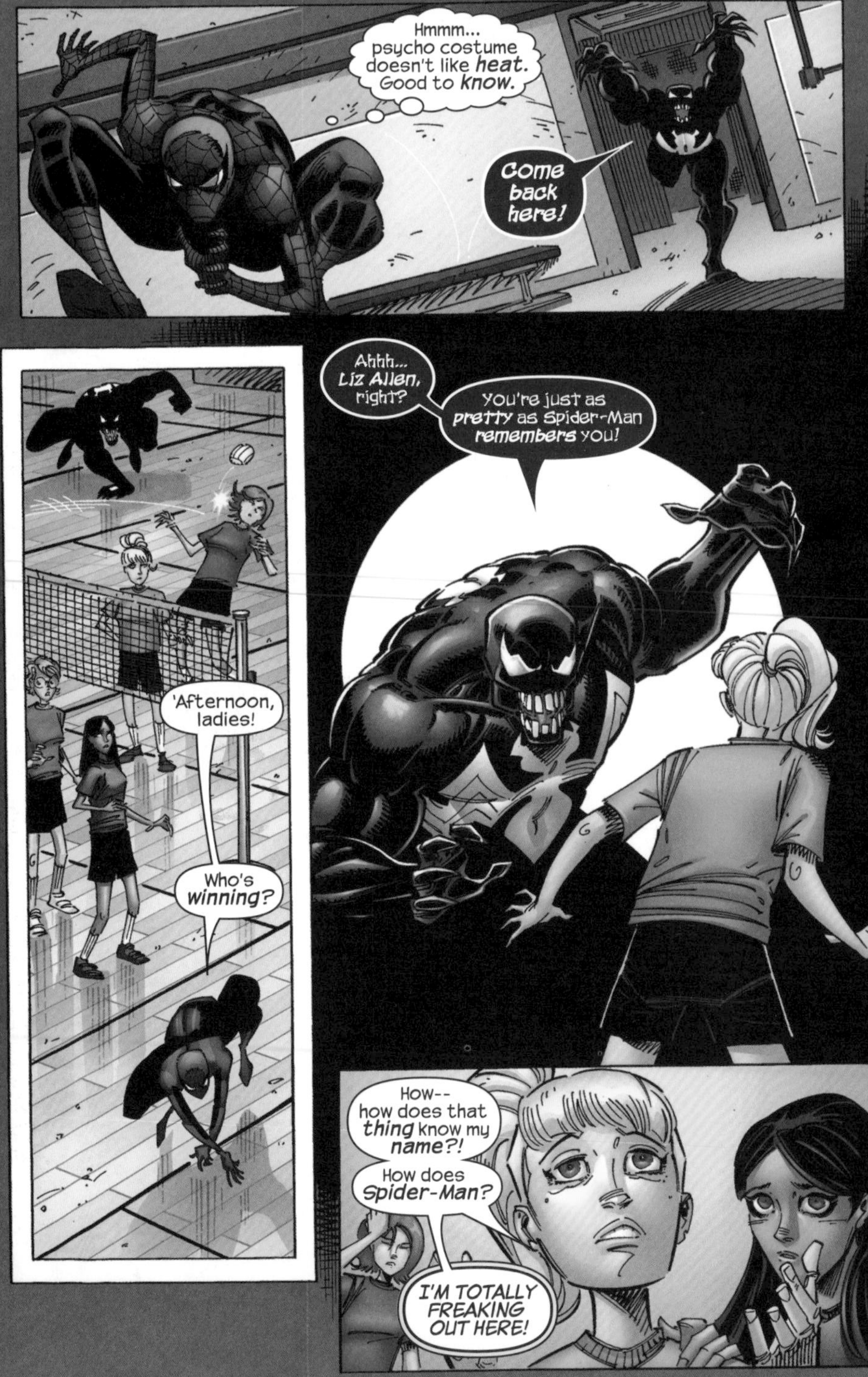
Hmmm... psycho costume doesn't like *heat*. Good to *know*.
Come back here!
'Afternoon, ladies!
Who's *winning*?
Ahhh... Liz Allen, right?
You're just as *pretty* as Spider-Man *remembers* you!
How-- how does that *thing* know my *name*?!
How does *Spider-Man*?
I'M TOTALLY FREAKING OUT HERE!

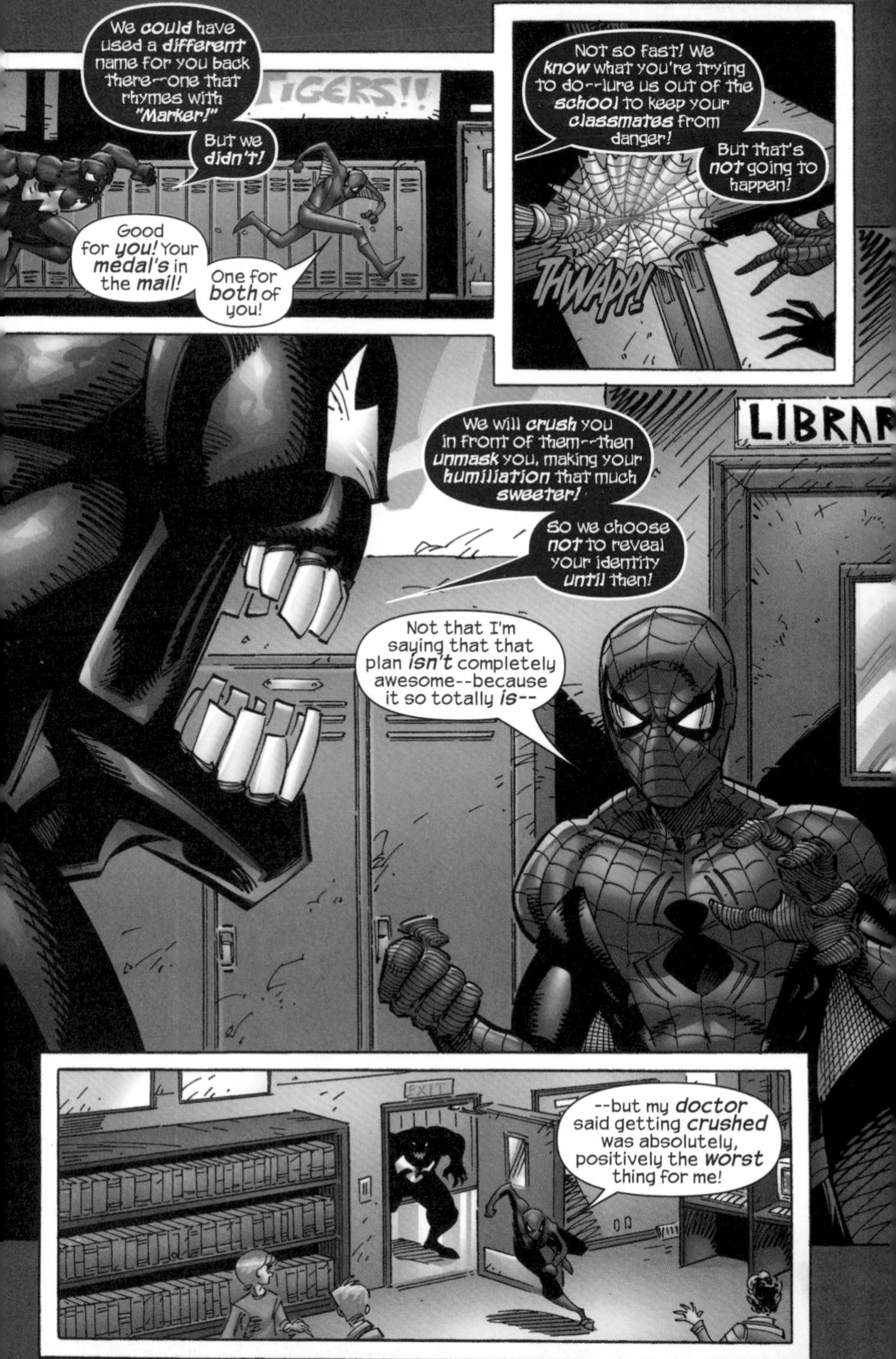
TIGERS!!
We could have used a different name for you back there--one that rhymes with "Marker!"
But we didn't!
Good for you! Your medal's in the mail!
One for both of you!
Not so fast! We know what you're trying to do--lure us out of the school to keep your classmates from danger!
But that's not going to happen!
THWAPP!
LIBRAR
We will crush you in front of them--then unmask you, making your humiliation that much sweeter!
So we choose not to reveal your identity until then!
Not that I'm saying that that plan isn't completely awesome--because it so totally is--
EXIT
--but my doctor said getting crushed was absolutely, positively the worst thing for me!

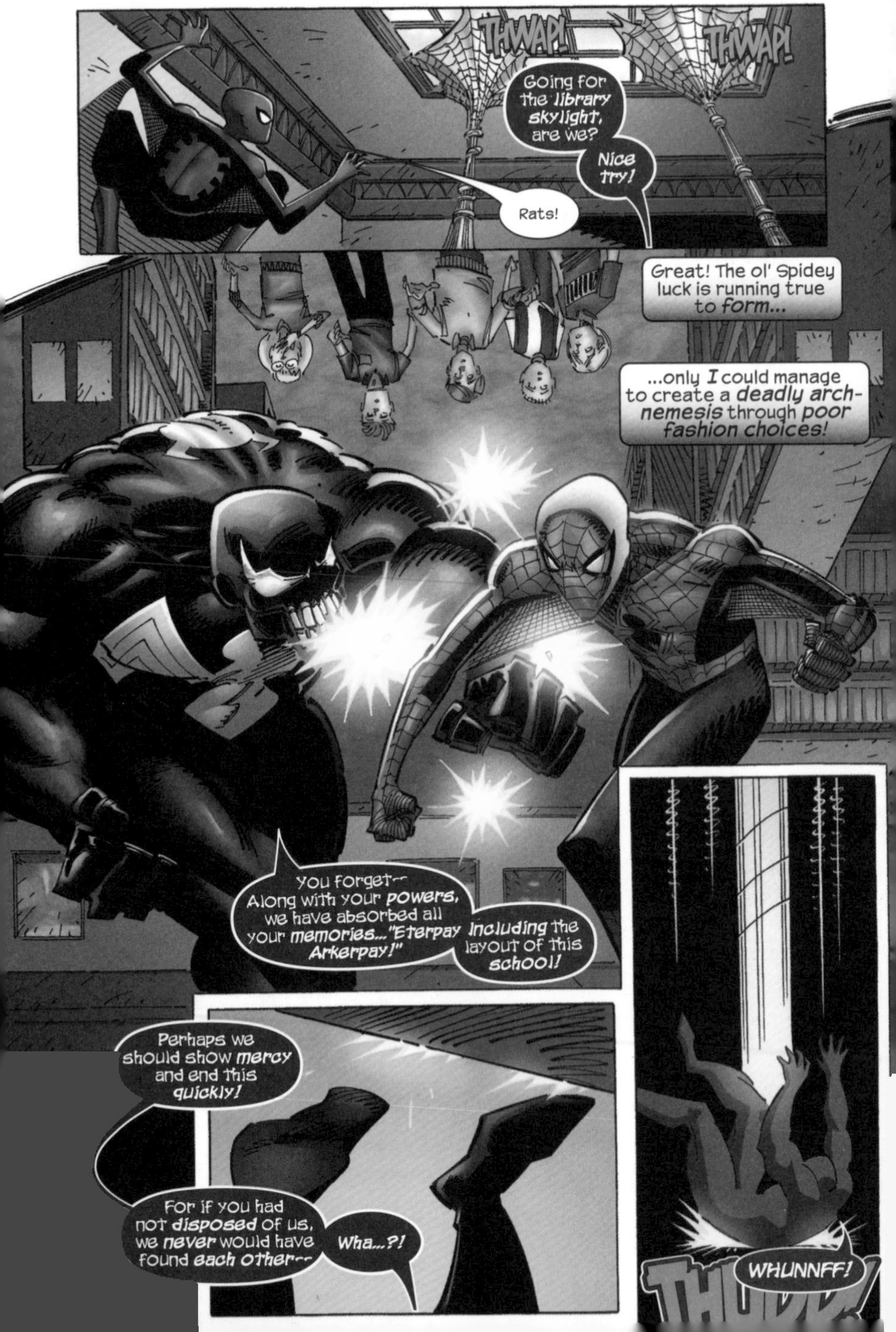
THWAP!
THWAP!
Going for the library skylight, are we?
Nice try!
Rats!
Great! The ol' Spidey luck is running true to form...
...only I could manage to create a deadly arch-nemesis through poor fashion choices!
You forget-- Along with your powers, we have absorbed all your memories..."Eterpay Arkerpay!"
Including the layout of this school!
Perhaps we should show mercy and end this quickly!
For if you had not disposed of us, we never would have found each other--
Wha...?!
WHUNNFF!
THUDD!

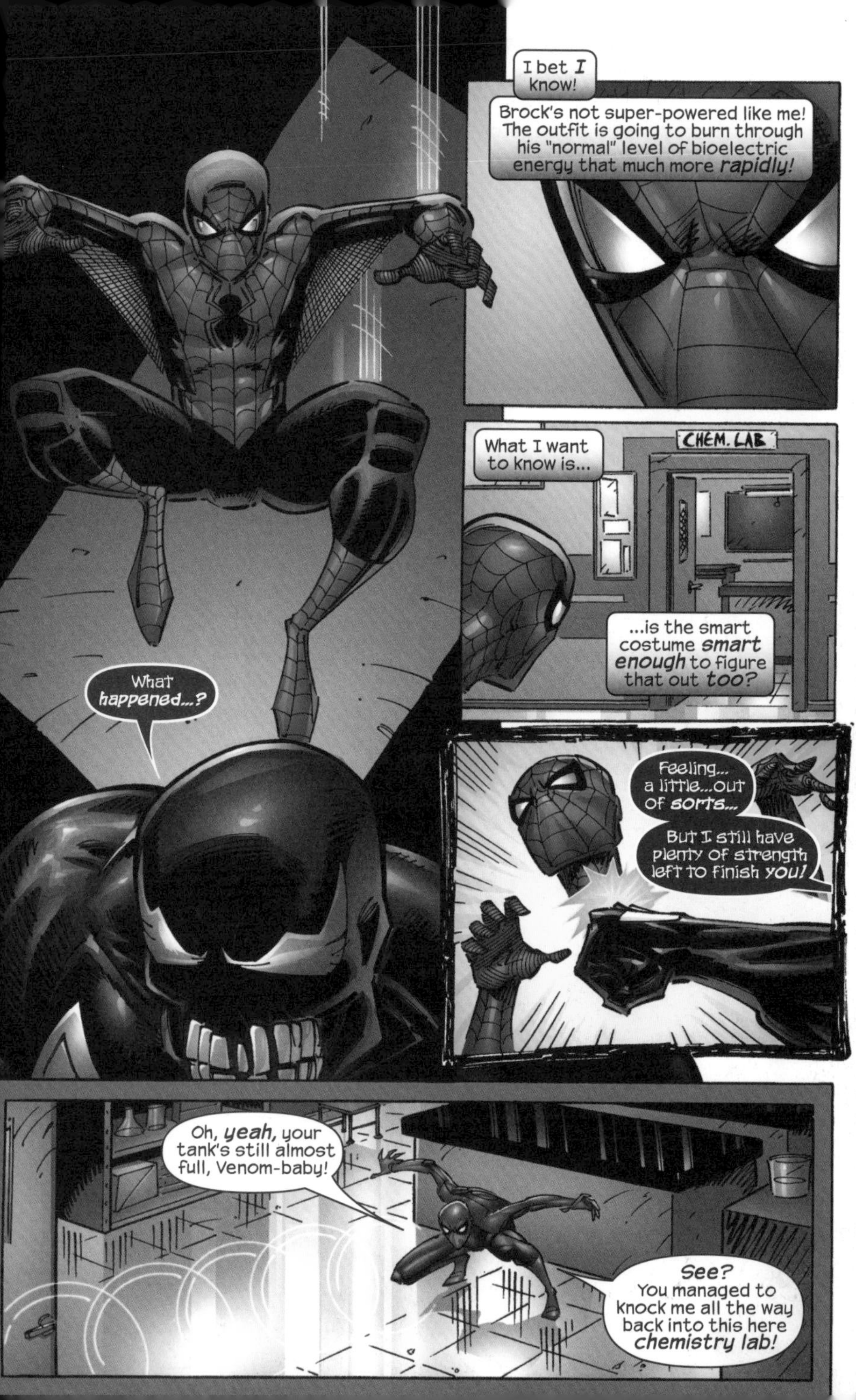
What happened...?
I bet I know!
Brock's not super-powered like me! The outfit is going to burn through his "normal" level of bioelectric energy that much more rapidly!
CHEM. LAB
What I want to know is...
...is the smart costume smart enough to figure that out too?
Feeling... a little...out of sorts...
But I still have plenty of strength left to finish you!
Oh, yeah, your tank's still almost full, Venom-baby!
See? You managed to knock me all the way back into this here chemistry lab!

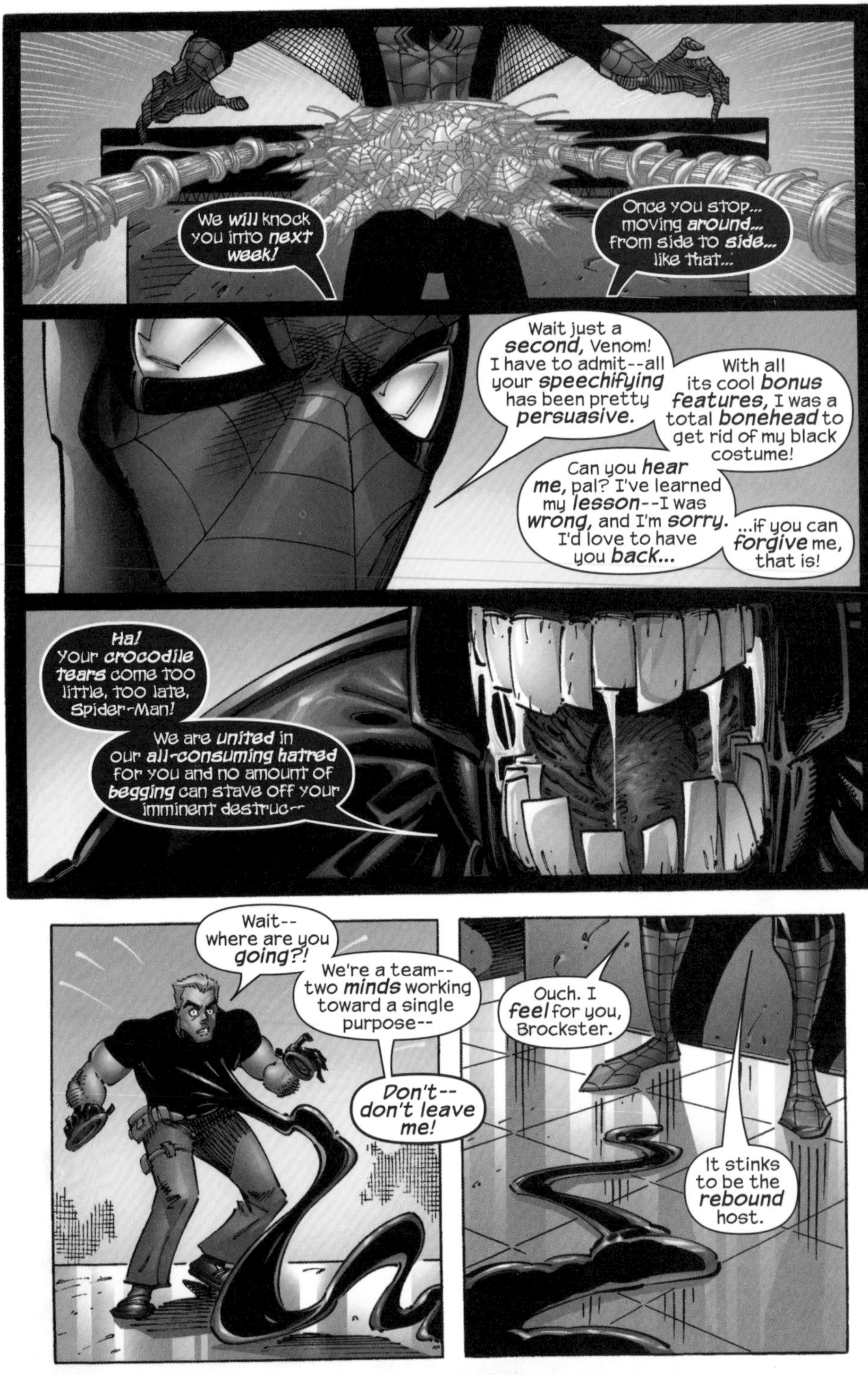

Once you stop... moving around... from side to side... like that...
We will knock you into next week!
Wait just a second, Venom! I have to admit--all your speechifying has been pretty persuasive.
With all its cool bonus features, I was a total bonehead to get rid of my black costume!
Can you hear me, pal? I've learned my lesson--I was wrong, and I'm sorry. I'd love to have you back...
...if you can forgive me, that is!
Ha! Your crocodile tears come too little, too late, Spider-Man!
We are united in our all-consuming hatred for you and no amount of begging can stave off your imminent destruc--
Wait--where are you going?!
We're a team--two minds working toward a single purpose--
Don't--don't leave me!
Ouch. I feel for you, Brockster.
It stinks to be the rebound host.

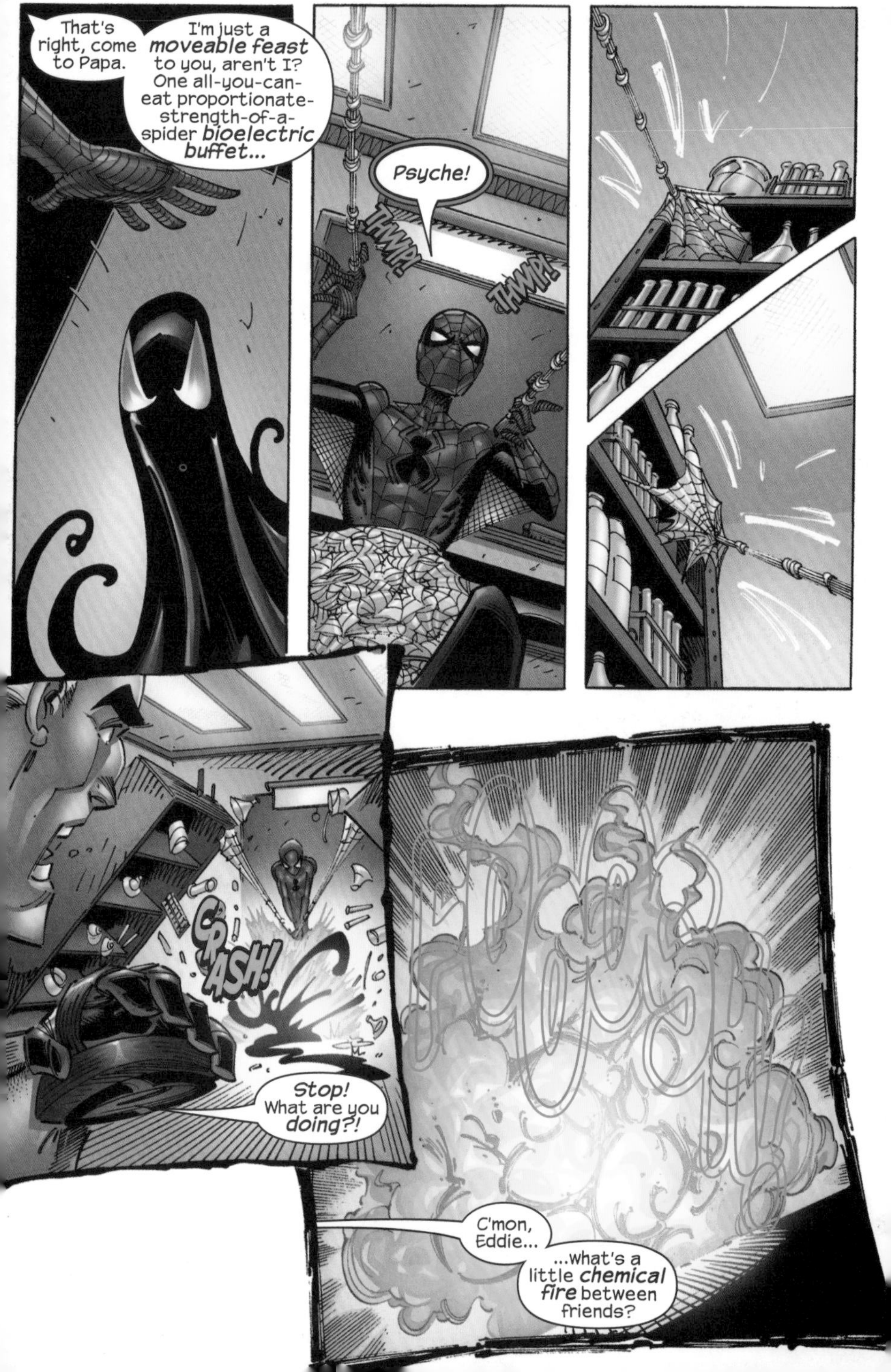
That's right, come to Papa.
I'm just a *moveable feast* to you, aren't I? One all-you-can-eat proportionate-strength-of-a-spider *bioelectric buffet...*
Psyche!
THWIP!
THWIP!
CRASH!
Stop! What are you *doing?!*
C'mon, Eddie...
...what's a little *chemical fire* between friends?

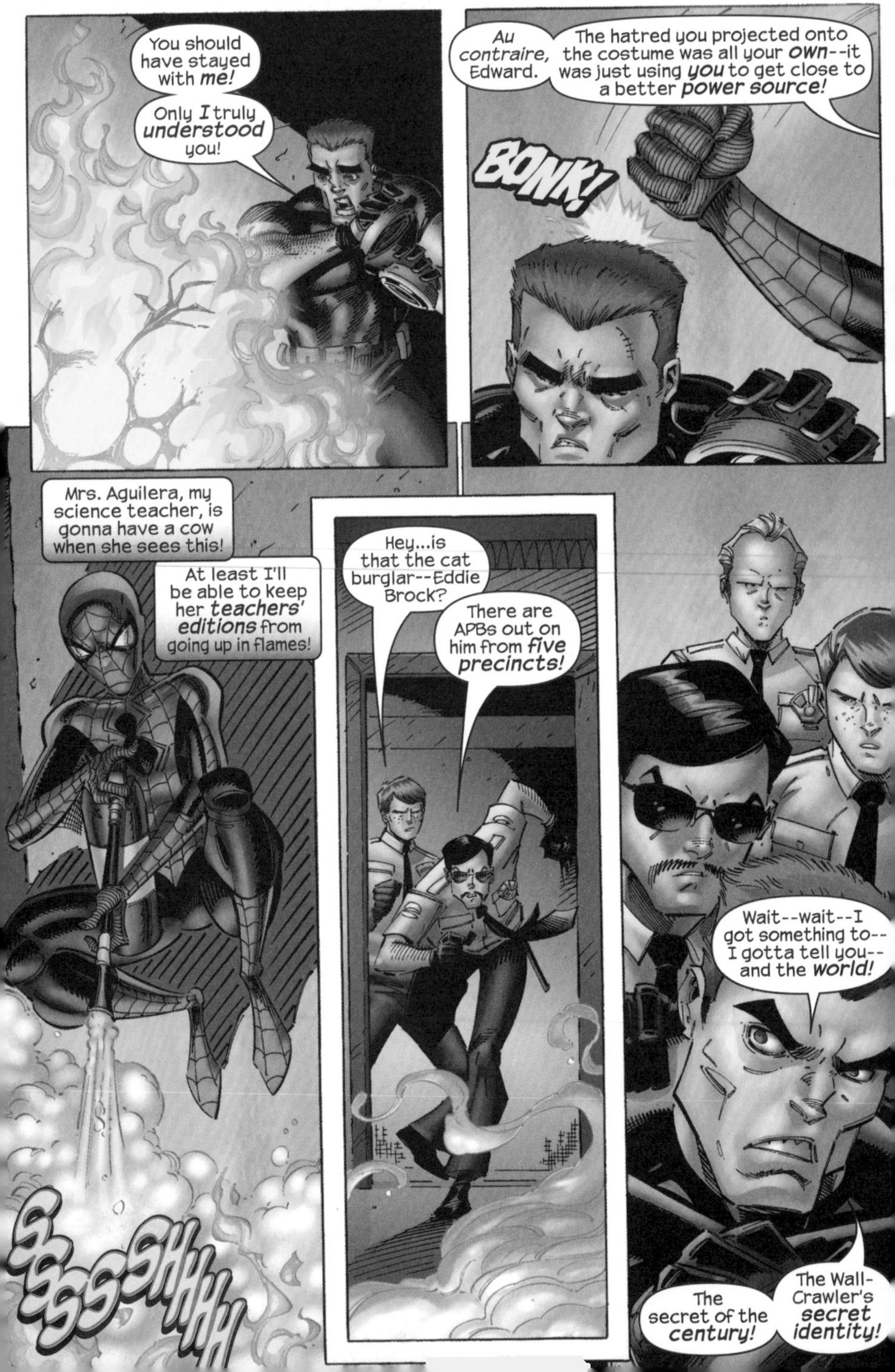
You should have stayed with *me!*
Only *I* truly *understood* you!
Au contraire, Edward.
The hatred you projected onto the costume was all your *own*--it was just using *you* to get close to a better *power source!*
BONK!
Mrs. Aguilera, my science teacher, is gonna have a cow when she sees this!
At least I'll be able to keep her *teachers' editions* from going up in flames!
SSSSSHHHHH
Hey...is that the cat burglar--Eddie Brock?
There are APBs out on him from *five precincts!*
Wait--wait--I got something to--I gotta tell you--and the *world!*
The Wall-Crawler's *secret identity!*
The secret of the *century!*

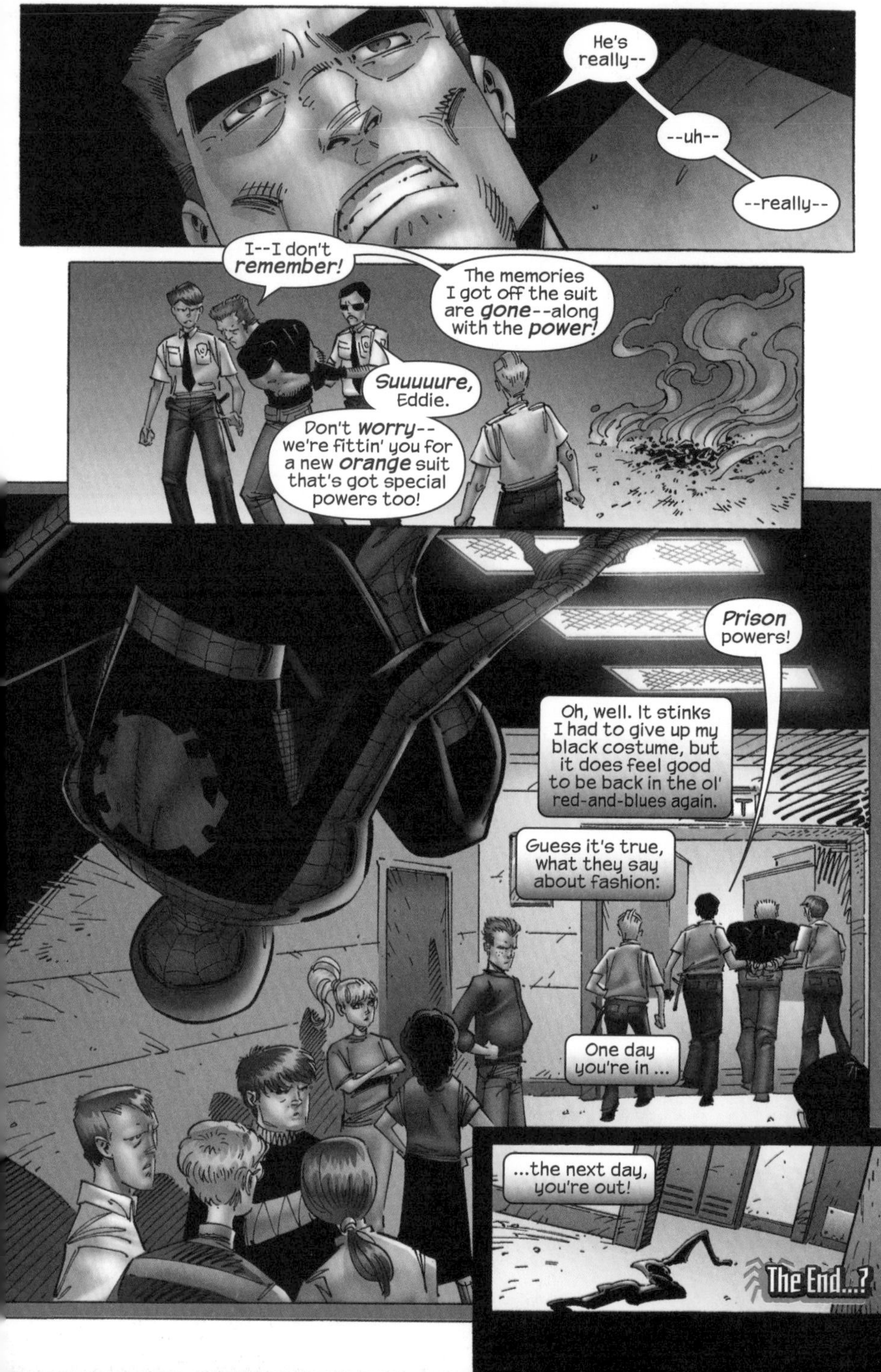
He's really--
--uh--
--really--
I--I don't *remember!*
The memories I got off the suit are *gone*--along with the *power!*
Suuuuure, Eddie.
Don't *worry*-- we're fittin' you for a new *orange* suit that's got special powers too!
Prison powers!
Oh, well. It stinks I had to give up my black costume, but it does feel good to be back in the ol' red-and-blues again.
Guess it's true, what they say about fashion:
One day you're in ...
...the next day, you're out!
The End...?

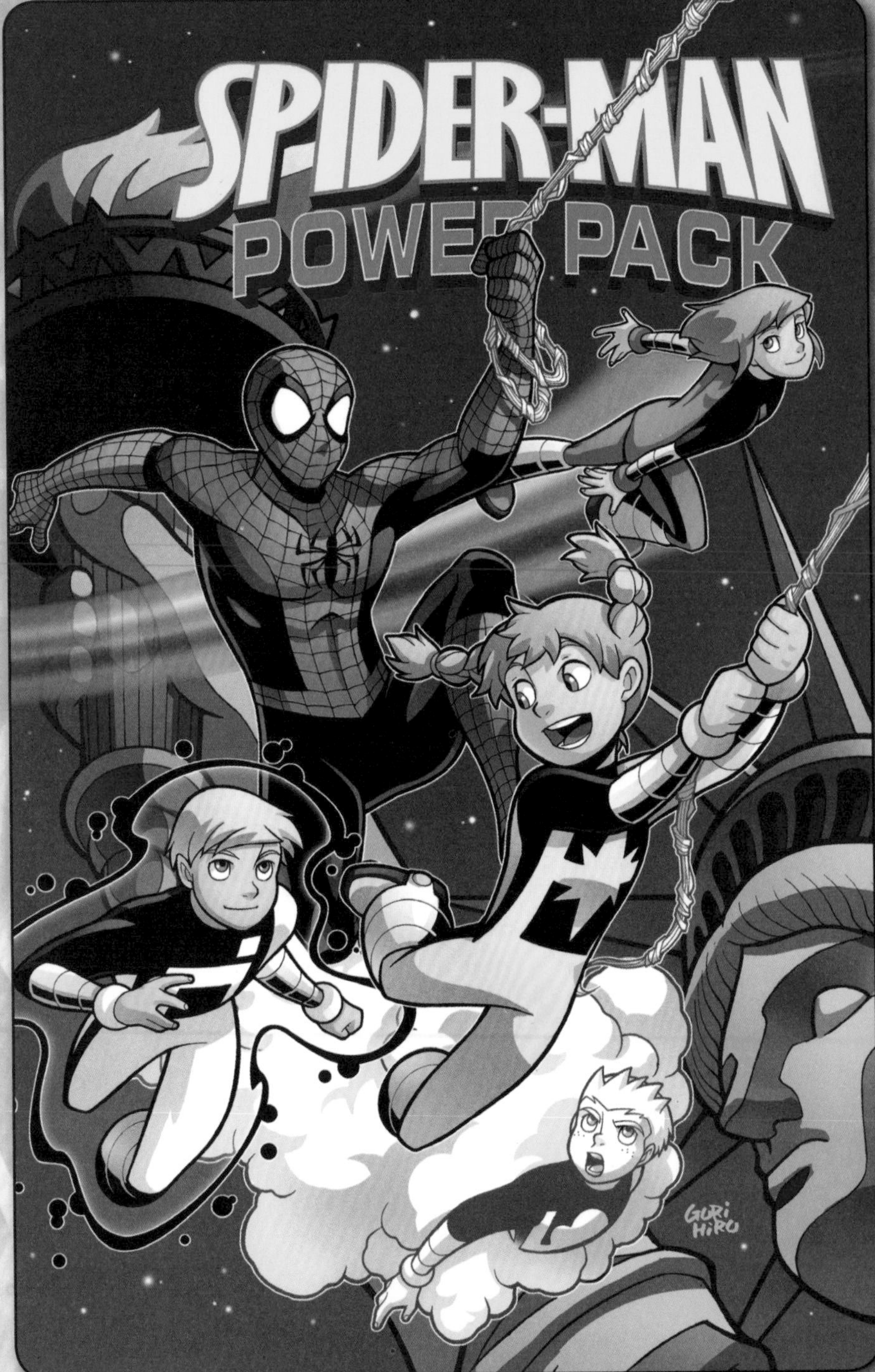
SPIDER-MAN
POWER PACK
GURI HIRU

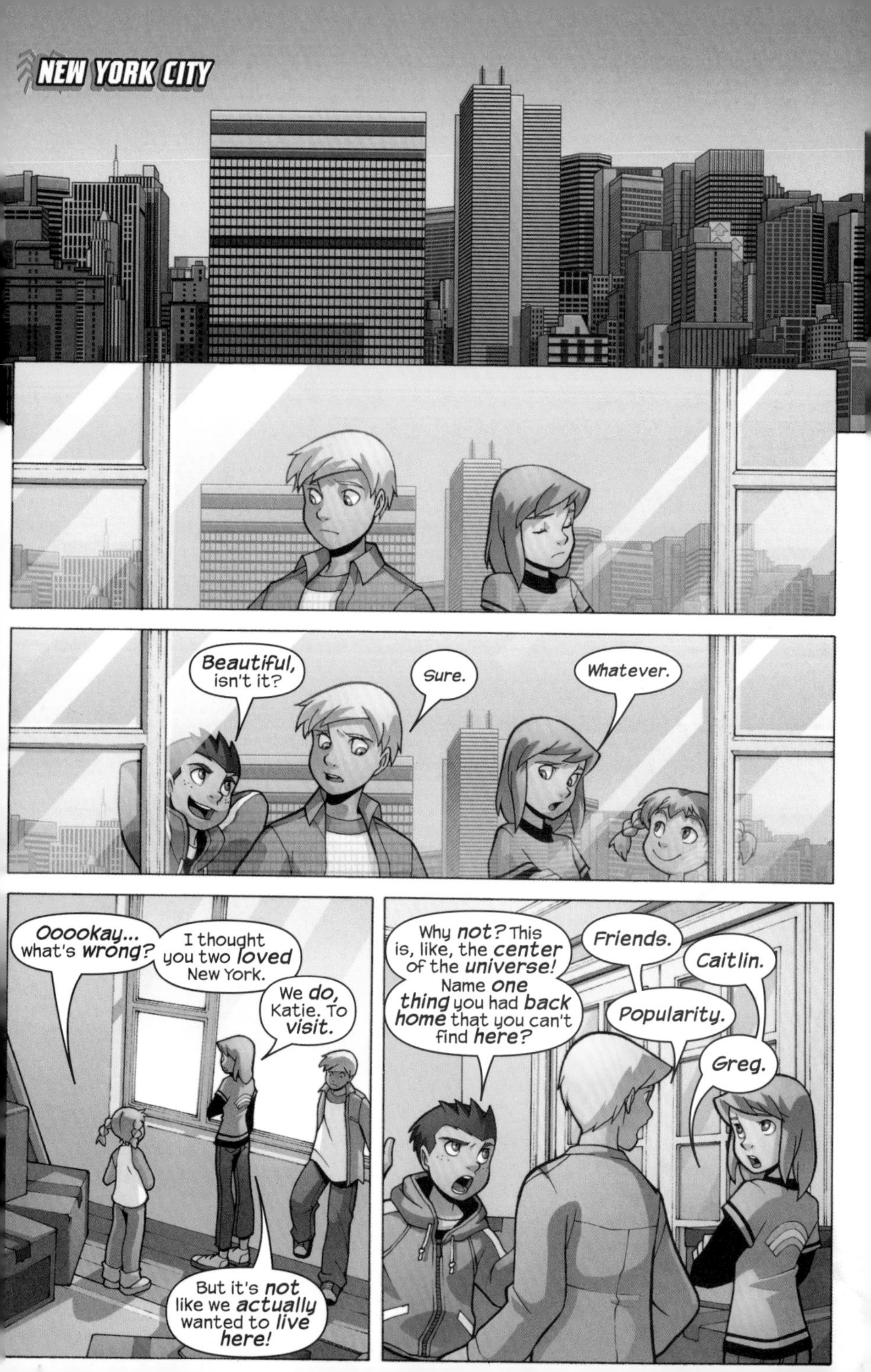
NEW YORK CITY
Beautiful, isn't it?
Sure.
Whatever.
Ooookay... what's wrong?
I thought you two loved New York.
We do, Katie. To visit.
But it's not like we actually wanted to live here!
Why not? This is, like, the center of the universe! Name one thing you had back home that you can't find here?
Friends.
Popularity.
Caitlin.
Greg.

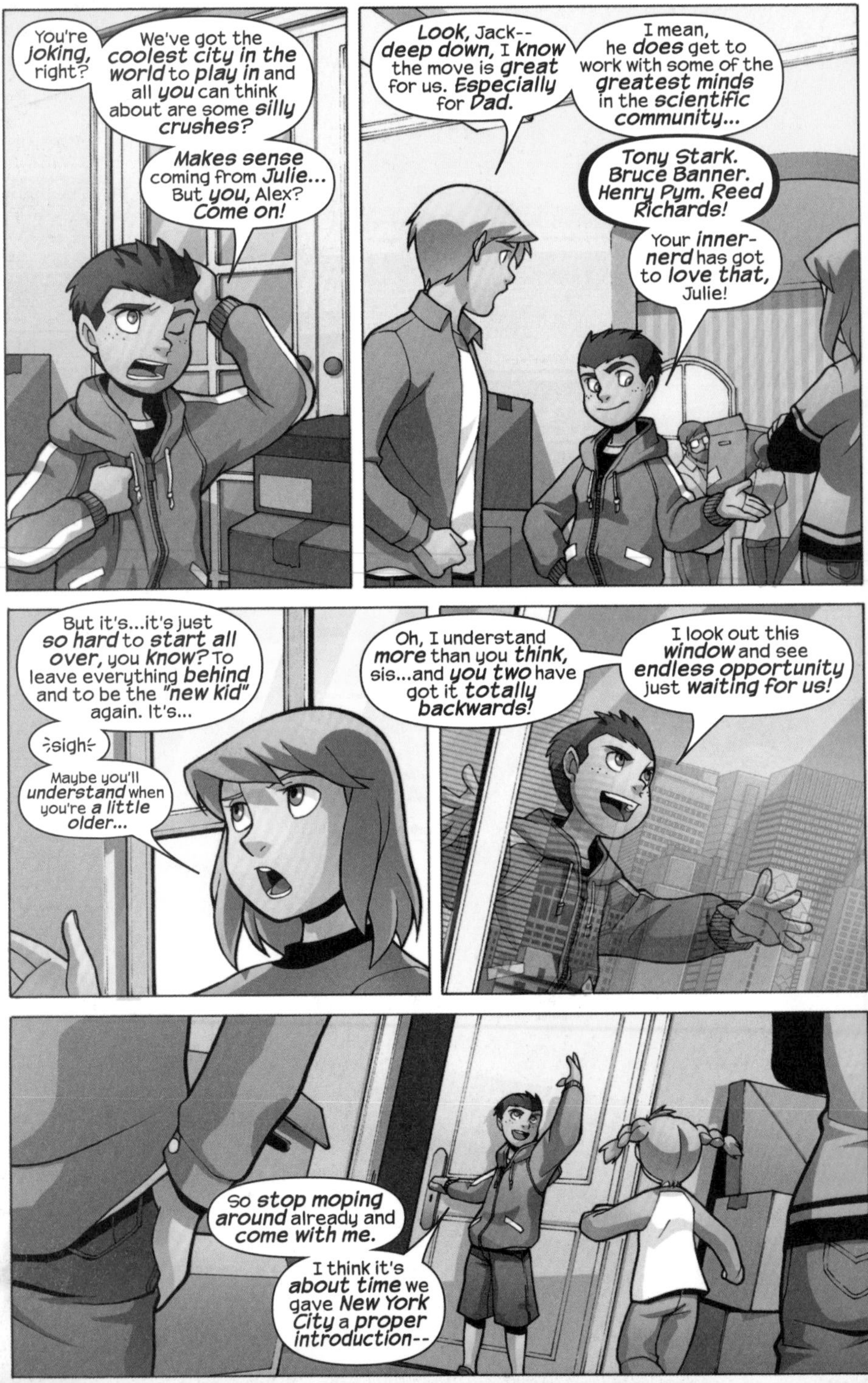
You're joking, right?
We've got the coolest city in the world to play in and all you can think about are some silly crushes?
Makes sense coming from Julie... But you, Alex? Come on!
Look, Jack-- deep down, I know the move is great for us. Especially for Dad.
I mean, he does get to work with some of the greatest minds in the scientific community...
Tony Stark. Bruce Banner. Henry Pym. Reed Richards!
Your inner-nerd has got to love that, Julie!
But it's...it's just so hard to start all over, you know? To leave everything behind and to be the "new kid" again. It's...
sigh
Maybe you'll understand when you're a little older...
Oh, I understand more than you think, sis...and you two have got it totally backwards!
I look out this window and see endless opportunity just waiting for us!
So stop moping around already and come with me.
I think it's about time we gave New York City a proper introduction--

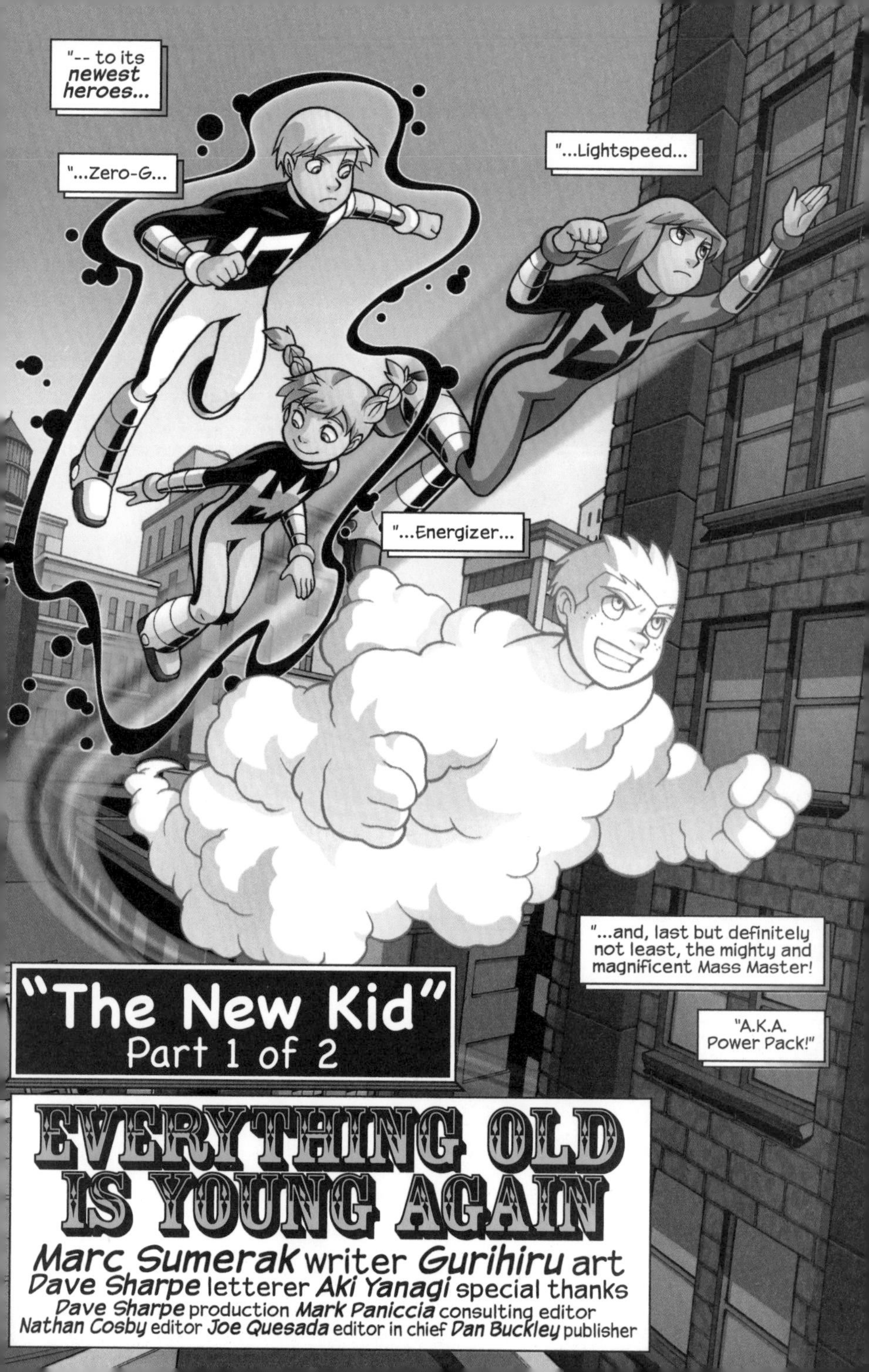
"-- to its newest heroes...
"...Zero-G...
"...Lightspeed...
"...Energizer...
"...and, last but definitely not least, the mighty and magnificent Mass Master!
"A.K.A. Power Pack!"
"The New Kid" Part 1 of 2
EVERYTHING OLD IS YOUNG AGAIN
Marc Sumerak writer Gurihiru art
Dave Sharpe letterer Aki Yanagi special thanks
Dave Sharpe production Mark Paniccia consulting editor
Nathan Cosby editor Joe Quesada editor in chief Dan Buckley publisher

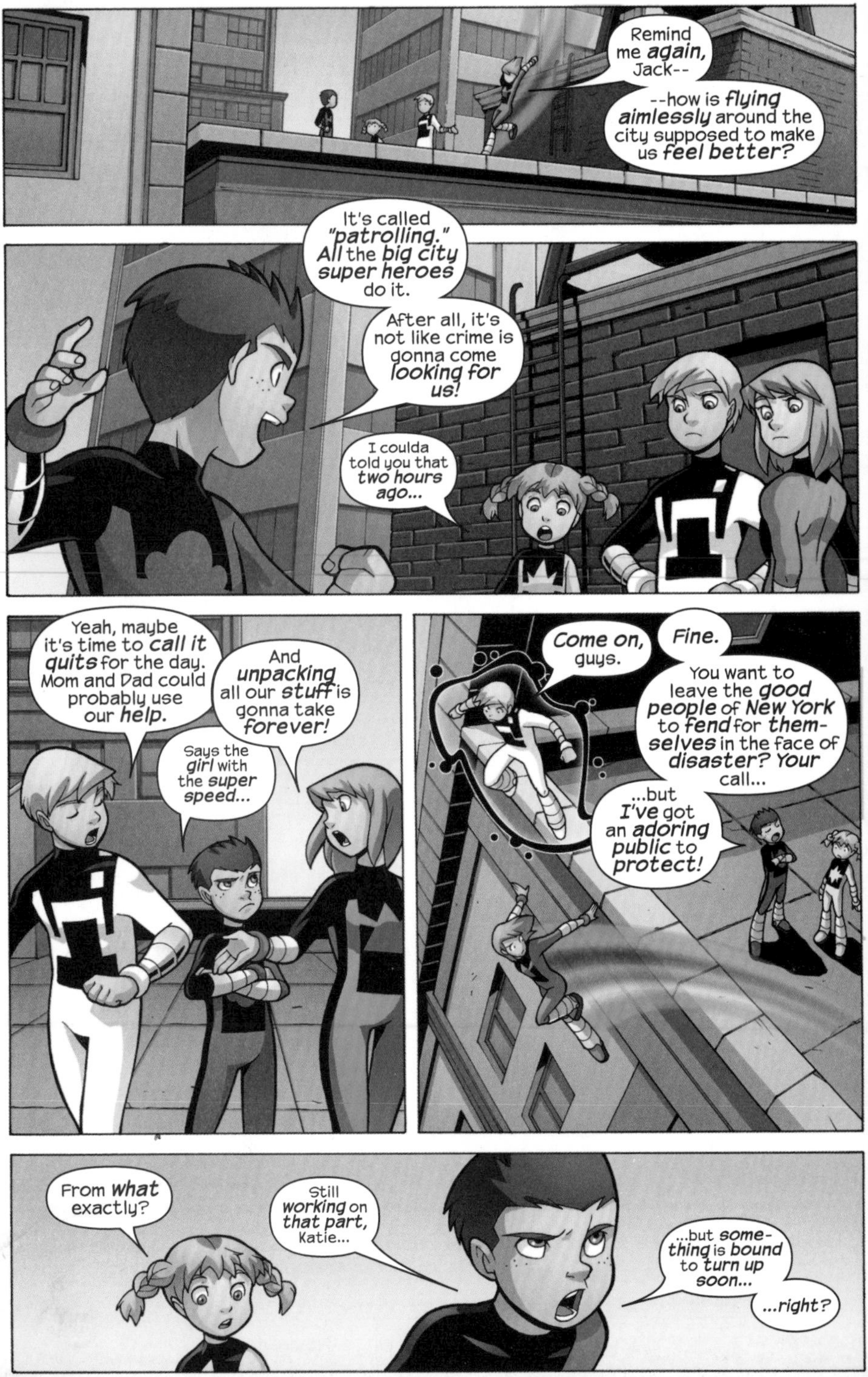
Remind me again, Jack--
--how is flying aimlessly around the city supposed to make us feel better?
It's called "patrolling." All the big city super heroes do it.
After all, it's not like crime is gonna come looking for us!
I coulda told you that two hours ago...
Yeah, maybe it's time to call it quits for the day. Mom and Dad could probably use our help.
And unpacking all our stuff is gonna take forever!
Says the girl with the super speed...
Come on, guys.
Fine.
You want to leave the good people of New York to fend for themselves in the face of disaster? Your call...
...but I've got an adoring public to protect!
From what exactly?
Still working on that part, Katie...
...but something is bound to turn up soon...
...right?

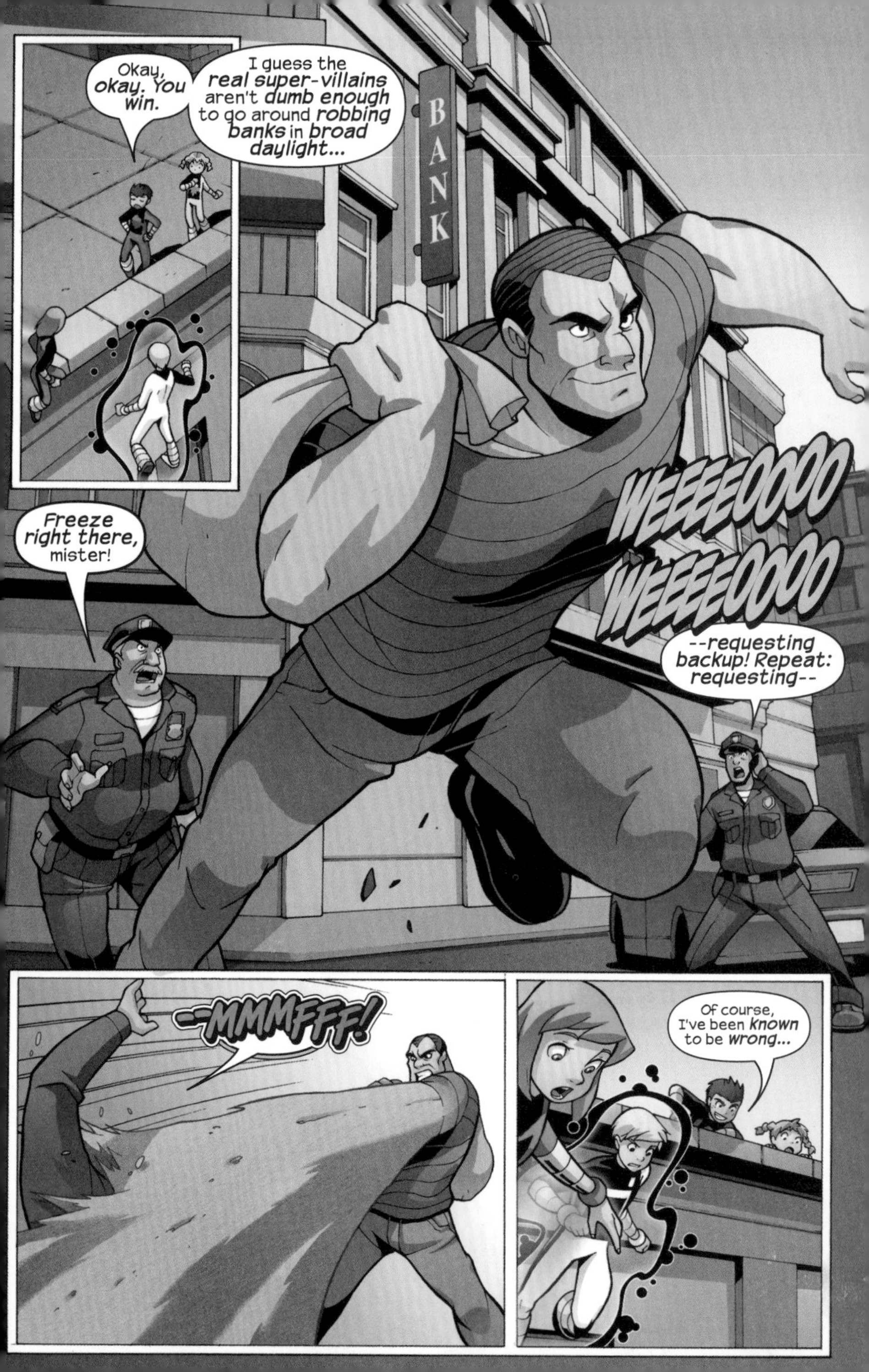
Okay, okay. You win.
I guess the real super-villains aren't dumb enough to go around robbing banks in broad daylight...
BANK
Freeze right there, mister!
WEEEEOOOO WEEEEOOOO
--requesting backup! Repeat: requesting--
--MMMFFF!
Of course, I've been known to be wrong...

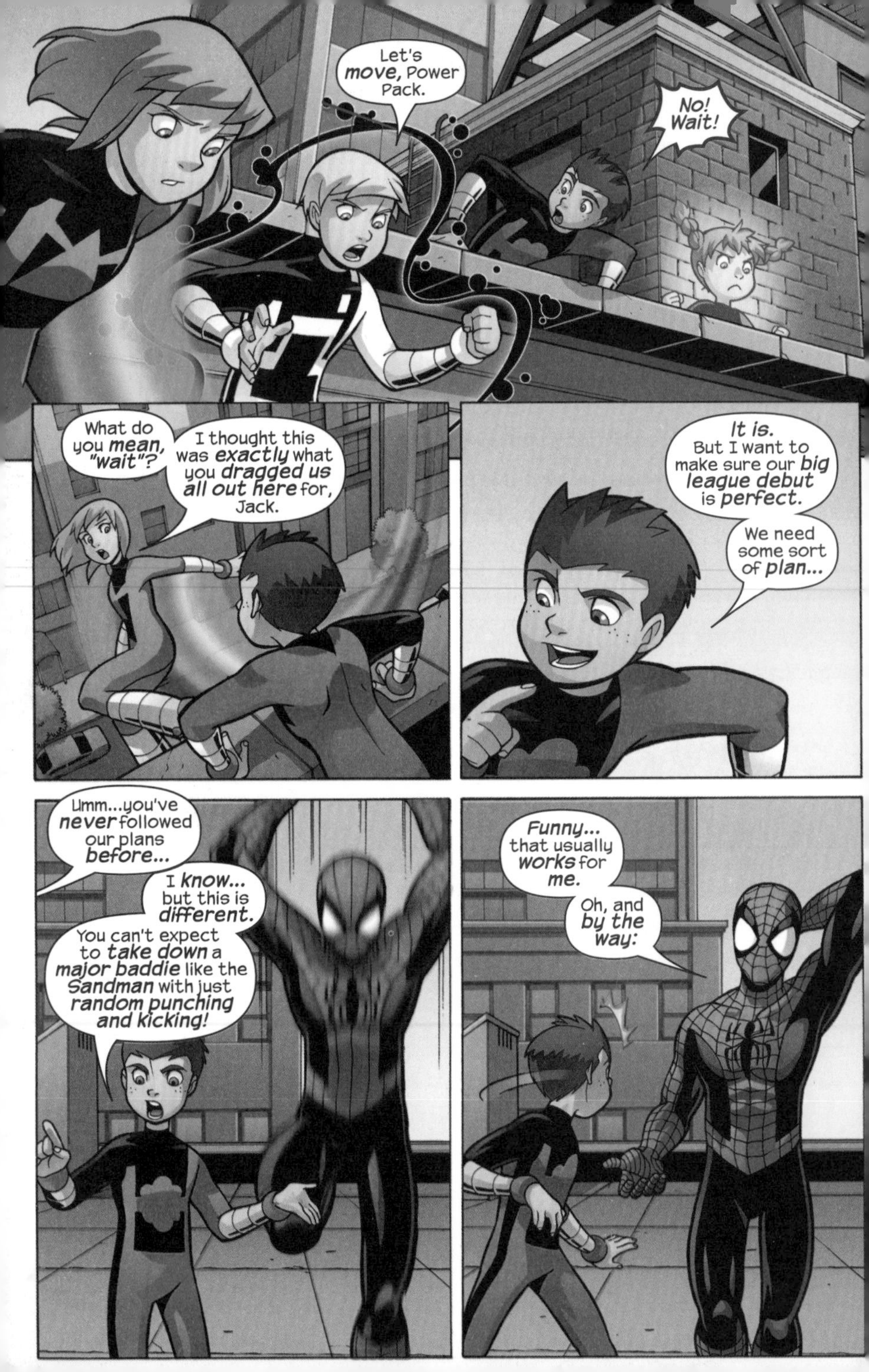
Let's move, Power Pack.
No! Wait!
What do you mean, "wait"?
I thought this was exactly what you dragged us all out here for, Jack.
It is. But I want to make sure our big league debut is perfect.
We need some sort of plan...
Umm...you've never followed our plans before...
I know... but this is different.
You can't expect to take down a major baddie like the Sandman with just random punching and kicking!
Funny... that usually works for me.
Oh, and by the way:

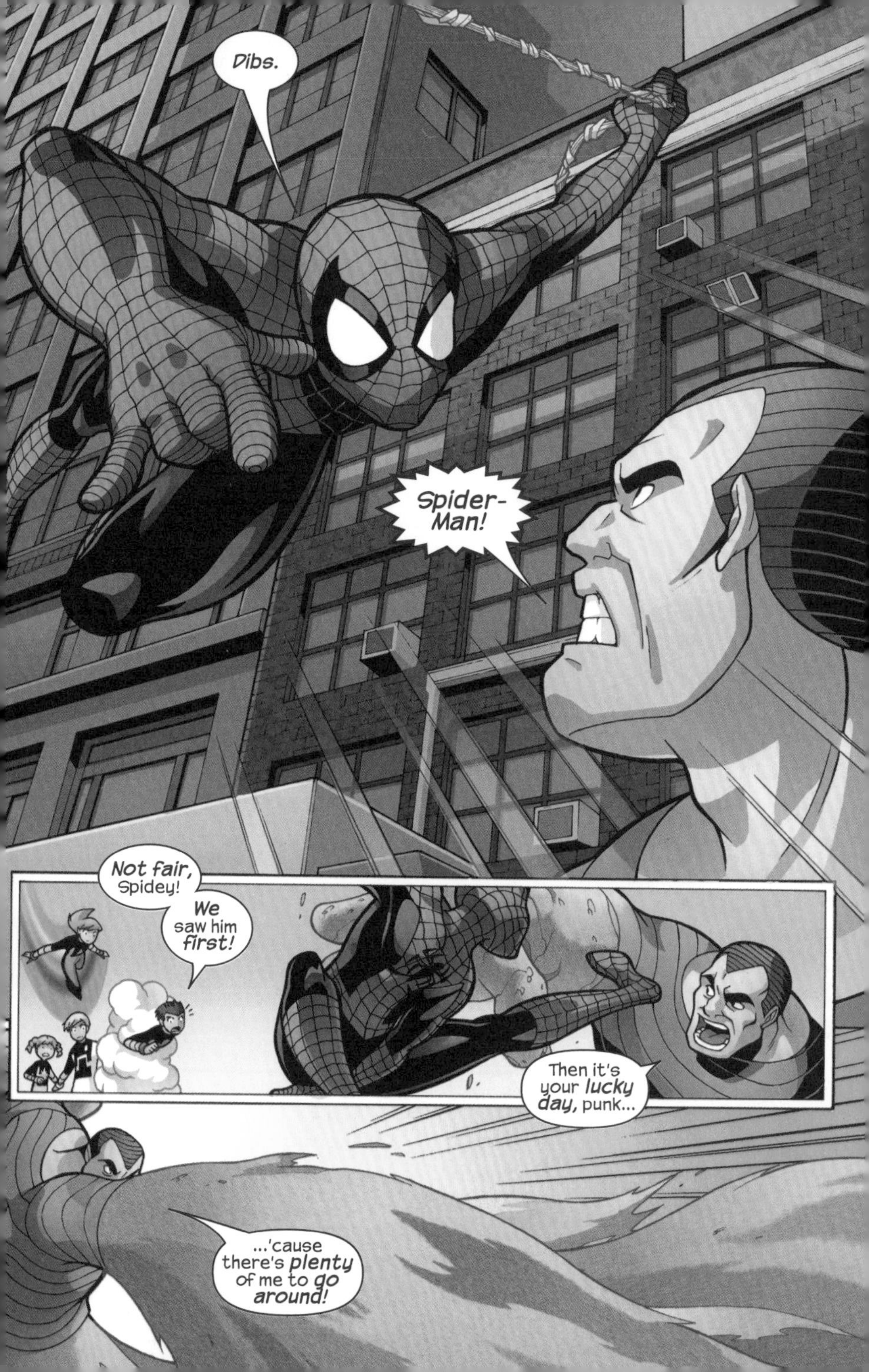
Dibs.
Spider-Man!
Not fair, Spidey!
We saw him first!
Then it's your lucky day, punk...
...'cause there's plenty of me to go around!

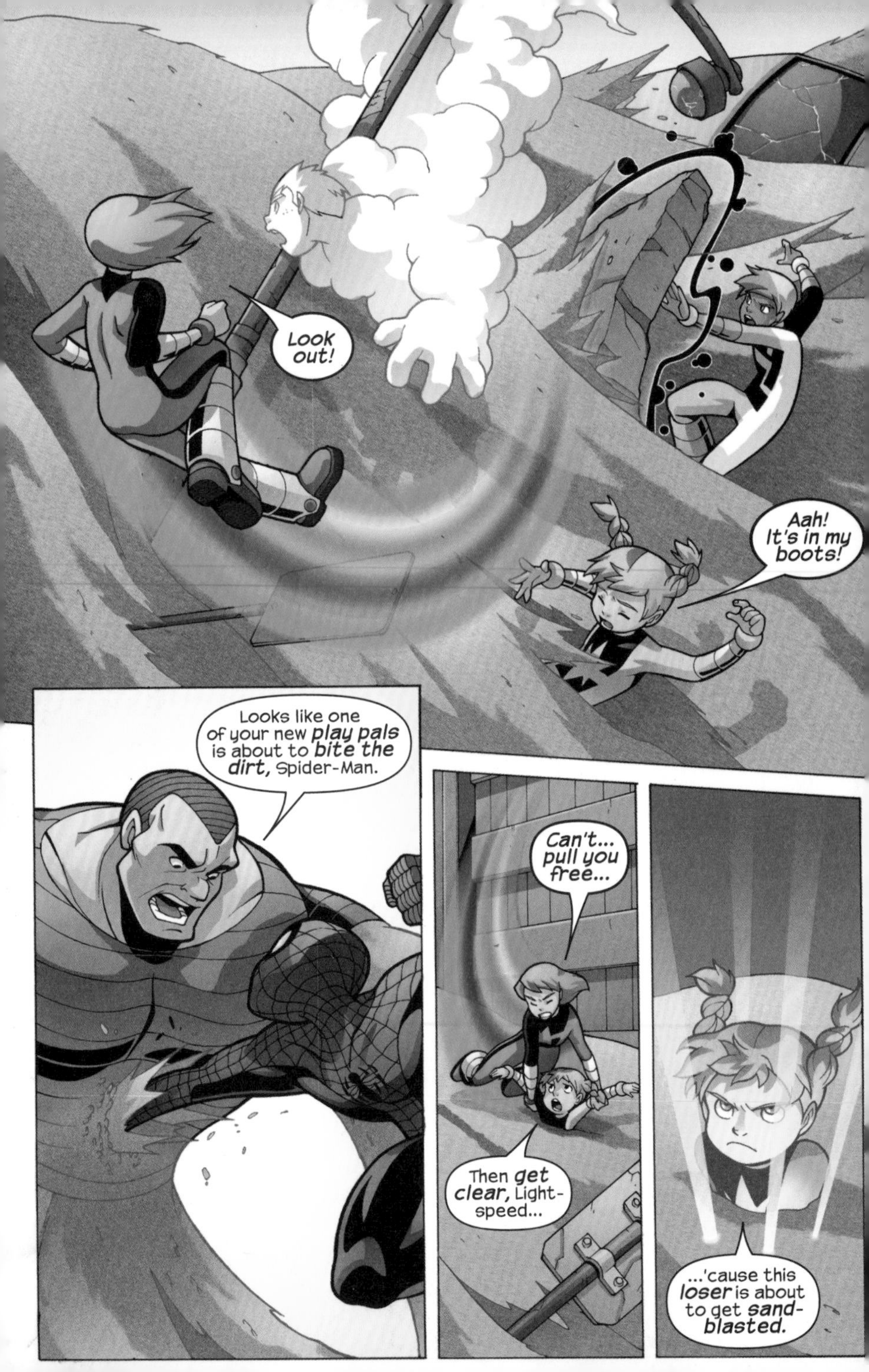
Look out!
Aah! It's in my boots!
Looks like one of your new *play pals* is about to *bite the dirt,* Spider-Man.
Can't... pull you free...
Then *get clear,* Light-speed...
...'cause this *loser* is about to get *sand-blasted.*

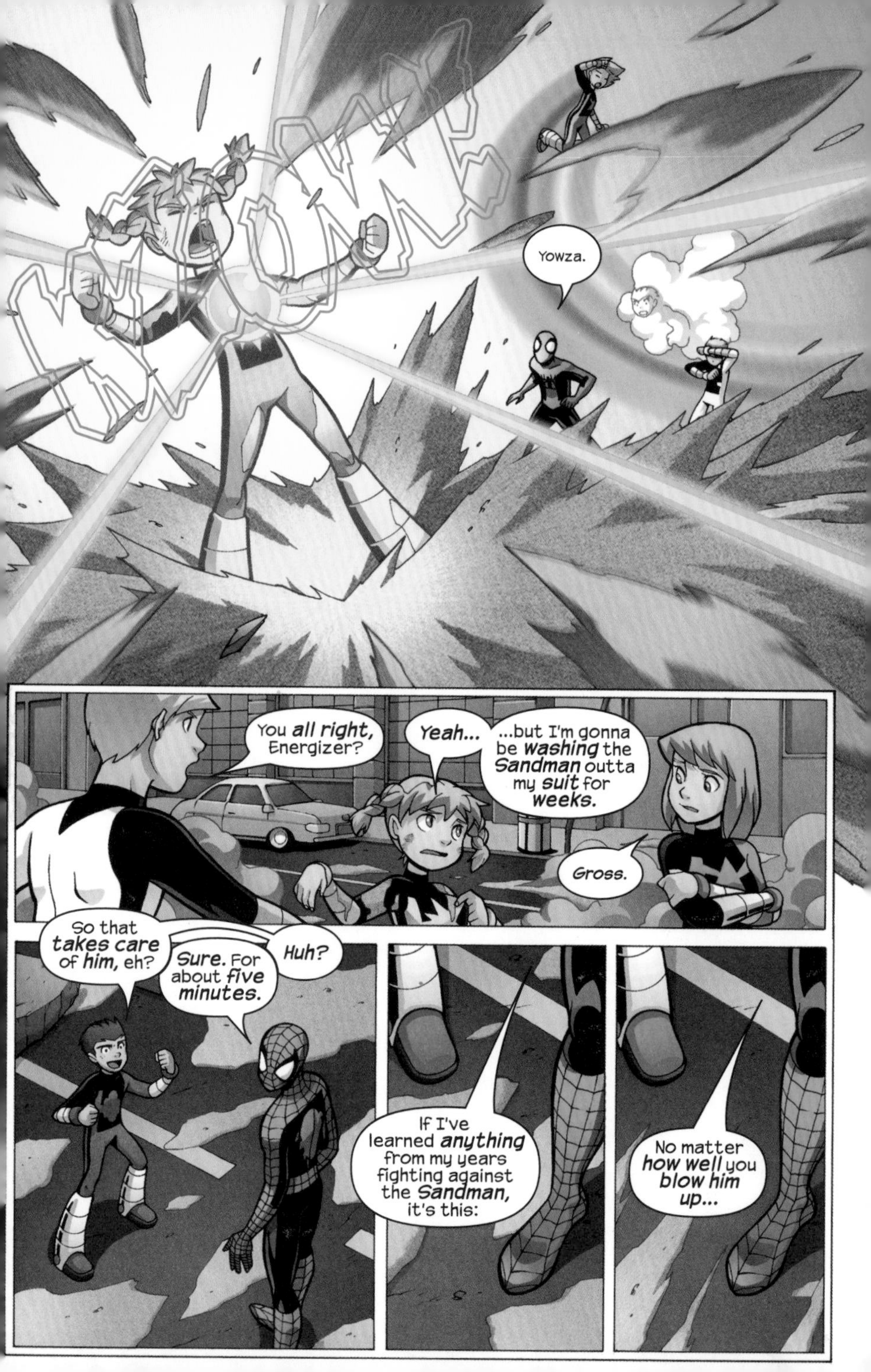
Yowza.
You all right, Energizer?
Yeah...
...but I'm gonna be washing the Sandman outta my suit for weeks.
Gross.
So that takes care of him, eh?
Sure. For about five minutes.
Huh?
If I've learned anything from my years fighting against the Sandman, it's this:
No matter how well you blow him up...

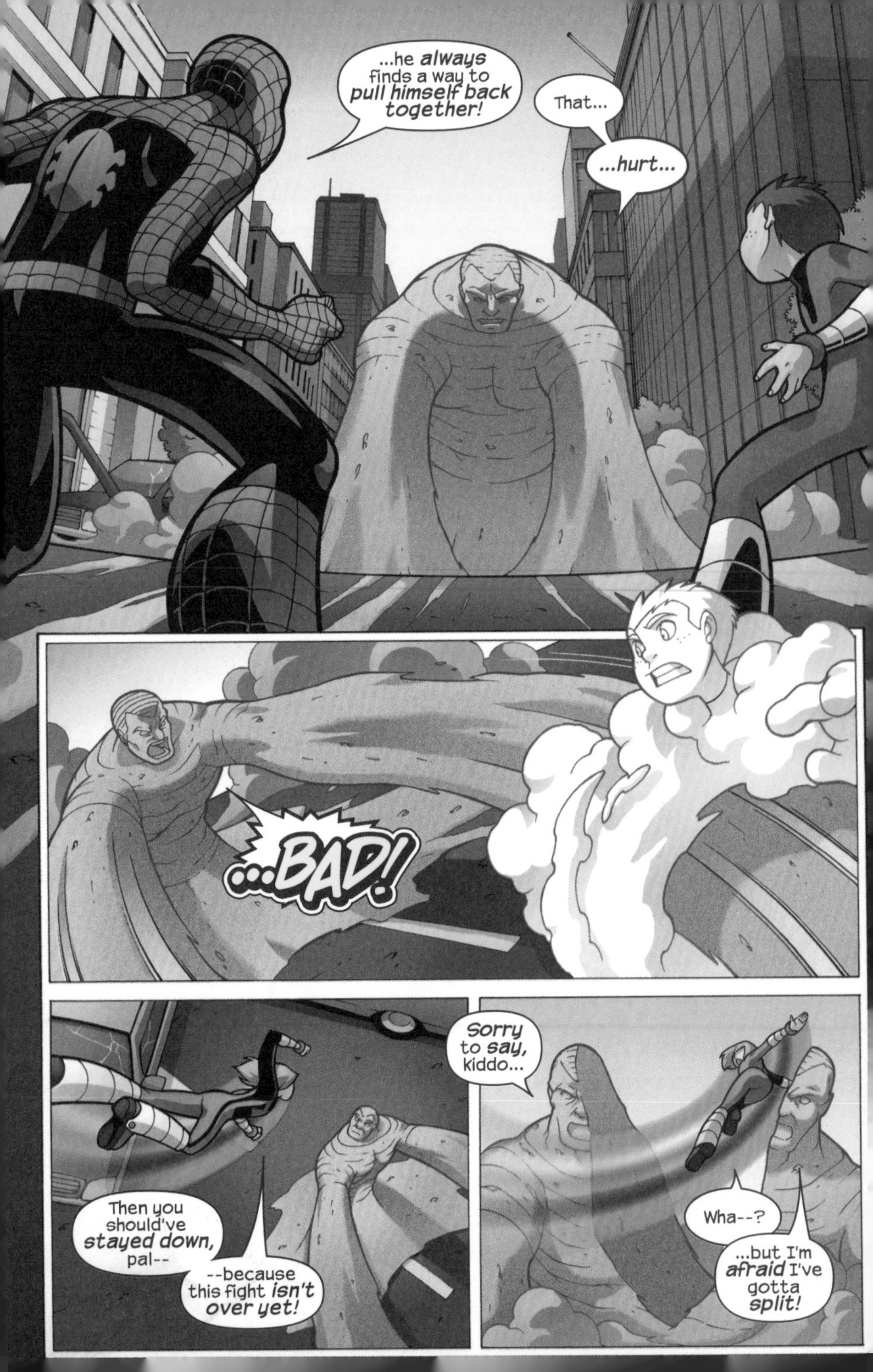
...he *always* finds a way to *pull himself back together!*
That...
...*hurt*...
...BAD!
Then you should've *stayed down*, pal--
--because this fight *isn't over yet!*
Sorry to *say*, kiddo...
Wha--?
...but I'm *afraid* I've gotta *split!*

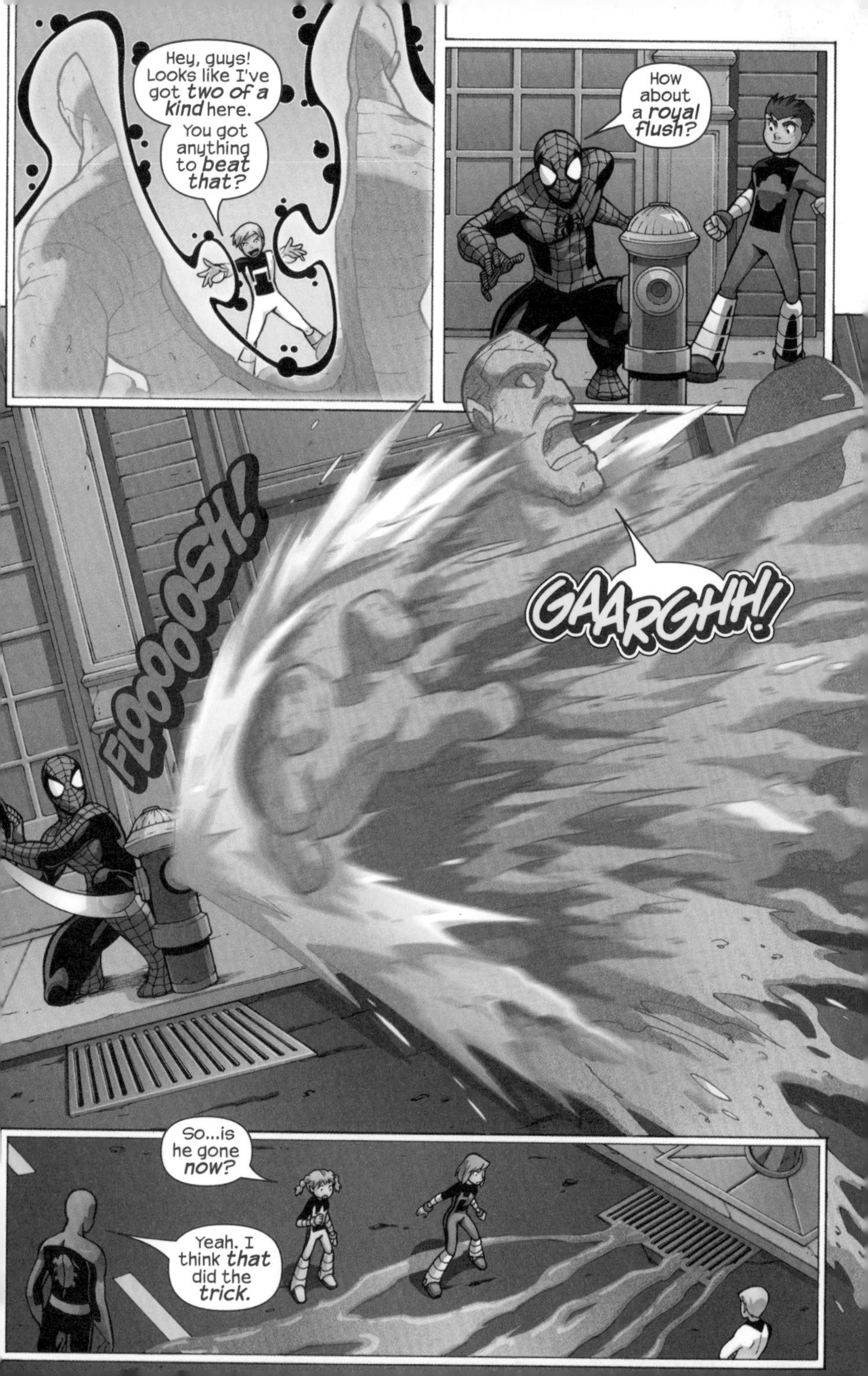

Hey, guys! Looks like I've got two of a kind here. You got anything to beat that?
How about a royal flush?
FLOOOOSH!
GAARGHH!
So...is he gone now?
Yeah. I think that did the trick.

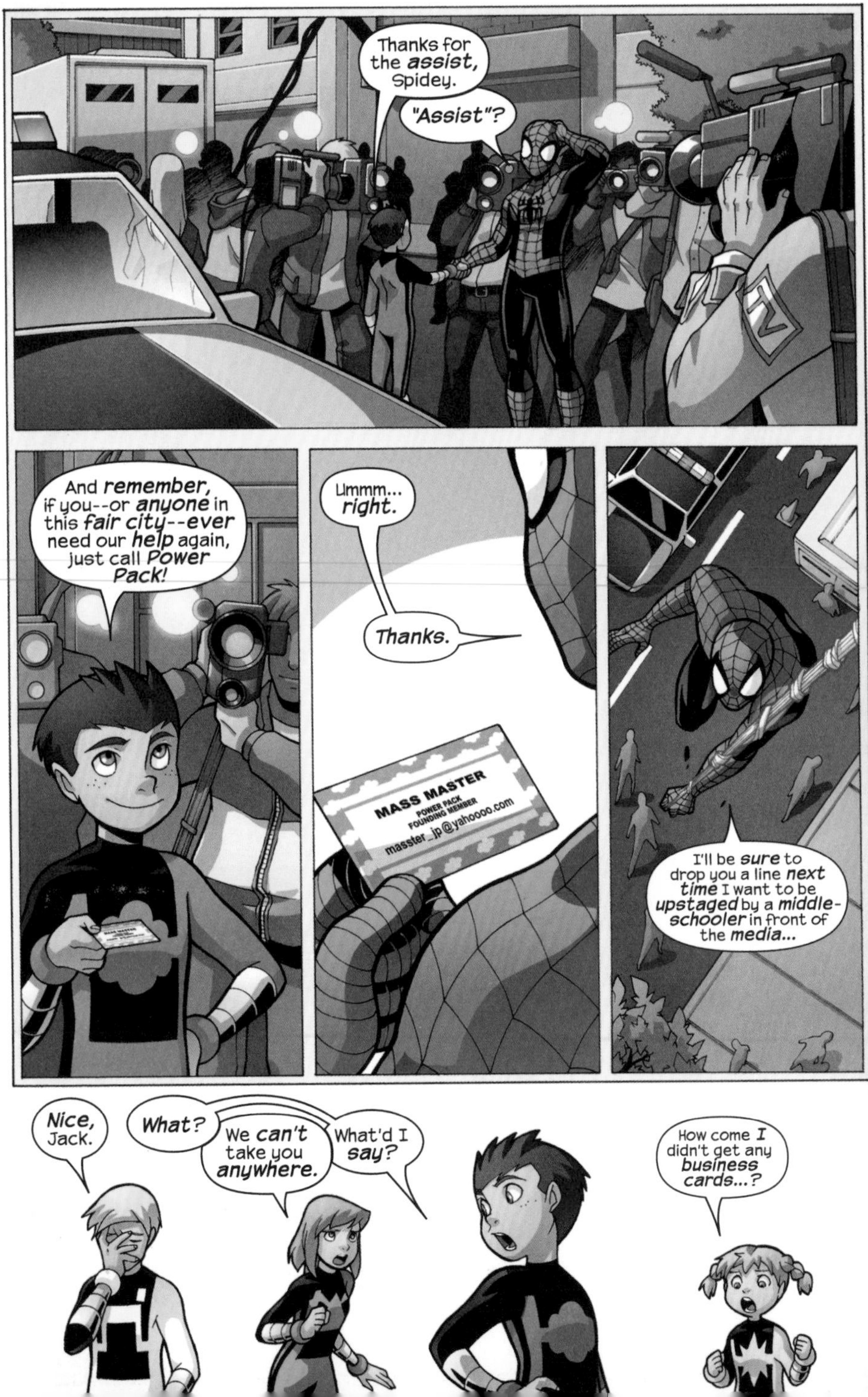
Thanks for the assist, Spidey.
"Assist"?
And remember, if you--or anyone in this fair city--ever need our help again, just call Power Pack!
Ummm... right.
Thanks.
MASS MASTER
POWER PACK
FOUNDING MEMBER
masster_jp@yahoooo.com
I'll be sure to drop you a line next time I want to be upstaged by a middle-schooler in front of the media...
Nice, Jack.
What?
We can't take you anywhere.
What'd I say?
How come I didn't get any business cards...?

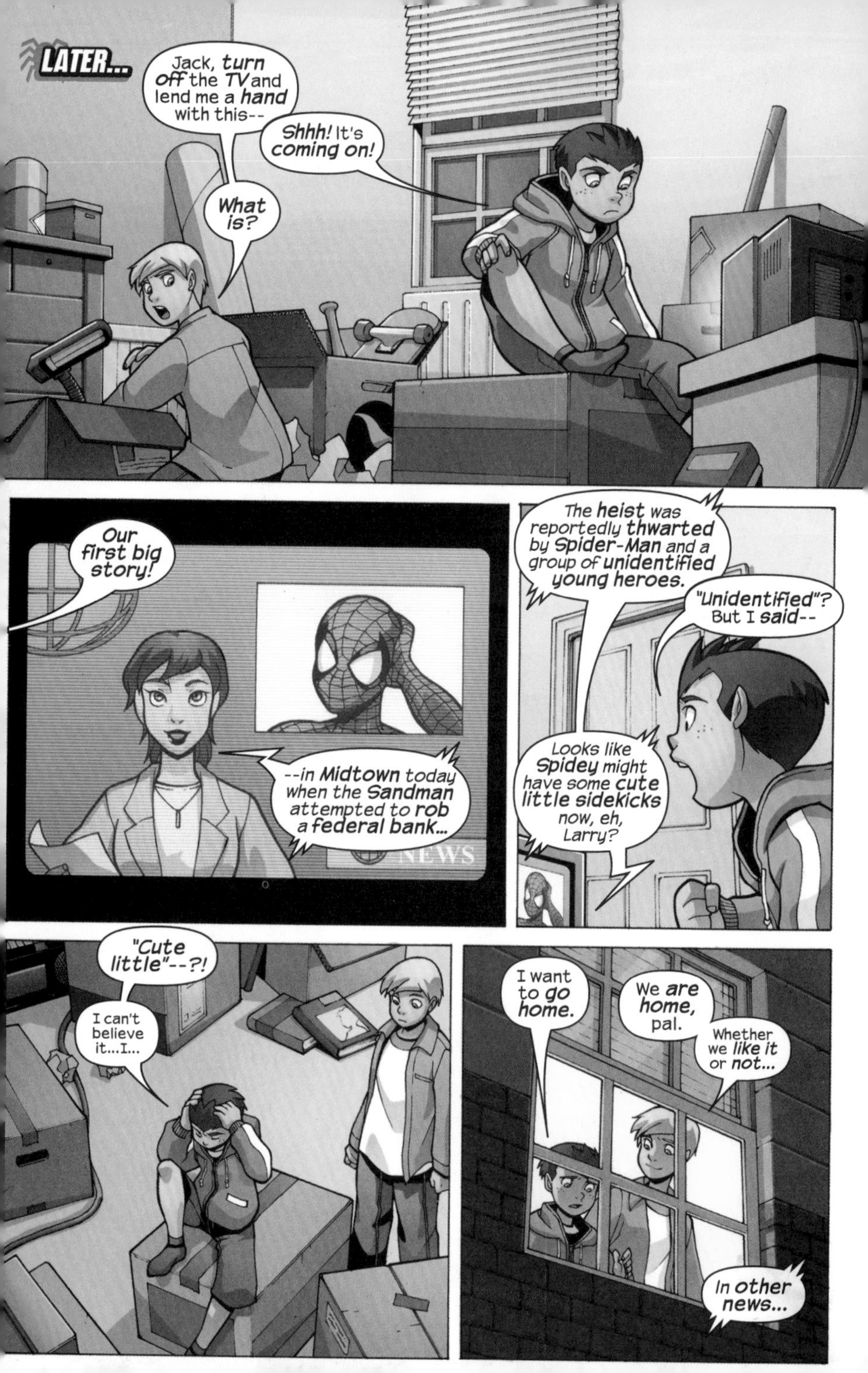
LATER...
Jack, turn off the TV and lend me a hand with this--
Shhh! It's coming on!
What is?
Our first big story!
--in Midtown today when the Sandman attempted to rob a federal bank...
NEWS
The heist was reportedly thwarted by Spider-Man and a group of unidentified young heroes.
"Unidentified"? But I said--
Looks like Spidey might have some cute little sidekicks now, eh, Larry?
"Cute little"--?!
I can't believe it...I...
I want to go home.
We are home, pal.
Whether we like it or not...
In other news...

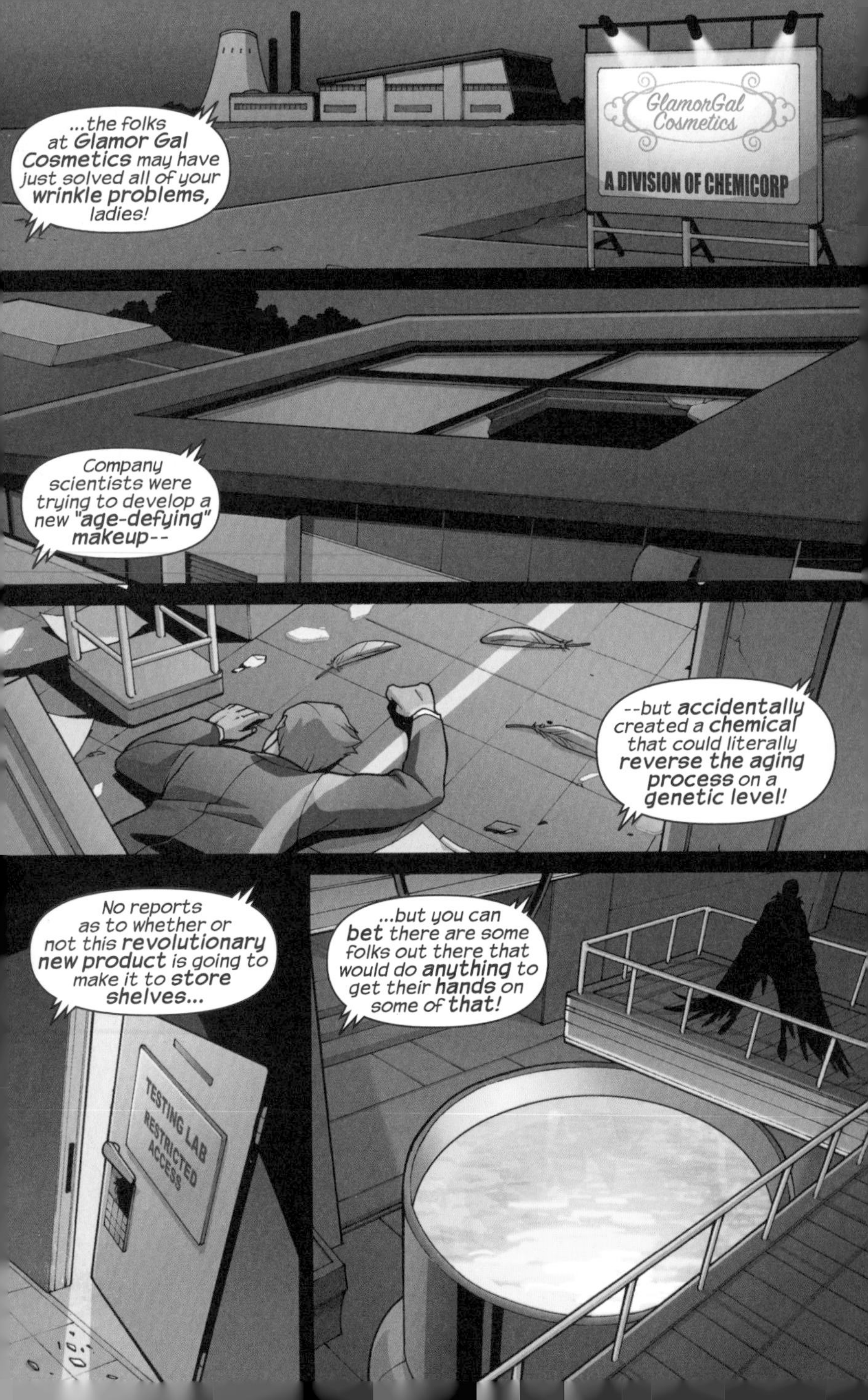
...the folks at Glamor Gal Cosmetics may have just solved all of your wrinkle problems, ladies!
GlamorGal Cosmetics
A DIVISION OF CHEMICORP
Company scientists were trying to develop a new "age-defying" makeup--
--but accidentally created a chemical that could literally reverse the aging process on a genetic level!
No reports as to whether or not this revolutionary new product is going to make it to store shelves...
...but you can bet there are some folks out there that would do anything to get their hands on some of that!
TESTING LAB RESTRICTED ACCESS

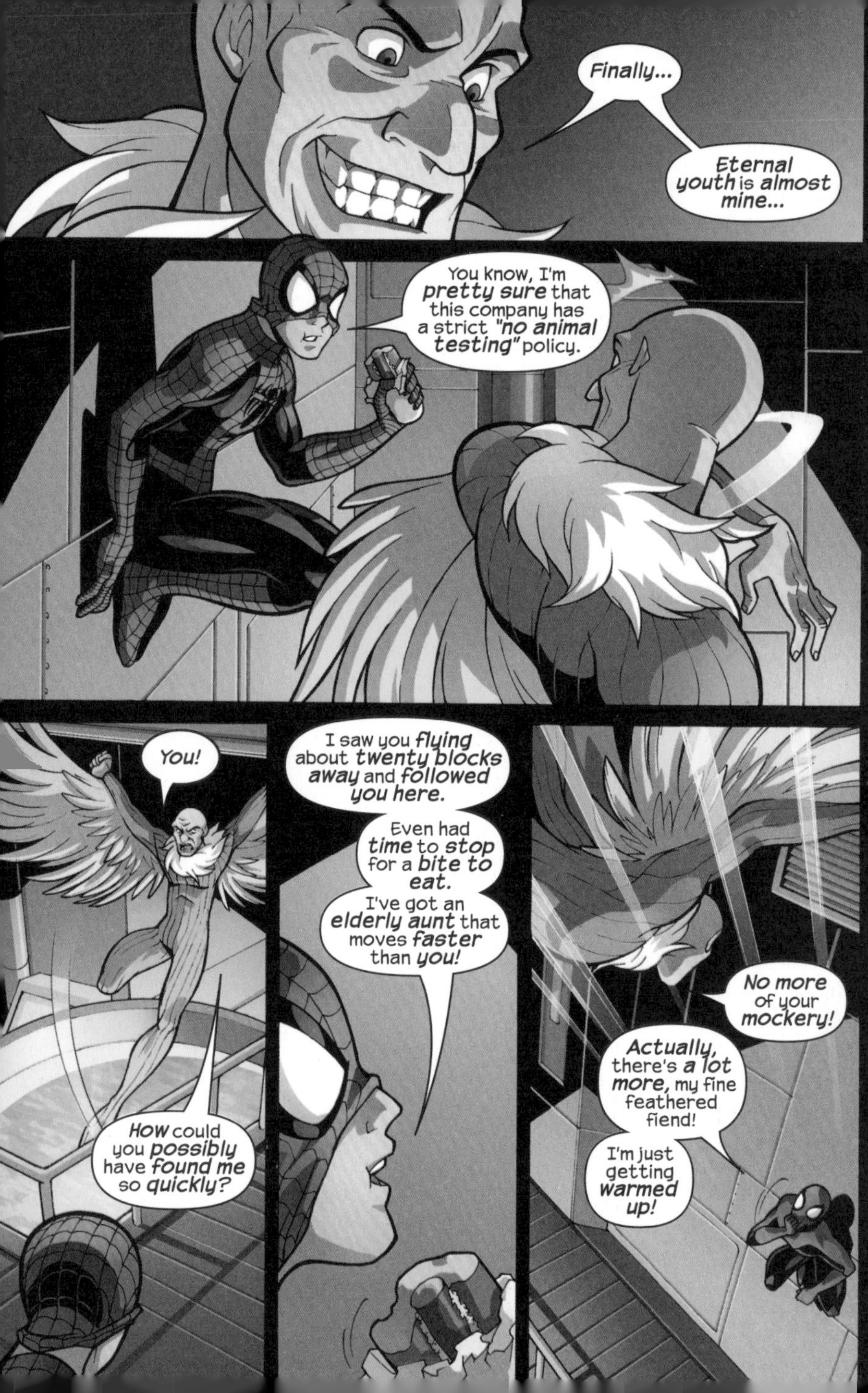
Finally...
Eternal youth is almost mine...
You know, I'm pretty sure that this company has a strict "no animal testing" policy.
You!
How could you possibly have found me so quickly?
I saw you flying about twenty blocks away and followed you here.
Even had time to stop for a bite to eat.
I've got an elderly aunt that moves faster than you!
No more of your mockery!
Actually, there's a lot more, my fine feathered fiend!
I'm just getting warmed up!

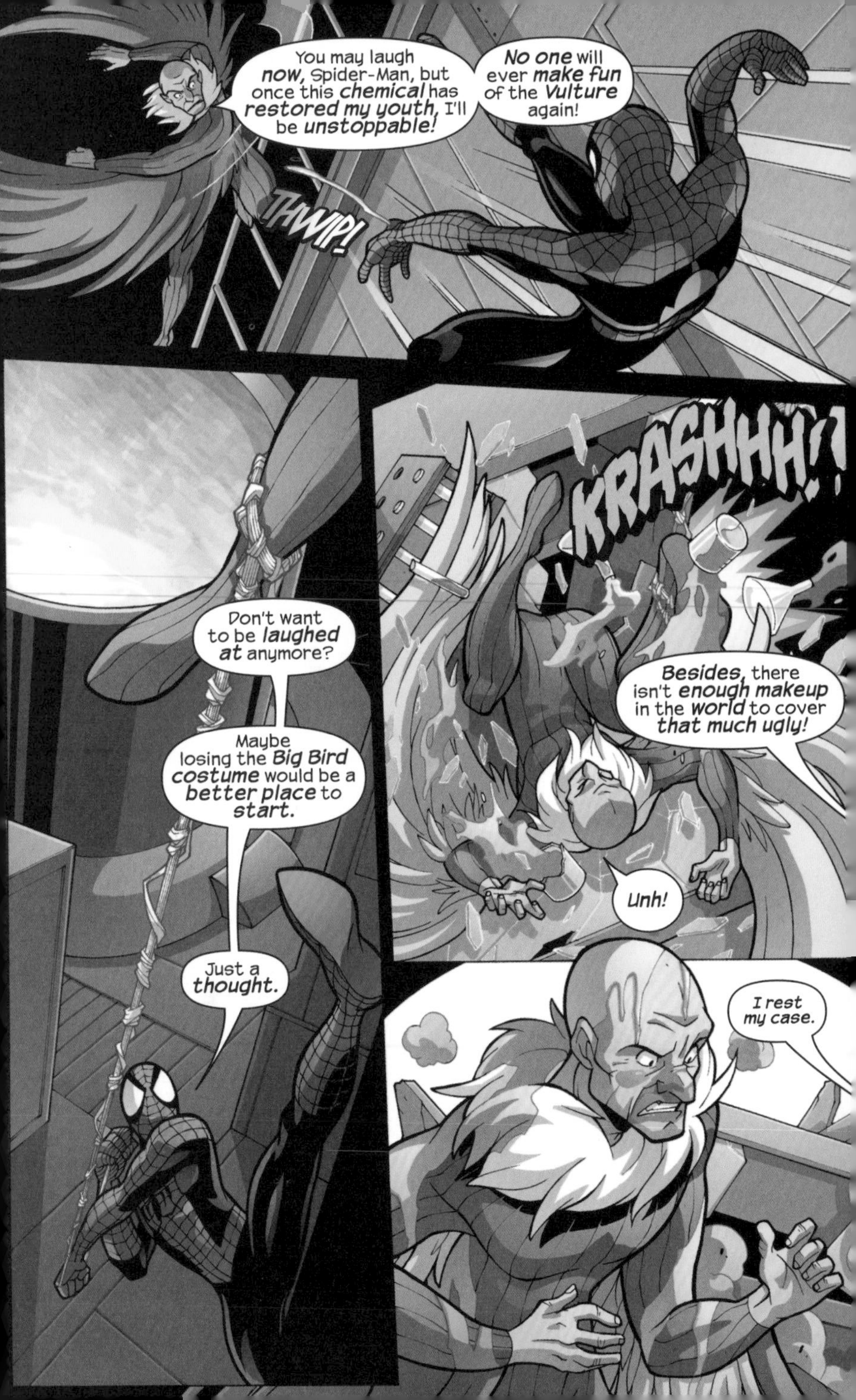
You may laugh now, Spider-Man, but once this chemical has restored my youth, I'll be unstoppable!
No one will ever make fun of the Vulture again!
THWIP!
Don't want to be laughed at anymore?
Maybe losing the Big Bird costume would be a better place to start.
Just a thought.
KRASHHH!!
Besides, there isn't enough makeup in the world to cover that much ugly!
Unh!
I rest my case.

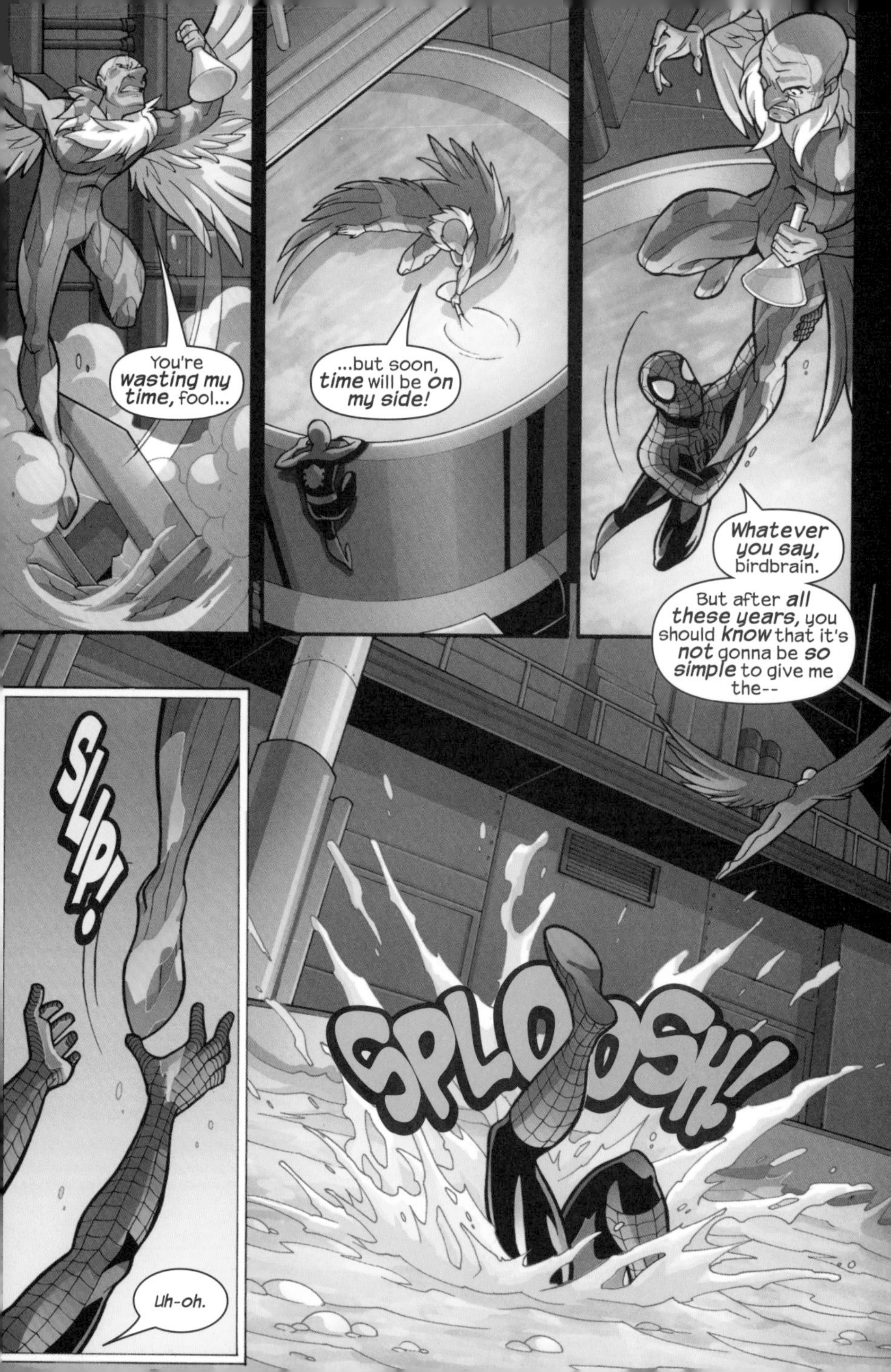
You're *wasting my time*, fool...
...but soon, *time* will be *on my side!*
Whatever you say, birdbrain.
But after *all these years*, you should *know* that it's *not* gonna be *so simple* to give me the--
SLIP!
Uh-oh.
SPLOOSH!

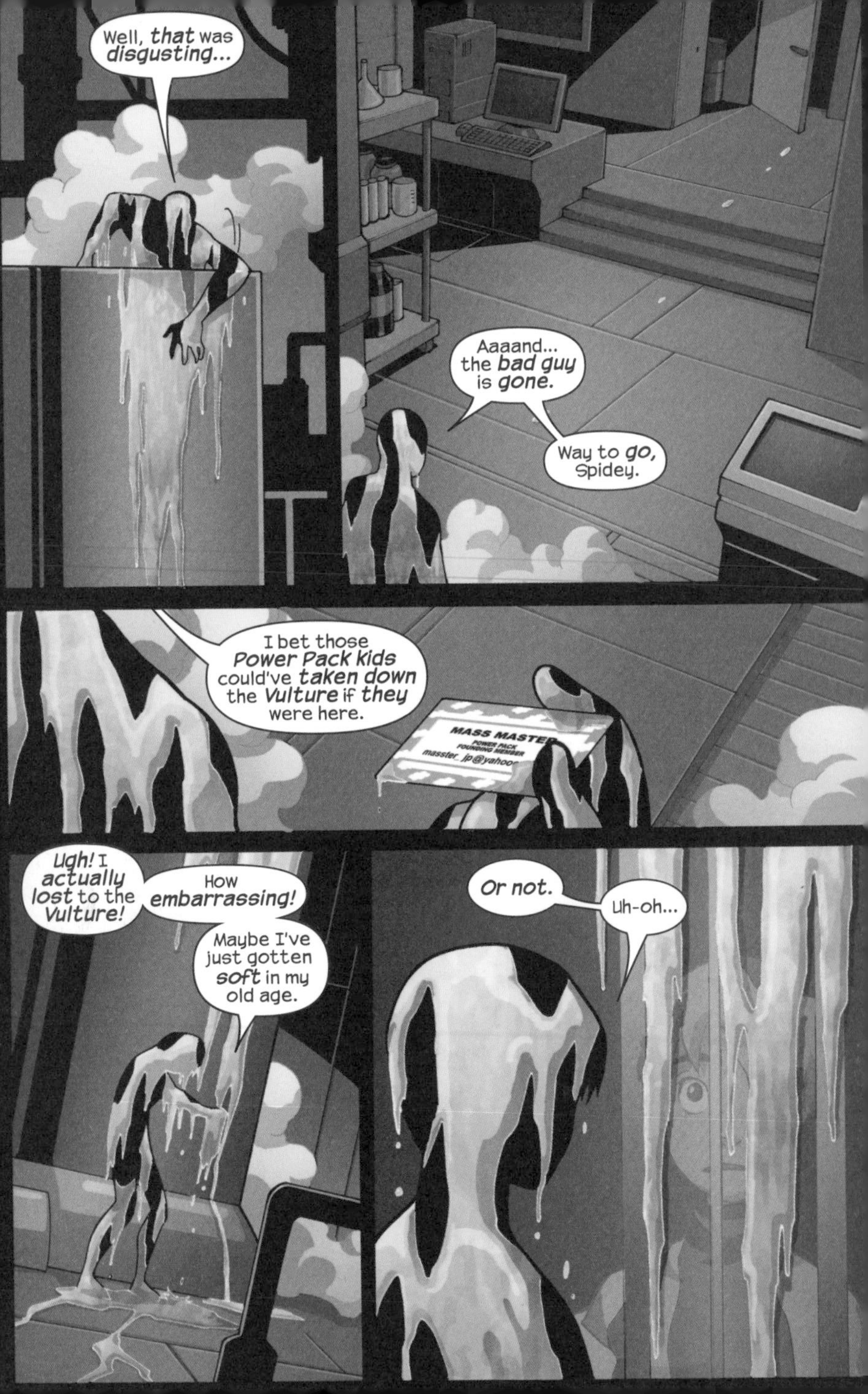
Well, that was disgusting...
Aaaand... the bad guy is gone.
Way to go, Spidey.
I bet those Power Pack kids could've taken down the Vulture if they were here.
MASS MASTER
POWER PACK FOUNDING MEMBER
masster. jp@yahoo
Ugh! I actually lost to the Vulture!
How embarrassing!
Maybe I've just gotten soft in my old age.
Or not.
Uh-oh...

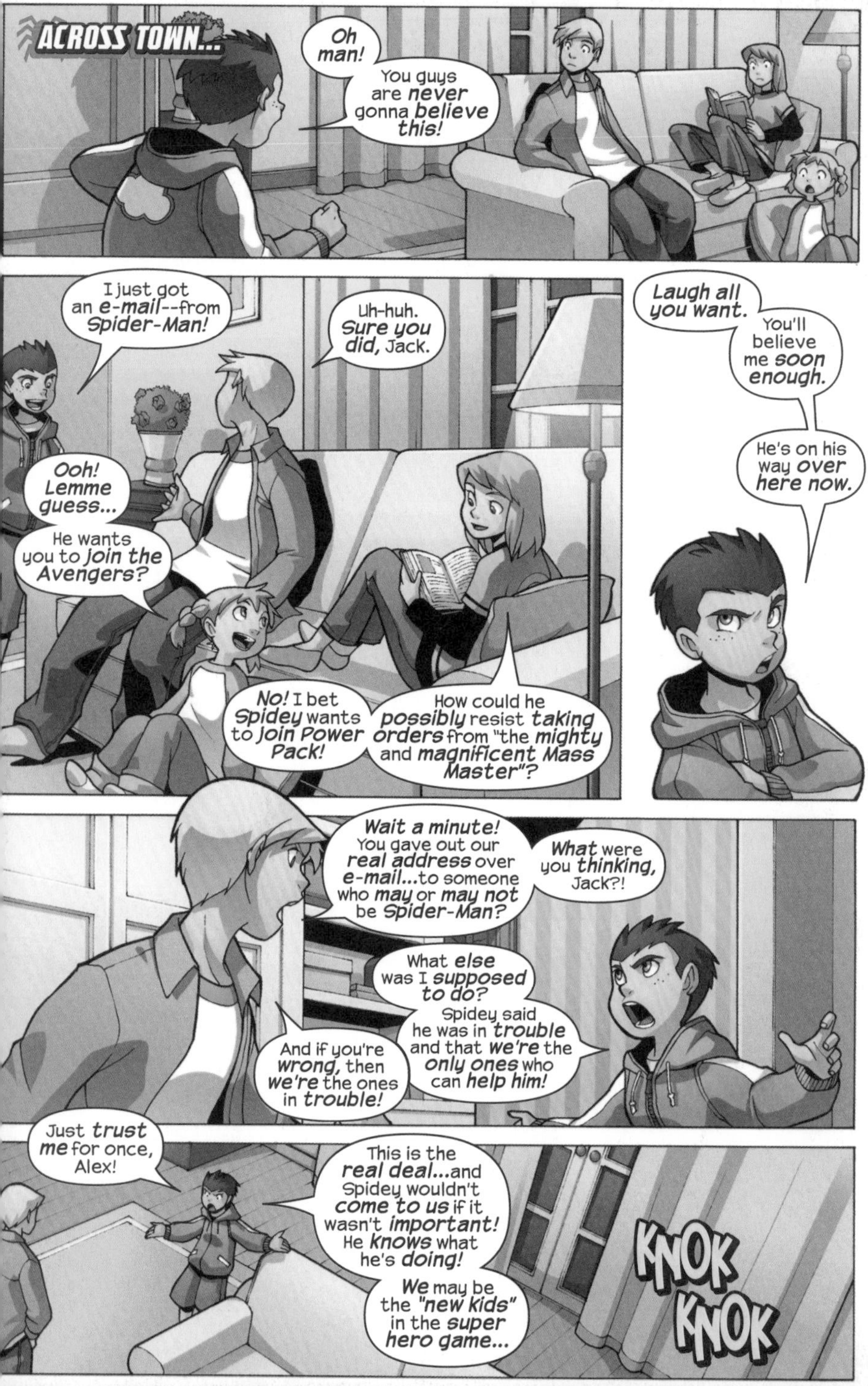
ACROSS TOWN...
Oh man!
You guys are never gonna believe this!
I just got an e-mail--from Spider-Man!
Uh-huh. Sure you did, Jack.
Ooh! Lemme guess...
He wants you to join the Avengers?
No! I bet Spidey wants to join Power Pack!
How could he possibly resist taking orders from "the mighty and magnificent Mass Master"?
Laugh all you want.
You'll believe me soon enough.
He's on his way over here now.
Wait a minute! You gave out our real address over e-mail...to someone who may or may not be Spider-Man?
What were you thinking, Jack?!
What else was I supposed to do?
Spidey said he was in trouble and that we're the only ones who can help him!
And if you're wrong, then we're the ones in trouble!
Just trust me for once, Alex!
This is the real deal...and Spidey wouldn't come to us if it wasn't important! He knows what he's doing!
We may be the "new kids" in the super hero game...
KNOK KNOK

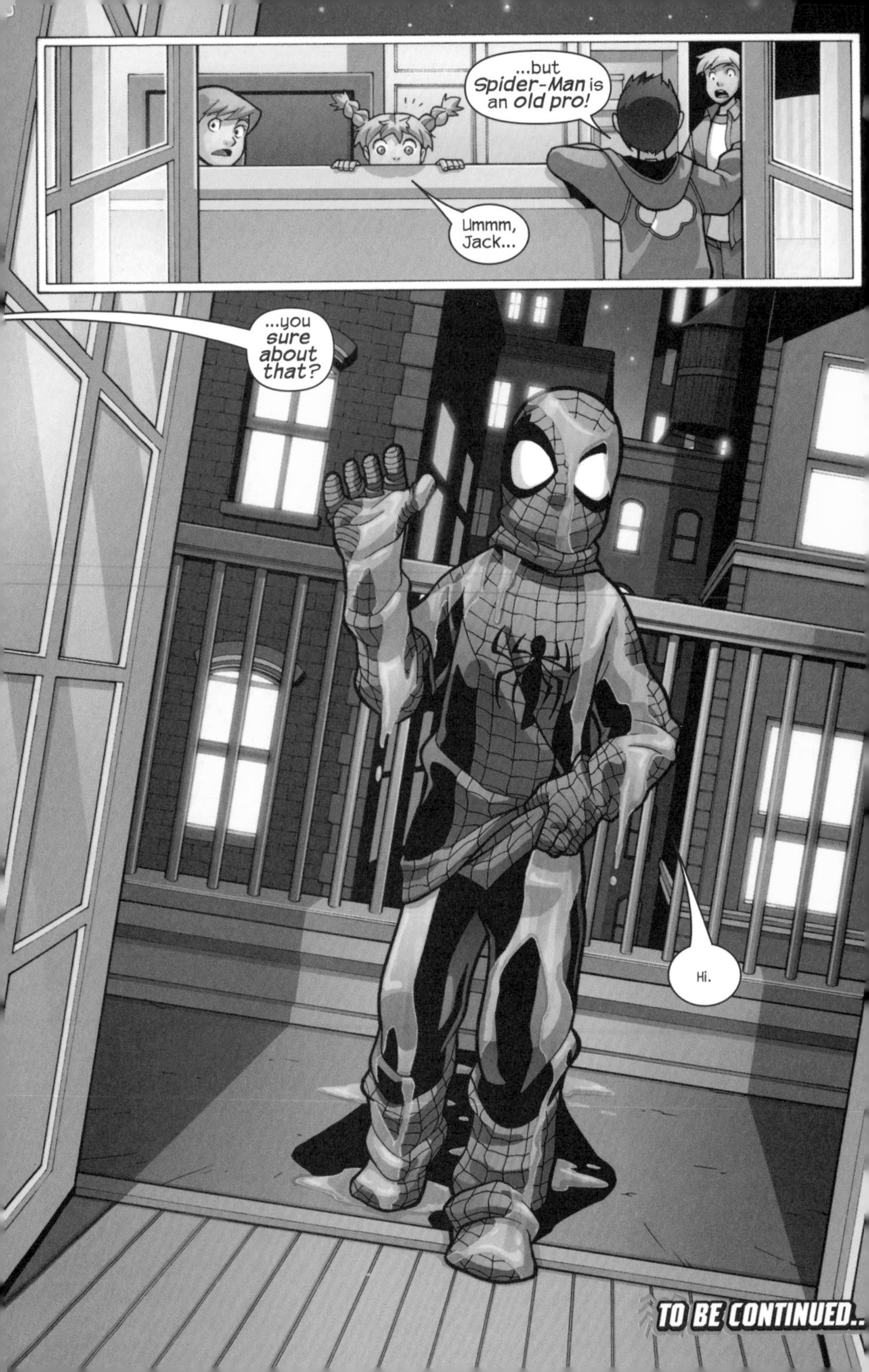
...but Spider-Man is an old pro!
Ummm, Jack...
...you sure about that?
Hi.
TO BE CONTINUED..

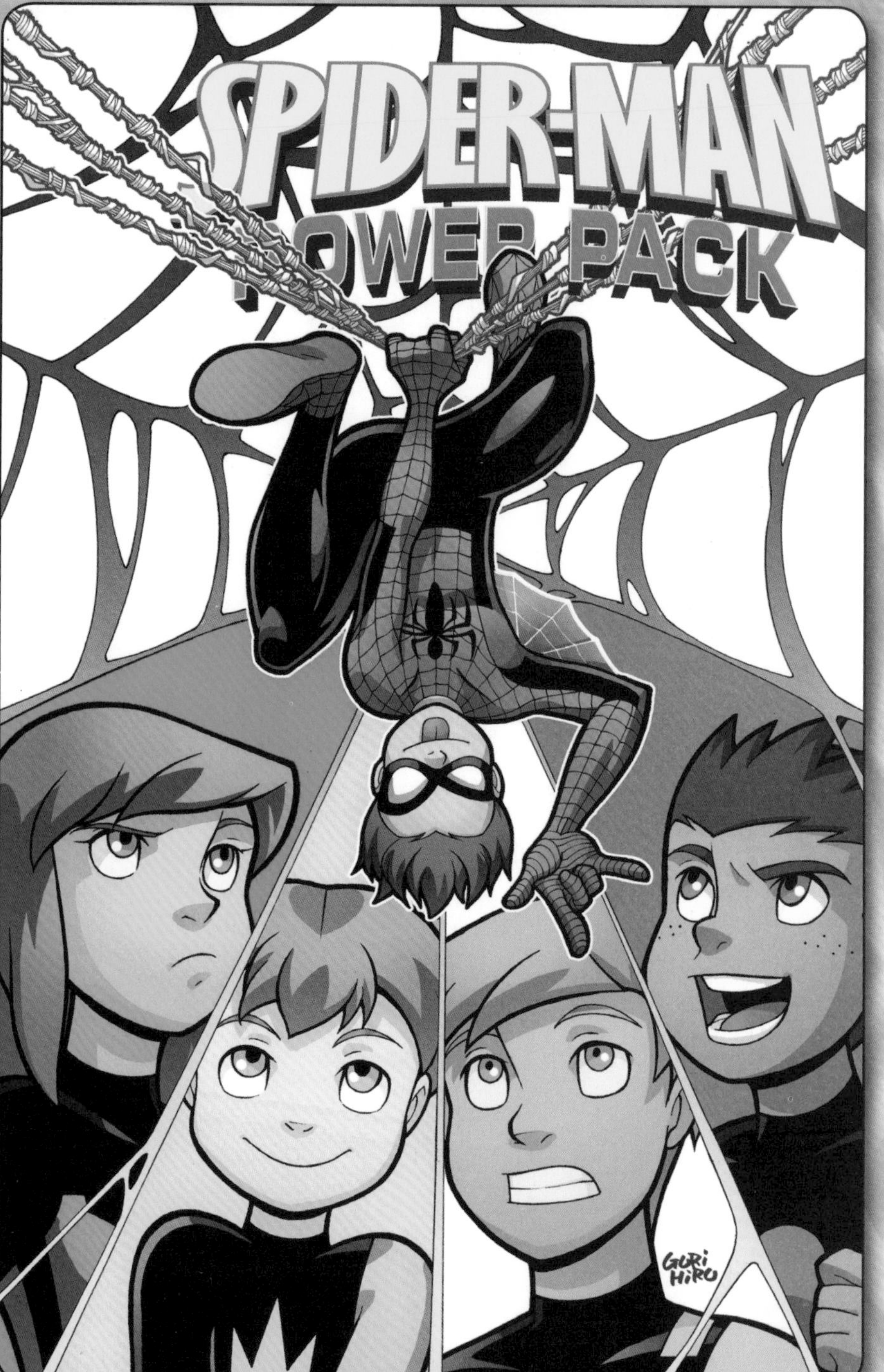
SPIDER-MAN
POWER PACK
GURI HIRU

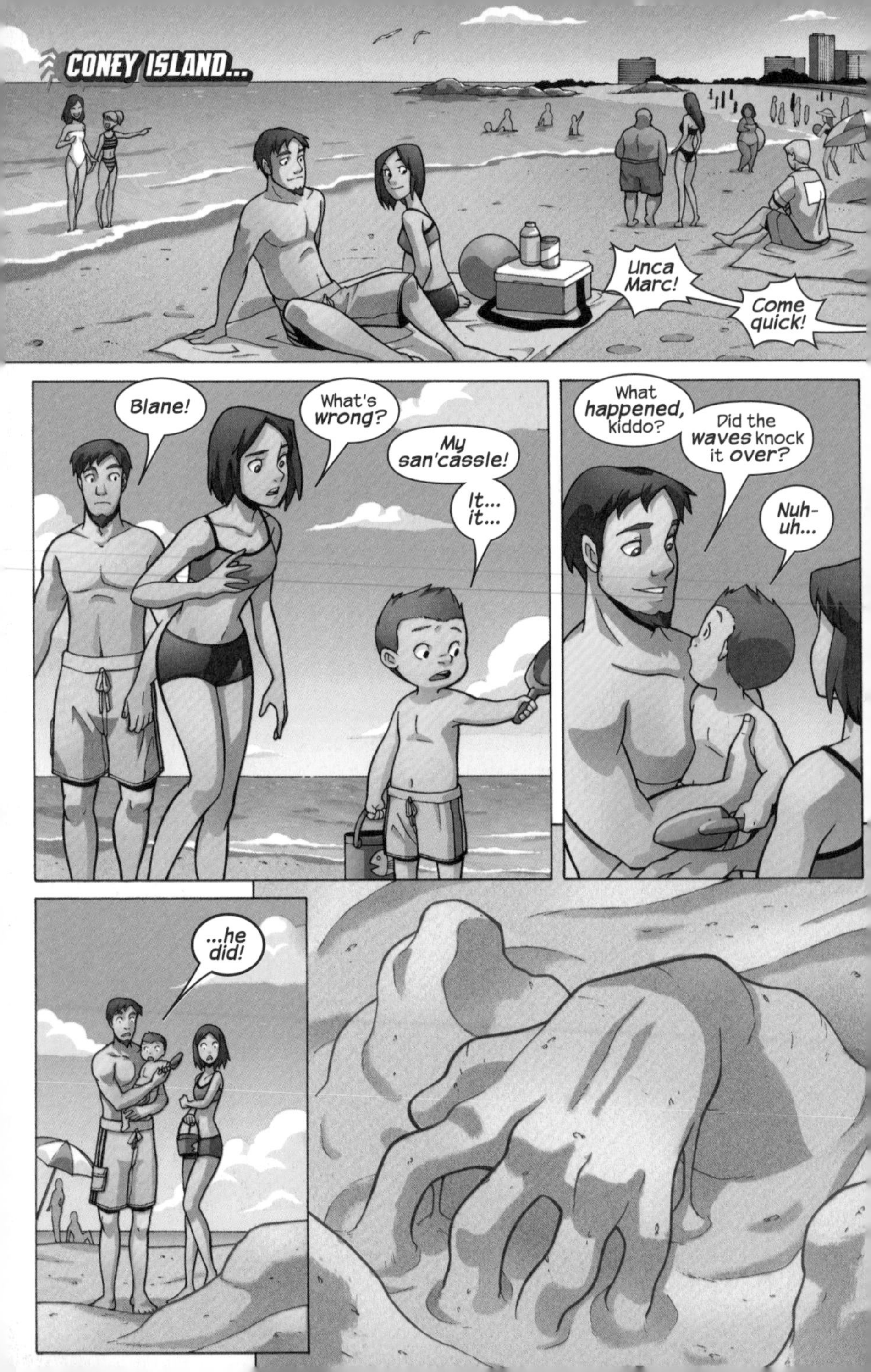
CONEY ISLAND...
Unca Marc!
Come quick!
Blane!
What's wrong?
My san'cassle!
It... it...
What happened, kiddo?
Did the waves knock it over?
Nuh-uh...
...he did!

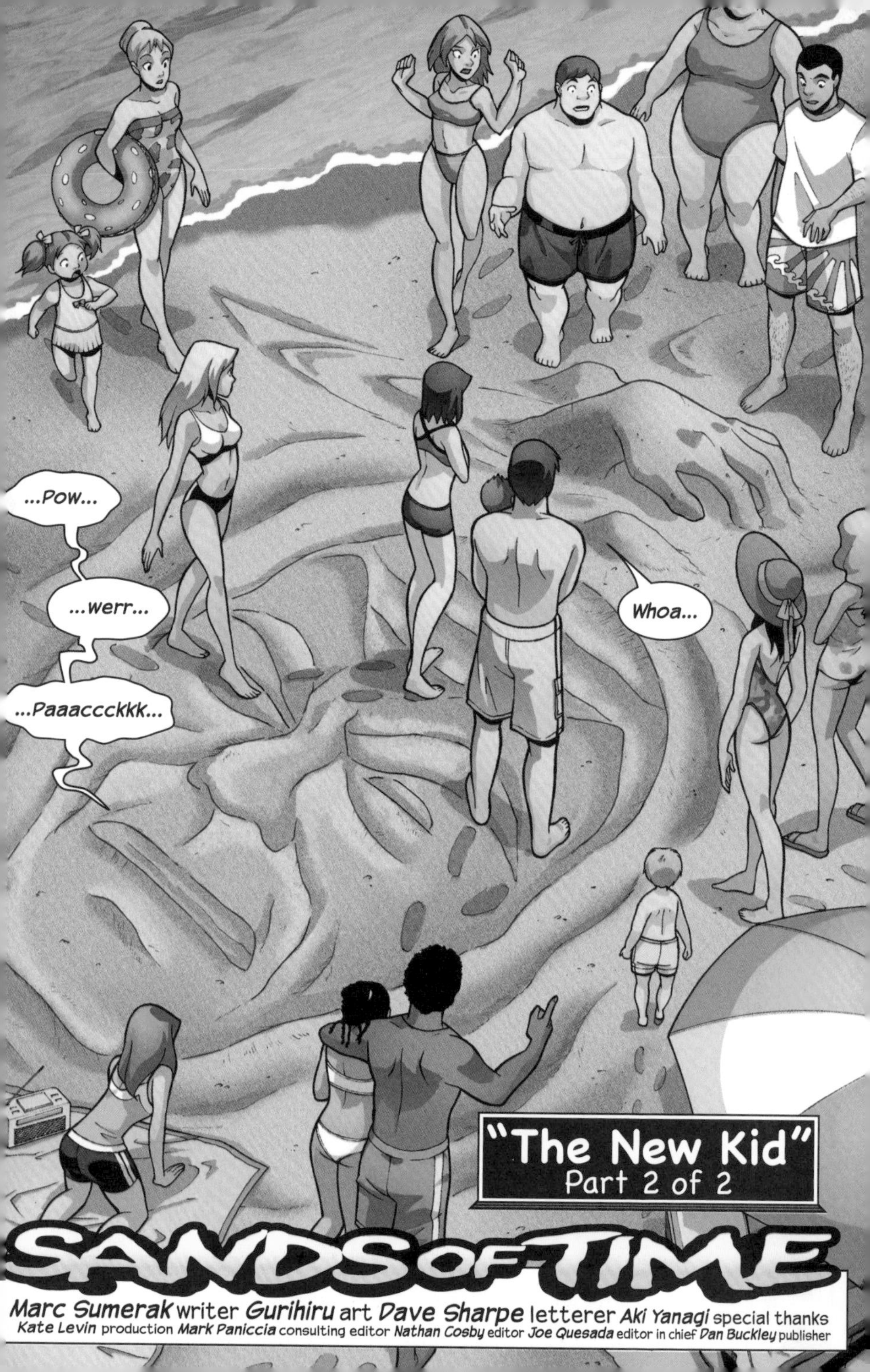
...Pow...
...werr...
...Paaaccckkk...
Whoa...
"The New Kid"
Part 2 of 2
SANDS OF TIME
Marc Sumerak writer Gurihiru art Dave Sharpe letterer Aki Yanagi special thanks
Kate Levin production Mark Paniccia consulting editor Nathan Cosby editor Joe Quesada editor in chief Dan Buckley publisher

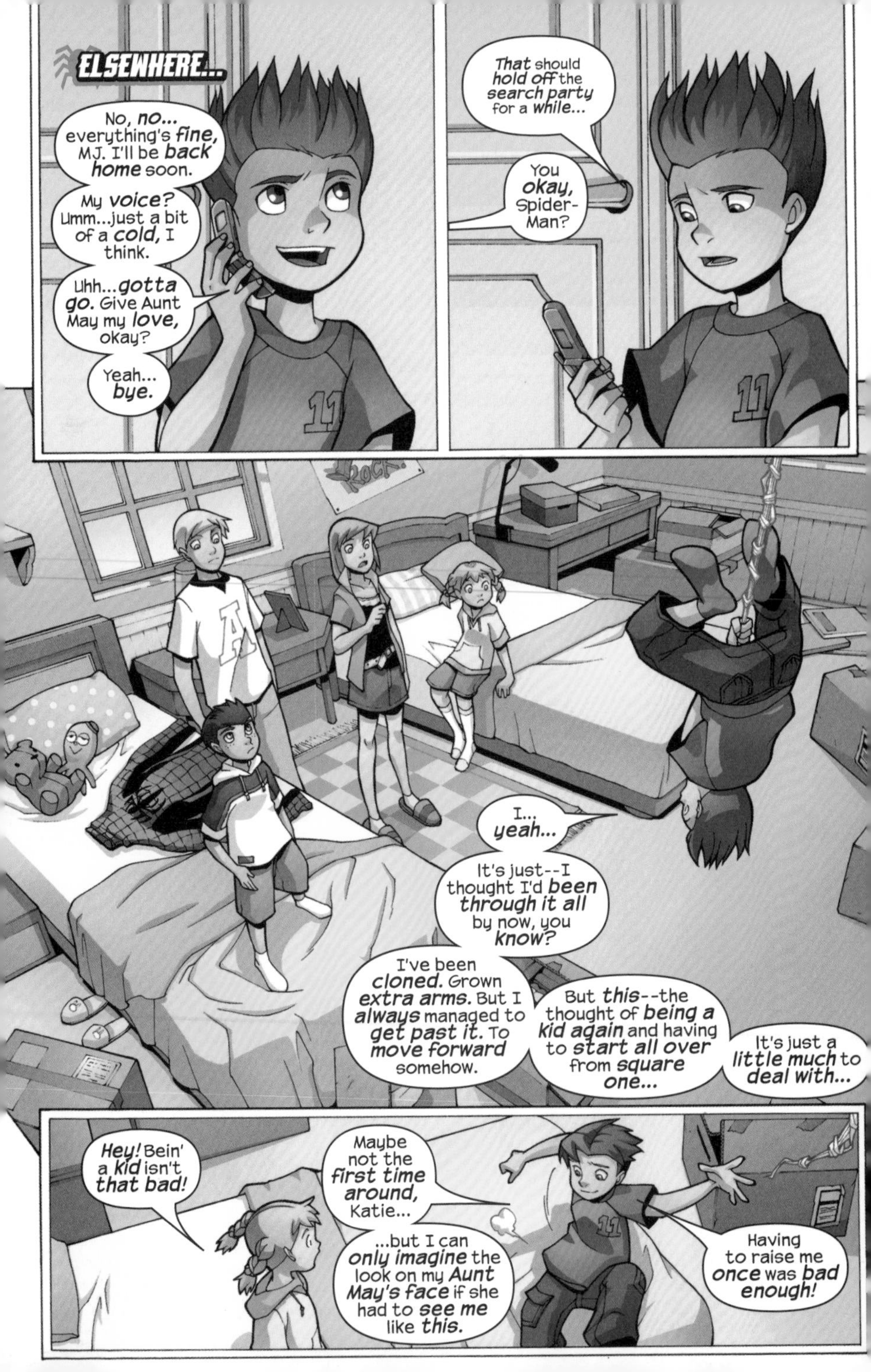
ELSEWHERE...
No, no... everything's fine, MJ. I'll be back home soon.
My voice? Umm...just a bit of a cold, I think.
Uhh...gotta go. Give Aunt May my love, okay?
Yeah... bye.
That should hold off the search party for a while...
You okay, Spider-Man?
I... yeah...
It's just--I thought I'd been through it all by now, you know?
I've been cloned. Grown extra arms. But I always managed to get past it. To move forward somehow.
But this--the thought of being a kid again and having to start all over from square one...
It's just a little much to deal with...
Hey! Bein' a kid isn't that bad!
Maybe not the first time around, Katie...
...but I can only imagine the look on my Aunt May's face if she had to see me like this.
Having to raise me once was bad enough!

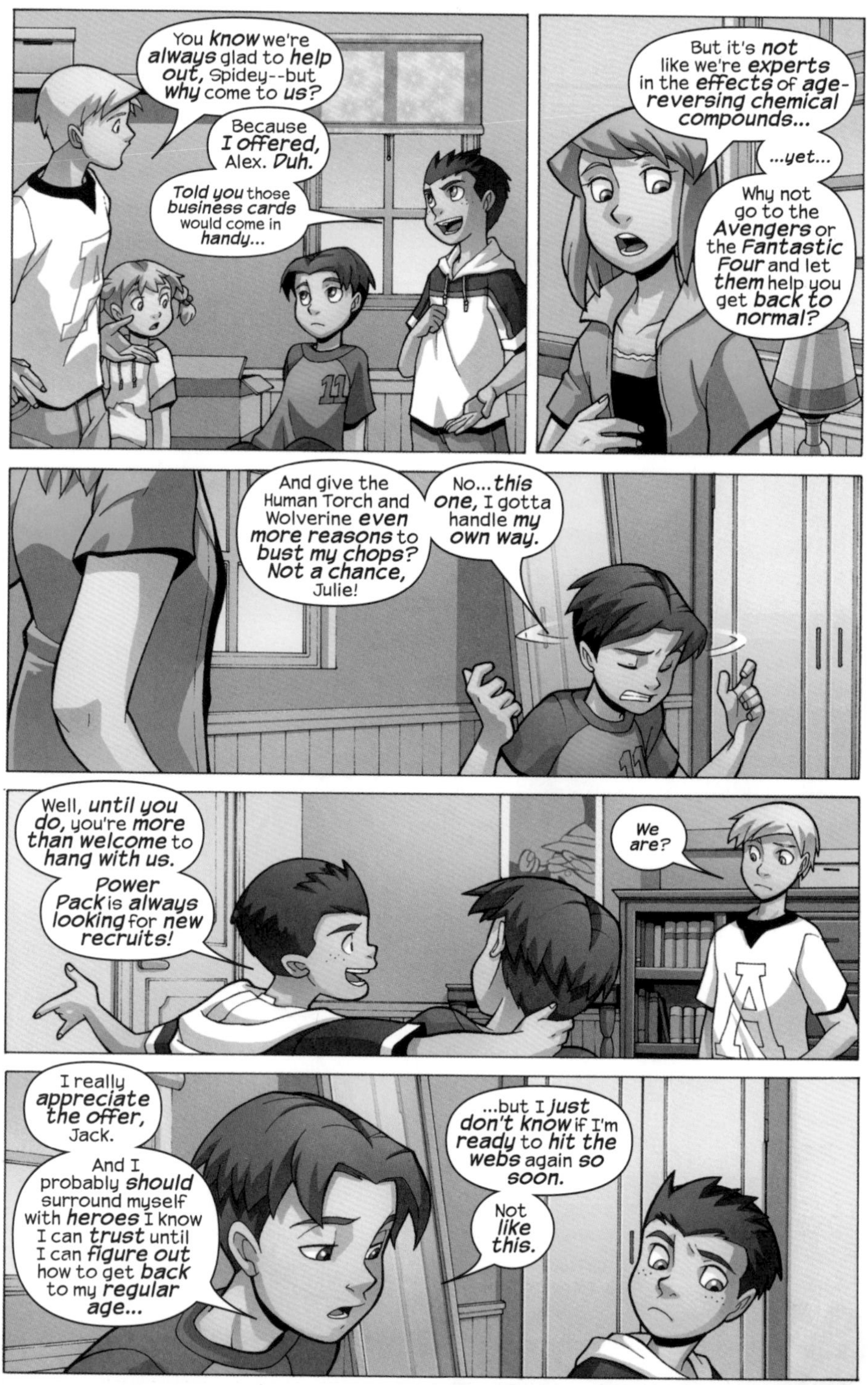
You **know** we're **always** glad to **help out,** Spidey--but **why** come to **us?**
Because **I offered,** Alex. **Duh.**
Told you those **business cards** would come in **handy...**
But it's **not** like we're **experts** in the **effects** of **age-reversing chemical compounds...**
...yet...
Why not go to the **Avengers** or the **Fantastic Four** and let **them** help you get **back to normal?**
And give the Human Torch and Wolverine **even more reasons** to **bust my chops? Not a chance,** Julie!
No... **this one,** I gotta handle **my own way.**
Well, **until you do,** you're **more than welcome** to **hang with us.**
Power Pack is **always looking** for **new recruits!**
We are?
I really **appreciate the offer,** Jack.
And I probably **should** surround myself with **heroes** I know I can **trust** until I can **figure out** how to get **back** to my **regular age...**
...but I **just don't know** if I'm **ready** to **hit the webs** again **so soon.**
Not **like this.**

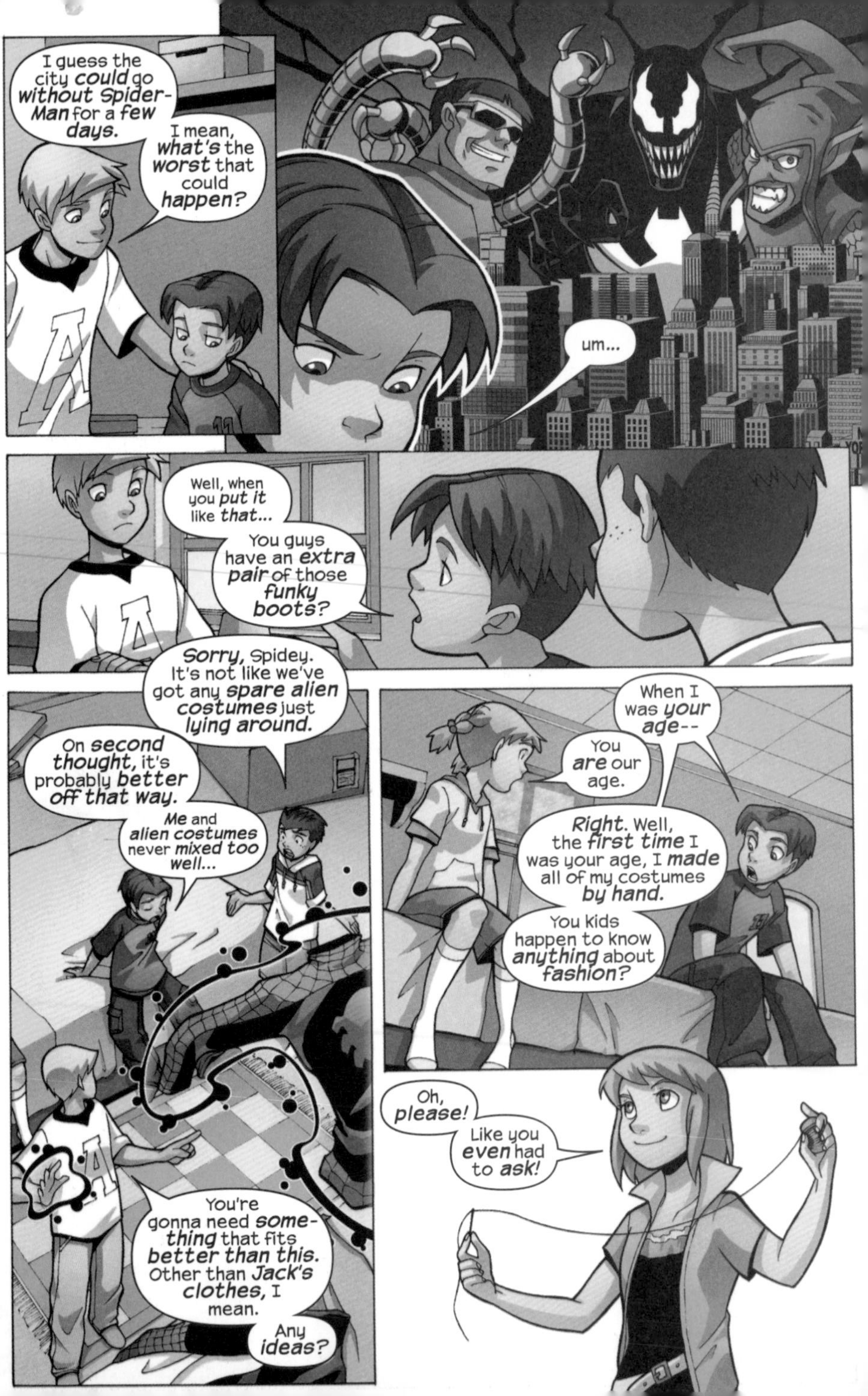

I guess the city could go without Spider-Man for a few days.
I mean, what's the worst that could happen?
um...
Well, when you put it like that...
You guys have an extra pair of those funky boots?
Sorry, Spidey. It's not like we've got any spare alien costumes just lying around.
On second thought, it's probably better off that way.
Me and alien costumes never mixed too well...
You're gonna need something that fits better than this. Other than Jack's clothes, I mean.
Any ideas?
When I was your age--
You are our age.
Right. Well, the first time I was your age, I made all of my costumes by hand.
You kids happen to know anything about fashion?
Oh, please!
Like you even had to ask!

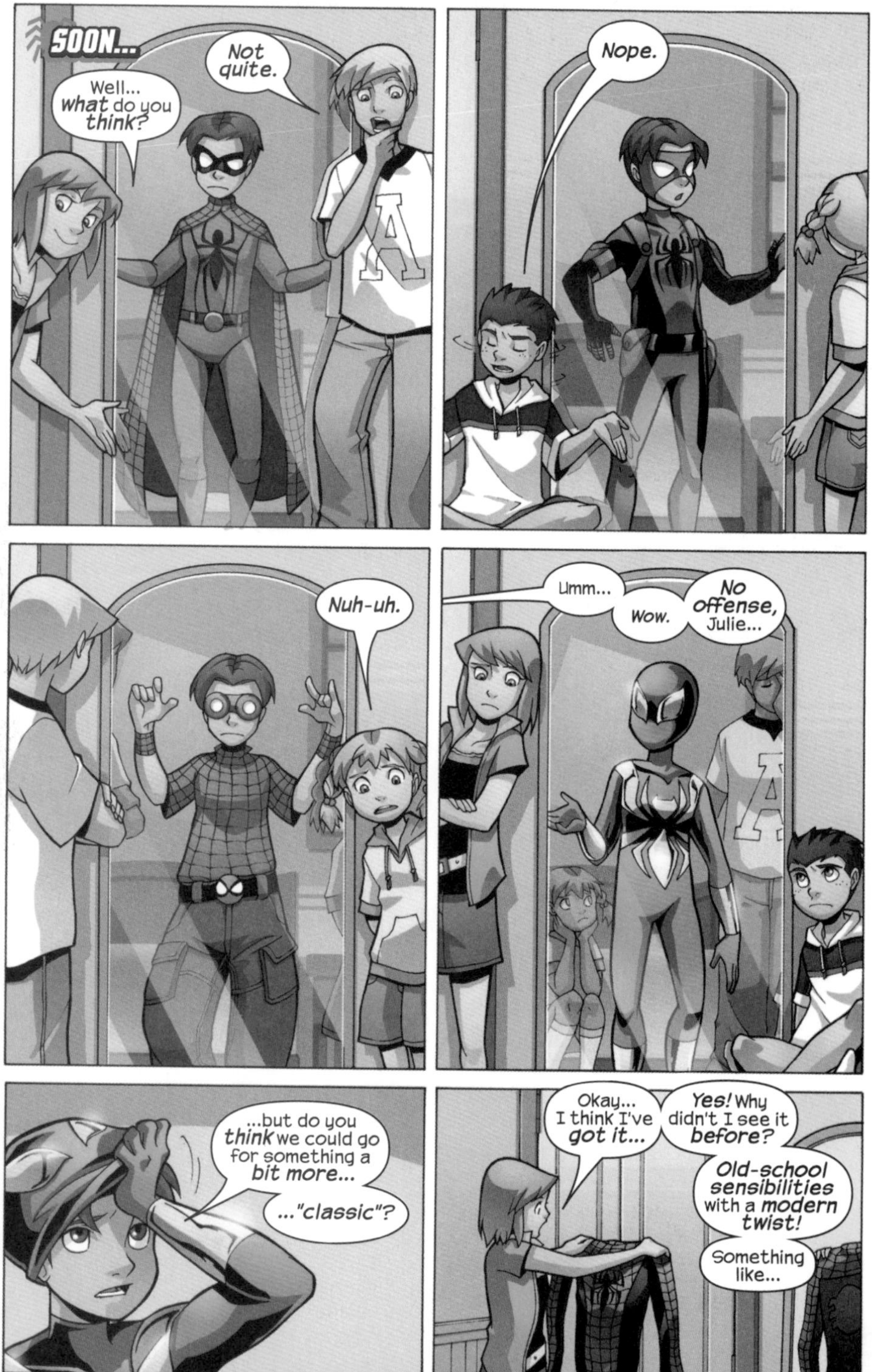
SOON...
Well... what do you think?
Not quite.
Nope.
Nuh-uh.
Umm...
Wow.
No offense, Julie...
...but do you think we could go for something a bit more...
..."classic"?
Okay... I think I've got it...
Yes! Why didn't I see it before?
Old-school sensibilities with a modern twist!
Something like...

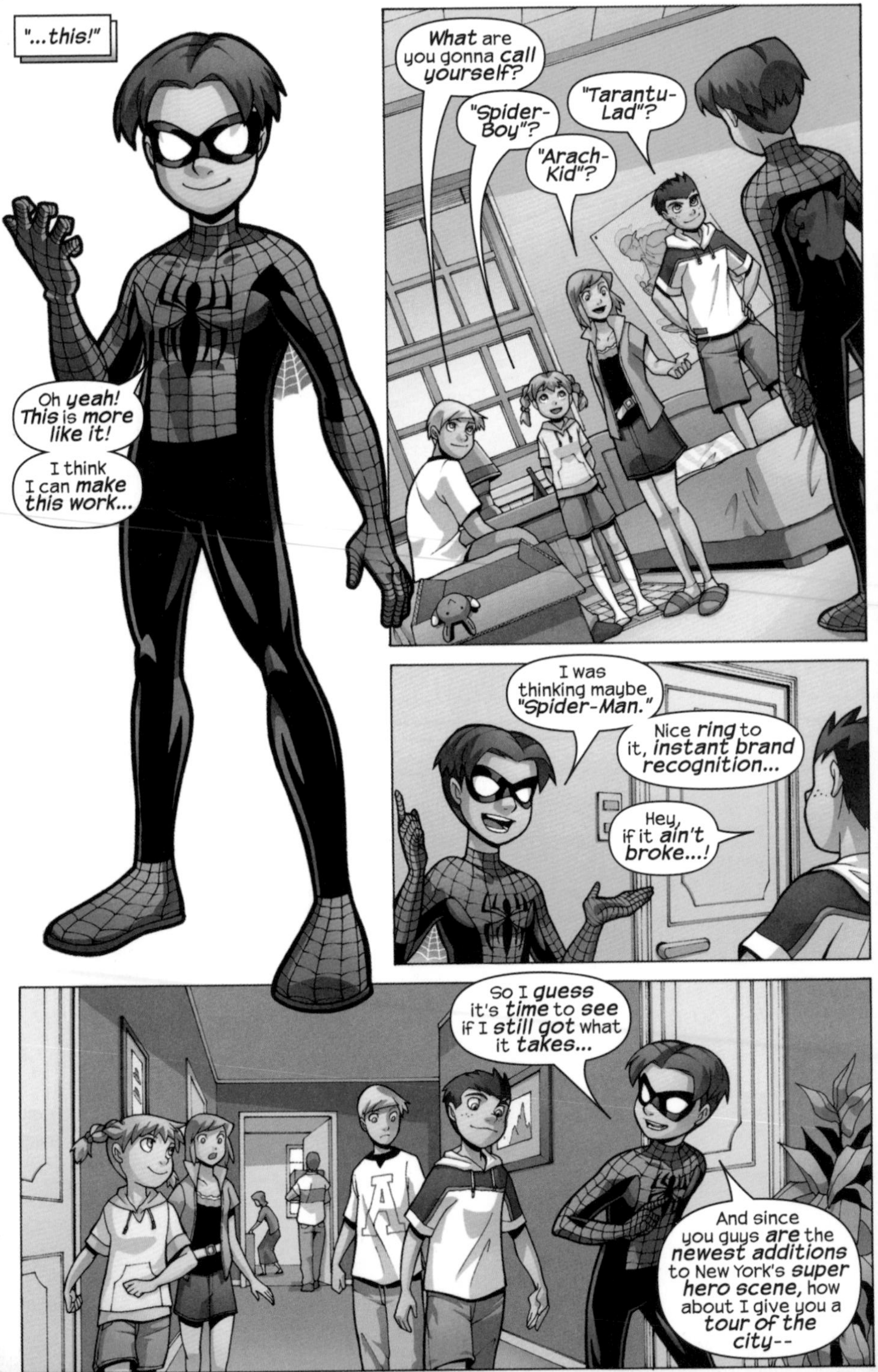
"...this!"
Oh *yeah!* *This* is *more like it!*
I think I can *make this work...*
What are you gonna *call yourself?*
"Spider-Boy"?
"Tarantu-Lad"?
"Arach-Kid"?
I was thinking maybe *"Spider-Man."*
Nice *ring* to it, *instant brand recognition...*
Hey, if it *ain't broke...!*
So I *guess* it's *time* to *see* if I *still got* what it *takes...*
And since you guys *are* the *newest additions* to New York's *super hero scene,* how about I give you a *tour of the city--*

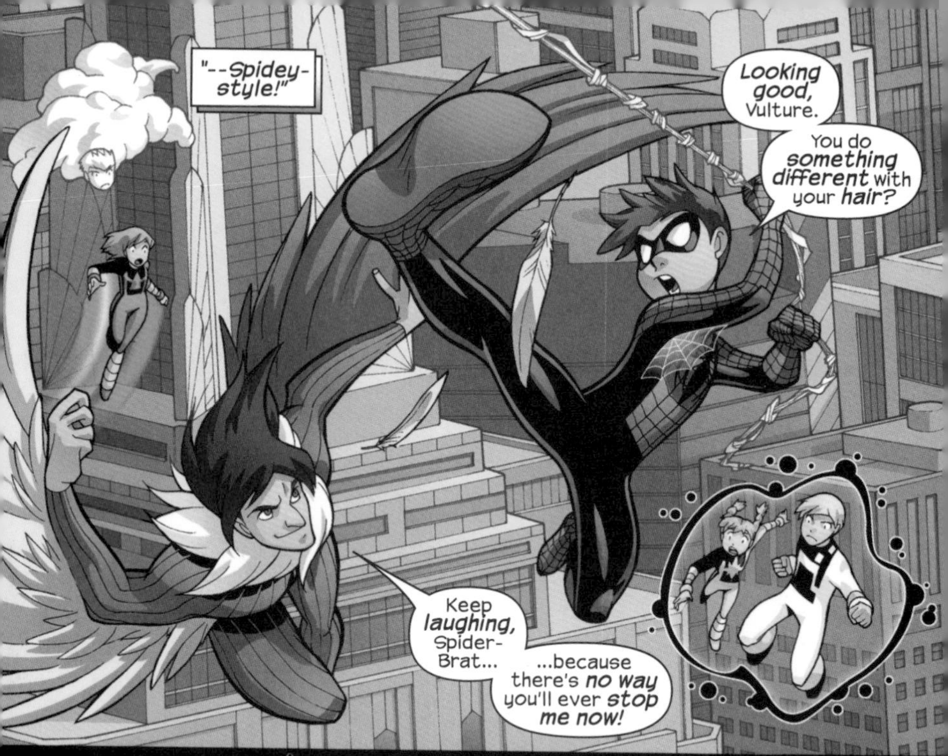
"--*Spidey-style!*"
Looking good, Vulture.
You do *something different* with your *hair?*
Keep *laughing,* Spider-Brat...
...because there's *no way* you'll ever *stop me now!*

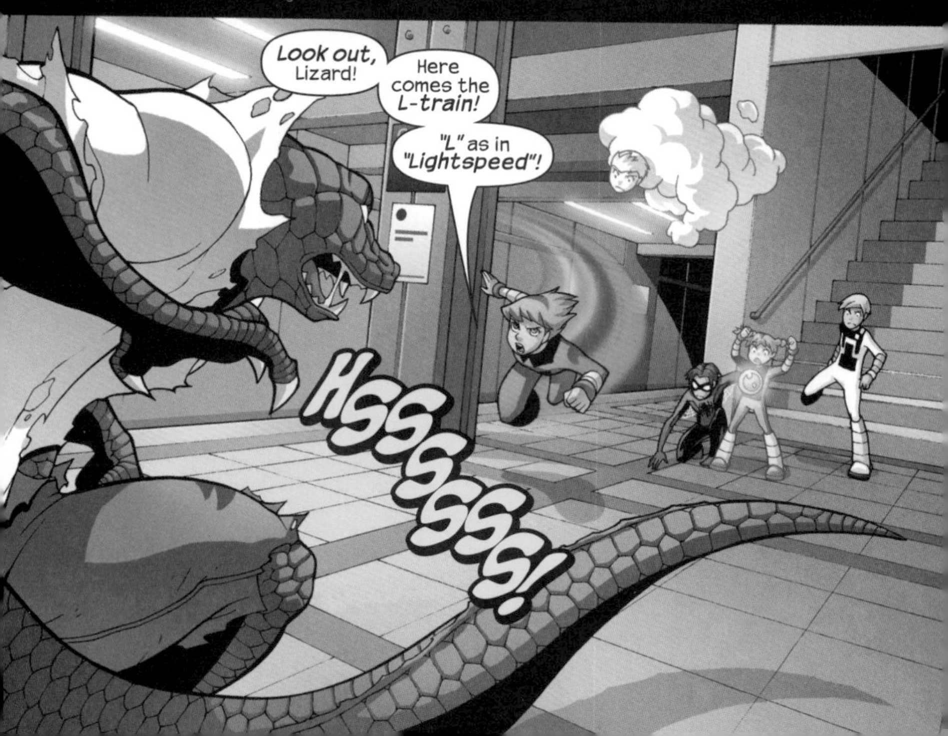
Look out, Lizard!
Here comes the *L-train!*
"L" as in *"Lightspeed"!*
HSSSSSS!

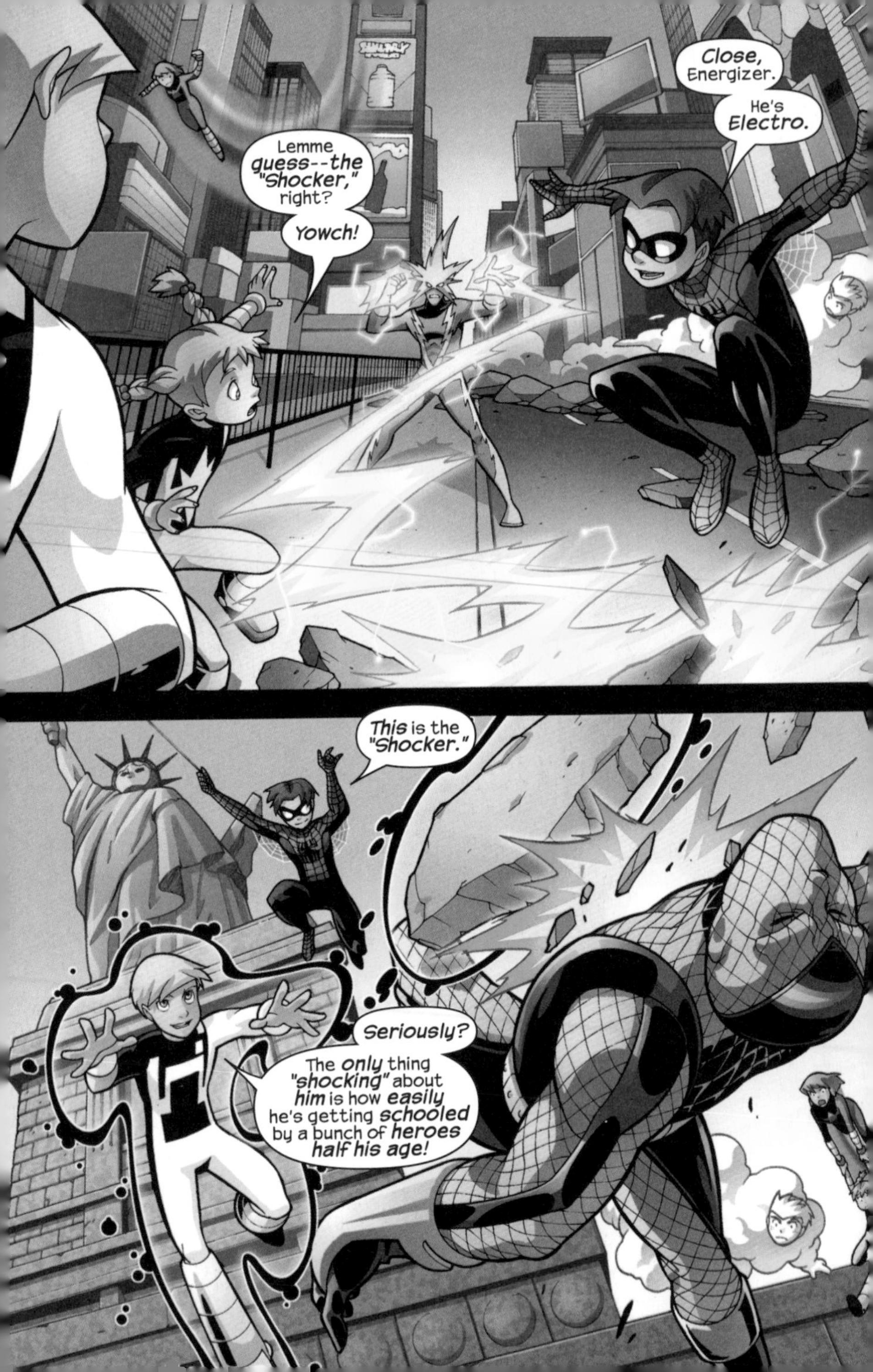
Lemme guess--the "Shocker," right?
Yowch!
Close, Energizer.
He's Electro.
This is the "Shocker."
Seriously?
The only thing "shocking" about him is how easily he's getting schooled by a bunch of heroes half his age!

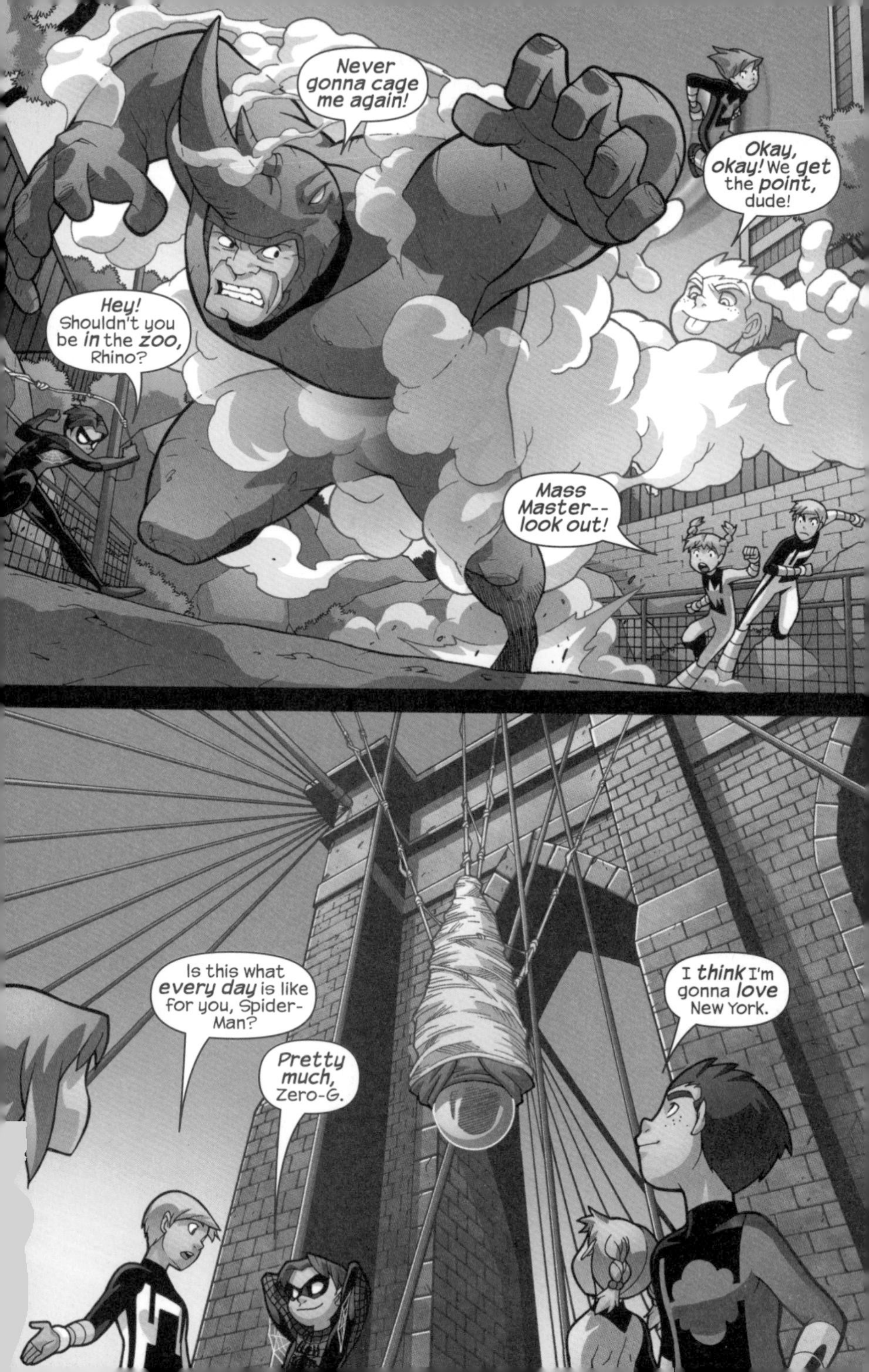
Never gonna cage me again!
Okay, okay! We get the point, dude!
Hey! Shouldn't you be in the zoo, Rhino?
Mass Master-- look out!
Is this what every day is like for you, Spider-Man?
Pretty much, Zero-G.
I think I'm gonna love New York.

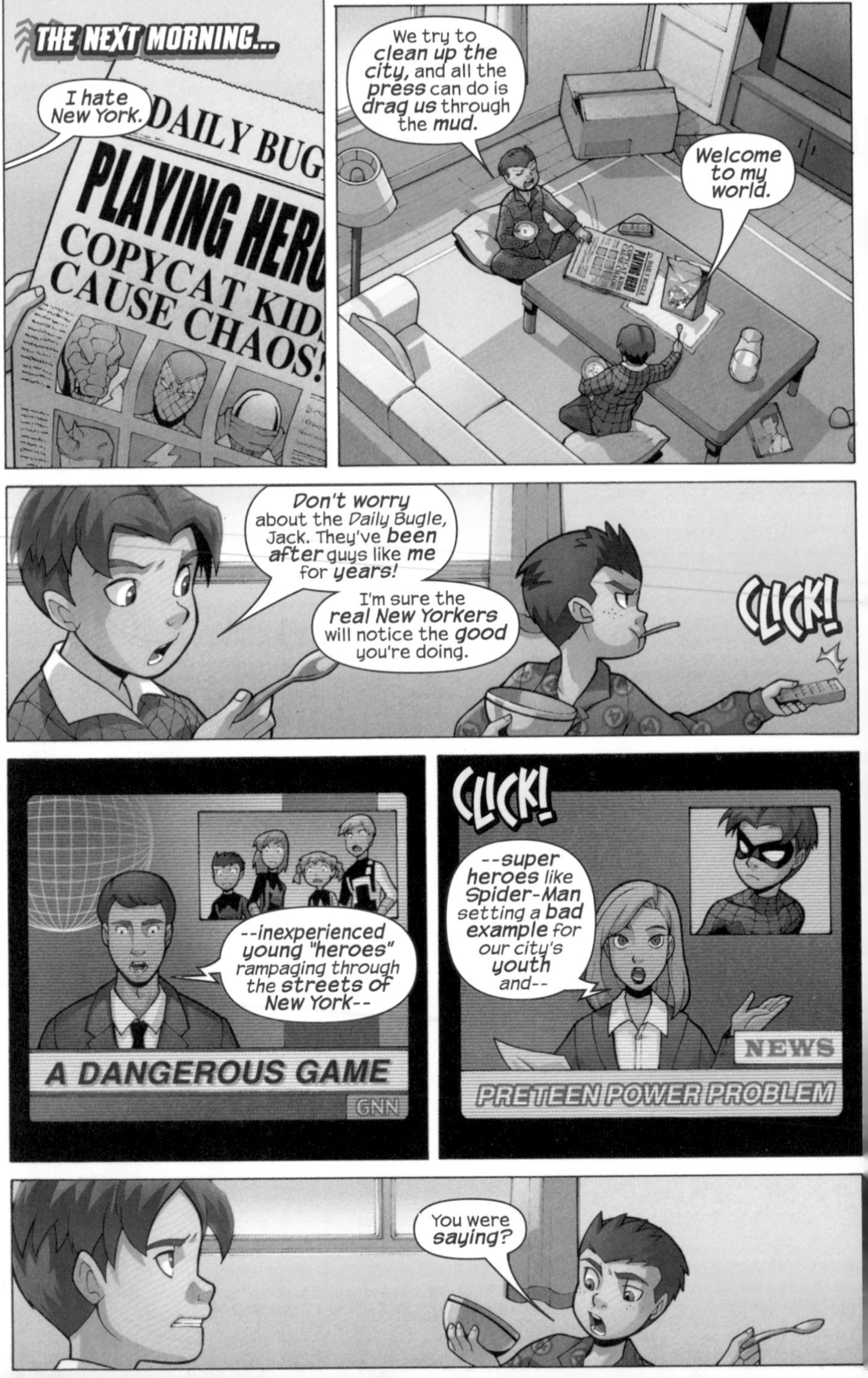
THE NEXT MORNING...
I hate New York.
DAILY BUG
PLAYING HERO
COPYCAT KID
CAUSE CHAOS!
We try to clean up the city, and all the press can do is drag us through the mud.
Welcome to my world.
Don't worry about the Daily Bugle, Jack. They've been after guys like me for years!
I'm sure the real New Yorkers will notice the good you're doing.
CLICK!
--inexperienced young "heroes" rampaging through the streets of New York--
A DANGEROUS GAME
GNN
CLICK!
--super heroes like Spider-Man setting a bad example for our city's youth and--
NEWS
PRETEEN POWER PROBLEM
You were saying?

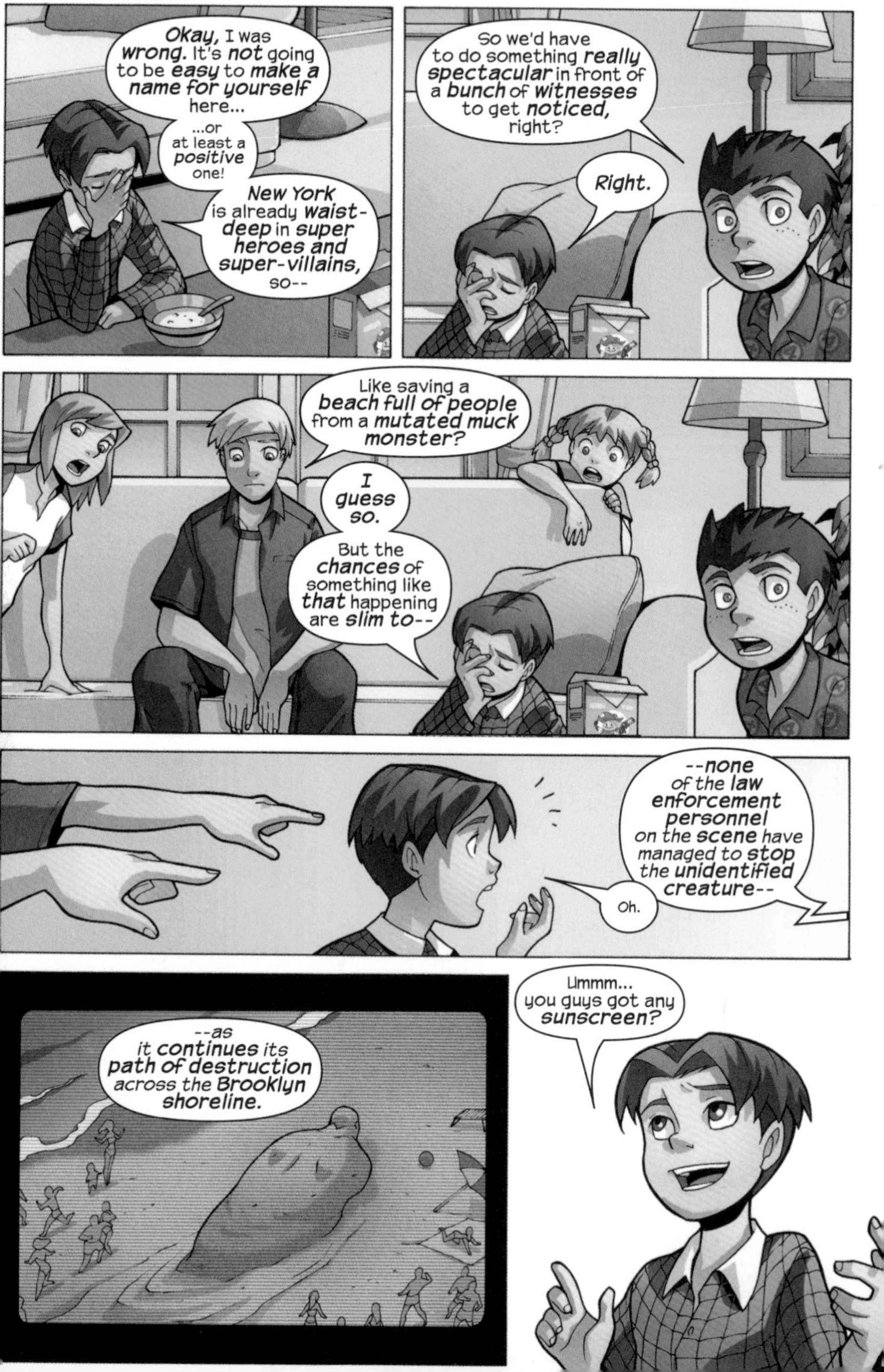

Okay, I was wrong. It's not going to be easy to make a name for yourself here...
...or at least a positive one!
New York is already waist-deep in super heroes and super-villains, so--
So we'd have to do something really spectacular in front of a bunch of witnesses to get noticed, right?
Right.
Like saving a beach full of people from a mutated muck monster?
I guess so.
But the chances of something like that happening are slim to--
--none of the law enforcement personnel on the scene have managed to stop the unidentified creature--
Oh.
--as it continues its path of destruction across the Brooklyn shoreline.
Ummm... you guys got any sunscreen?

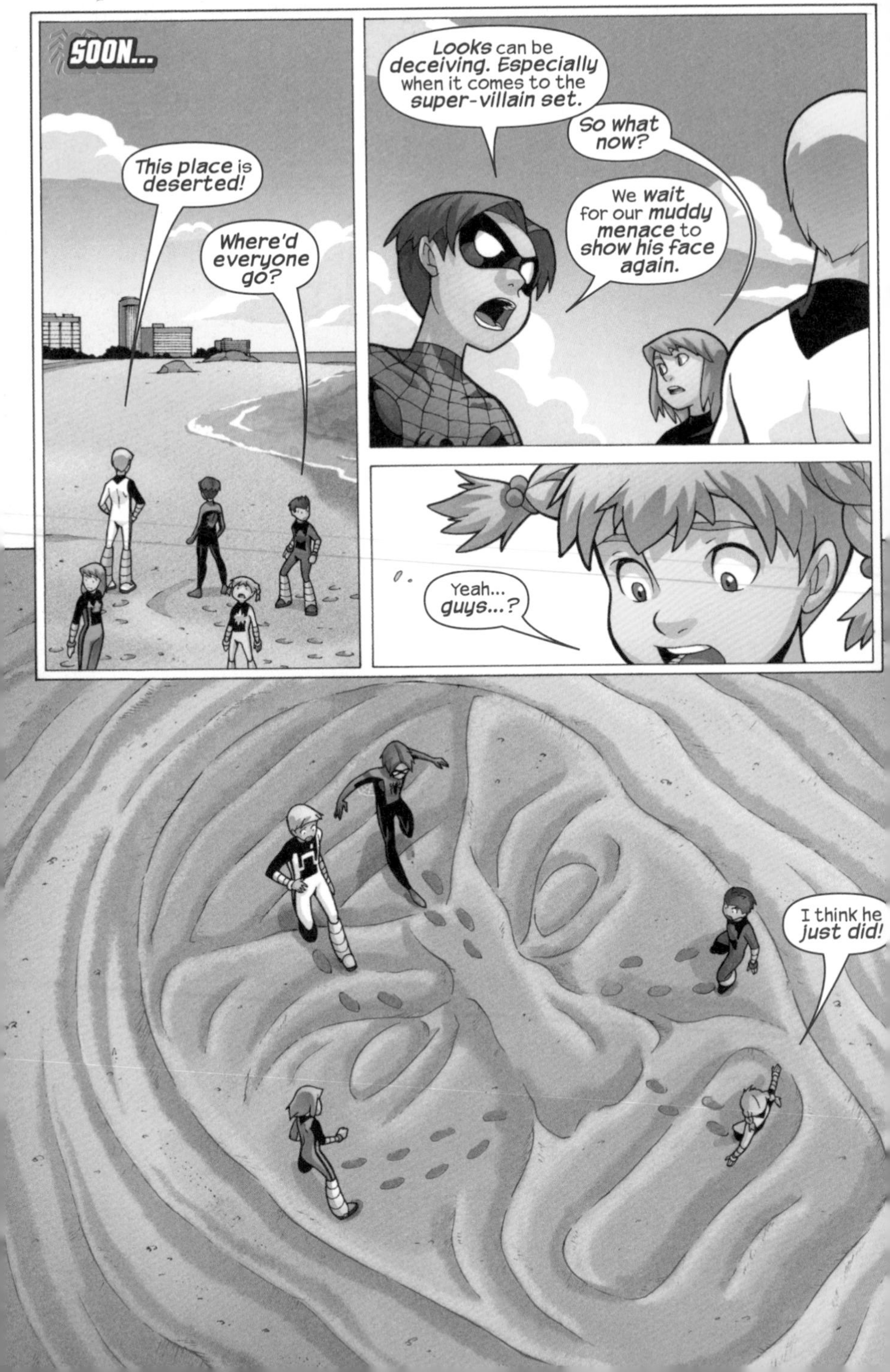
SOON...
This place is deserted!
Where'd everyone go?
Looks can be deceiving. Especially when it comes to the super-villain set.
So what now?
We wait for our muddy menace to show his face again.
Yeah... guys...?
I think he just did!

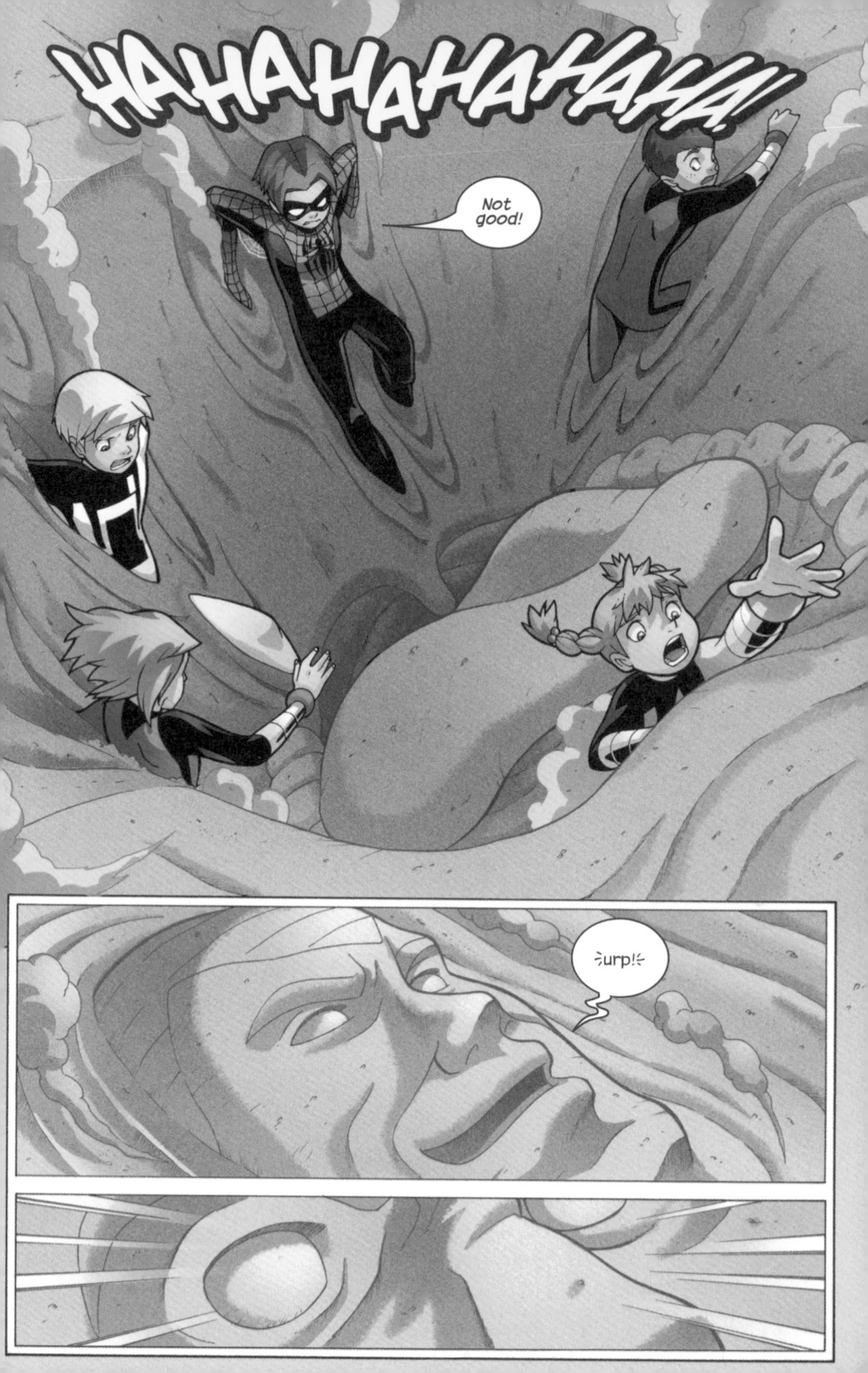
HAHAHAHAHAHAHA!
Not good!
urp!

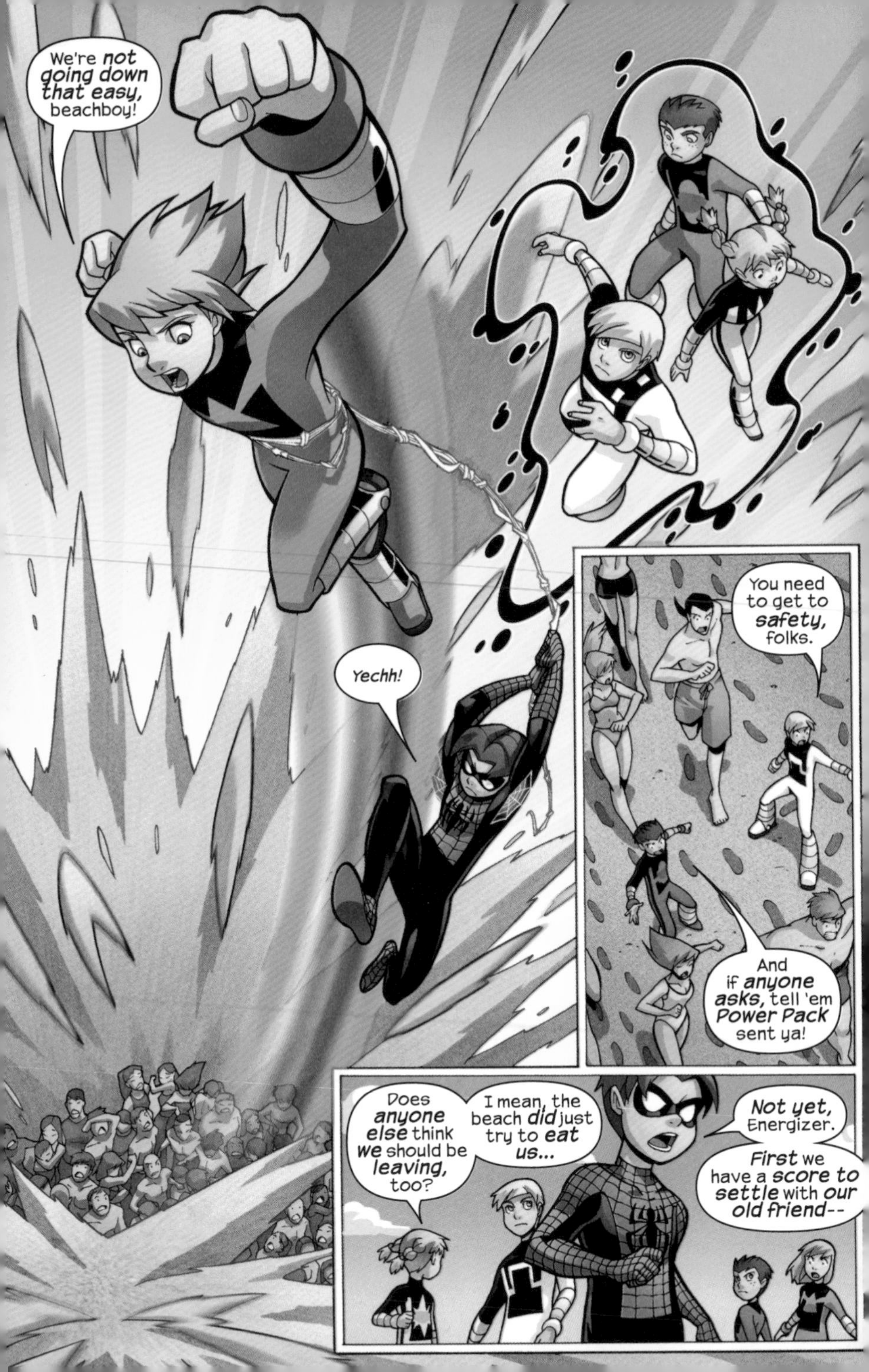
We're *not going down that easy,* beachboy!
Yechh!
You need to get to *safety,* folks.
And if *anyone asks,* tell 'em *Power Pack* sent ya!
Does *anyone else* think *we* should be *leaving,* too?
I mean, the beach *did* just try to *eat us...*
Not yet, Energizer.
First we have a *score to settle* with *our old friend*--

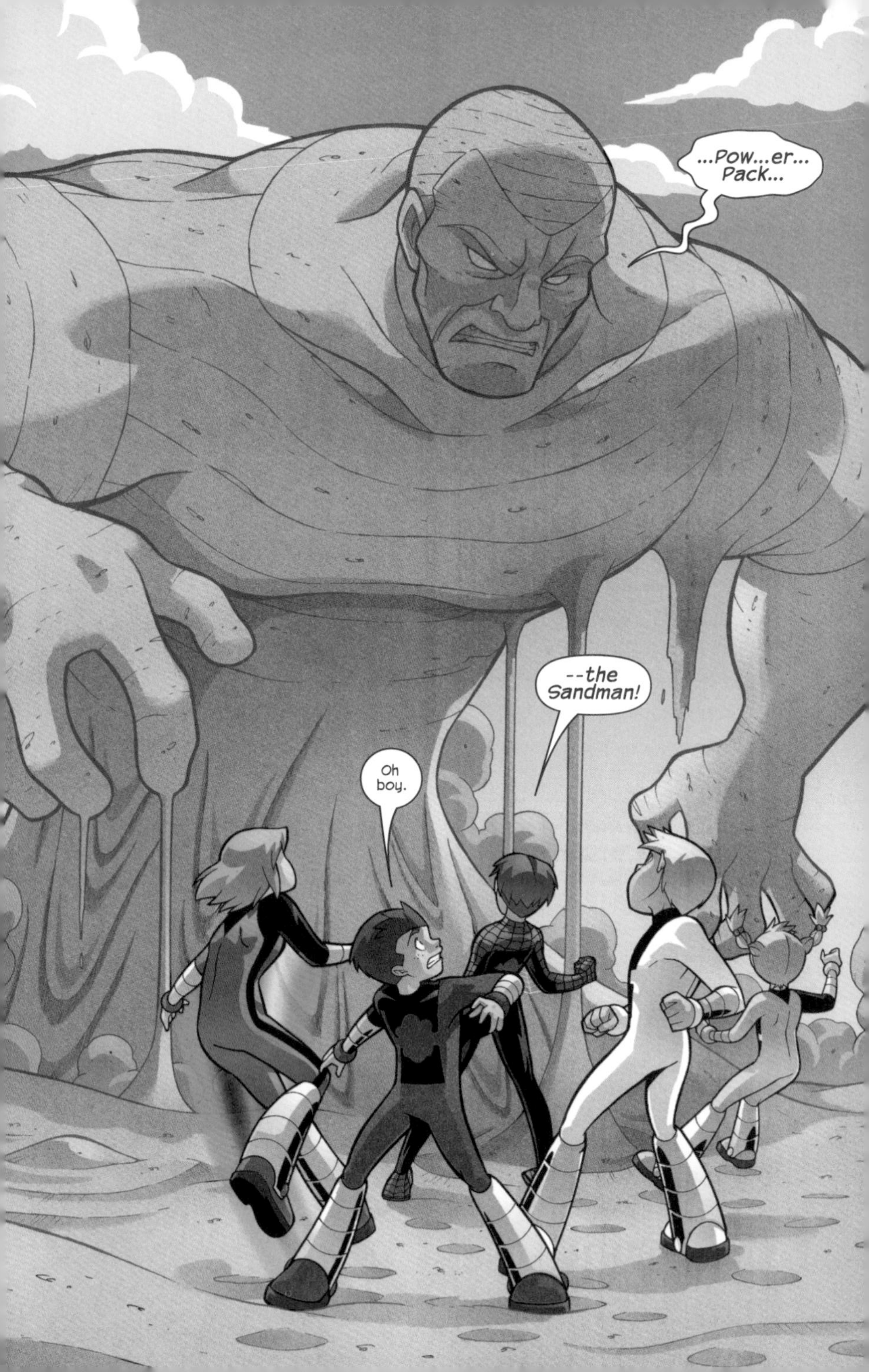
...Pow...er... Pack...
--the Sandman!
Oh boy.

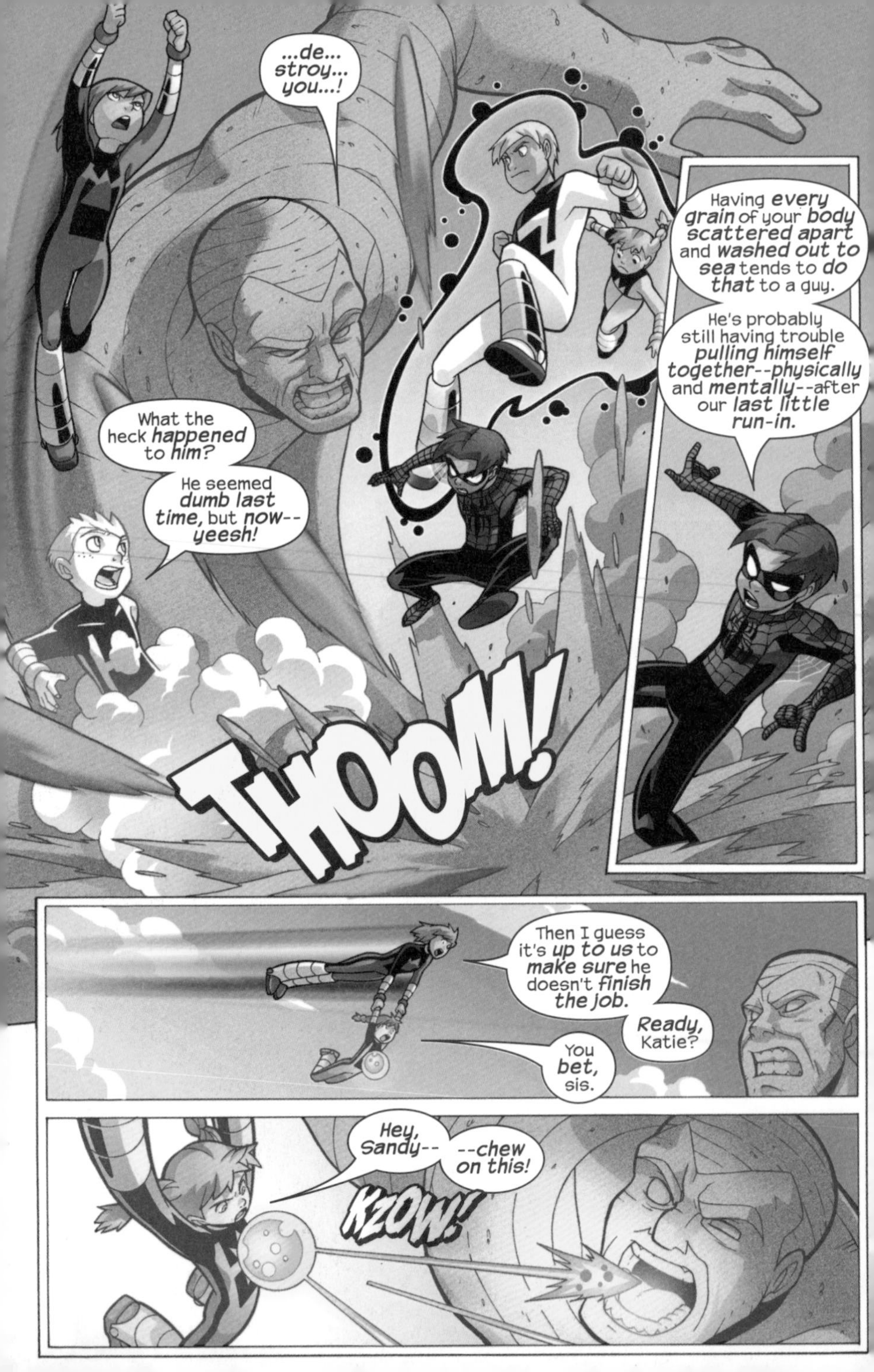
...de... stroy... you...!
Having every grain of your body scattered apart and washed out to sea tends to do that to a guy.
He's probably still having trouble pulling himself together--physically and mentally--after our last little run-in.
What the heck happened to him?
He seemed dumb last time, but now--yeesh!
THOOM!
Then I guess it's up to us to make sure he doesn't finish the job.
Ready, Katie?
You bet, sis.
Hey, Sandy--
--chew on this!
KZOW!

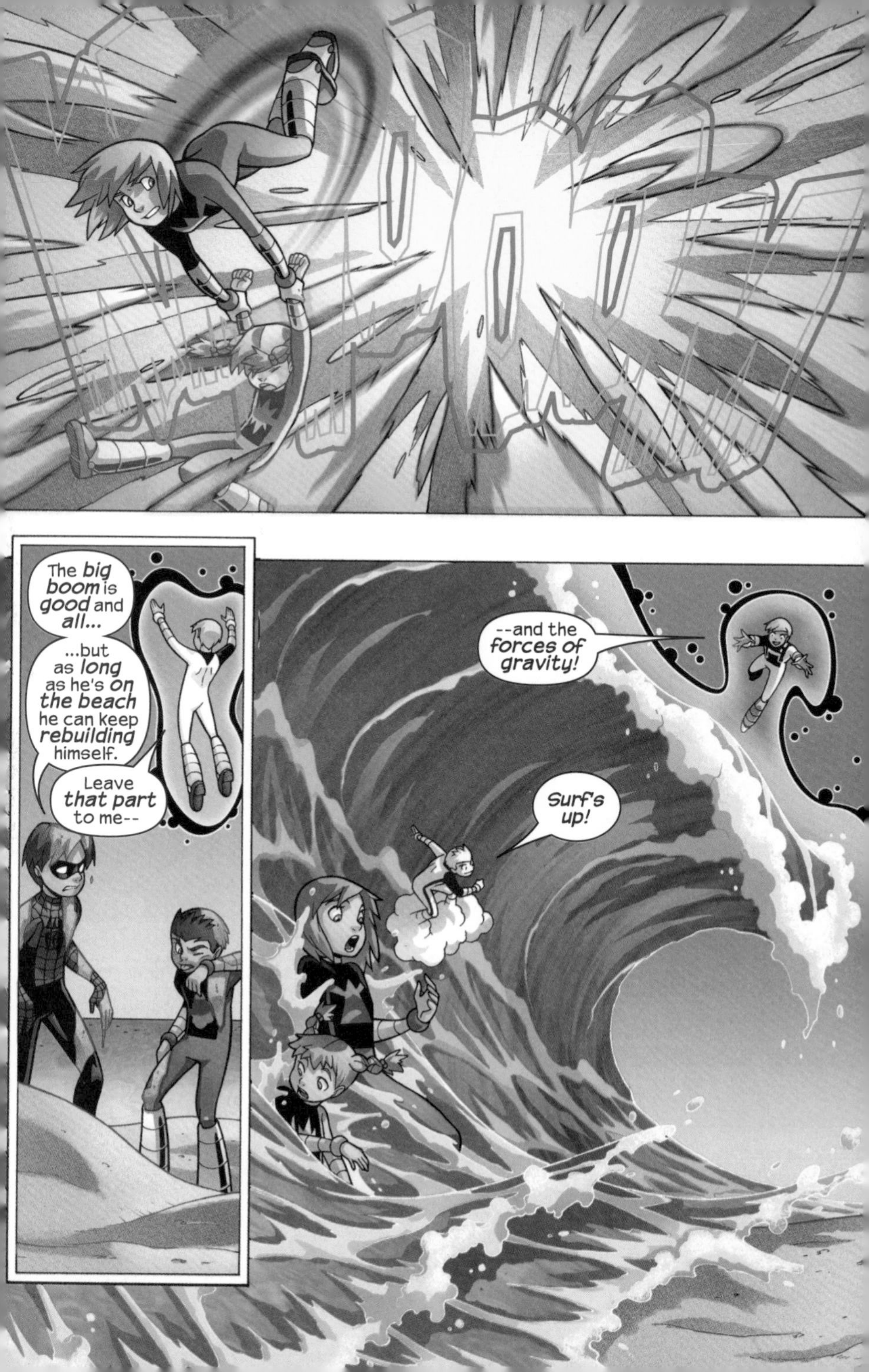
The big boom is good and all...
...but as long as he's on the beach he can keep rebuilding himself.
Leave that part to me--
--and the forces of gravity!
Surf's up!

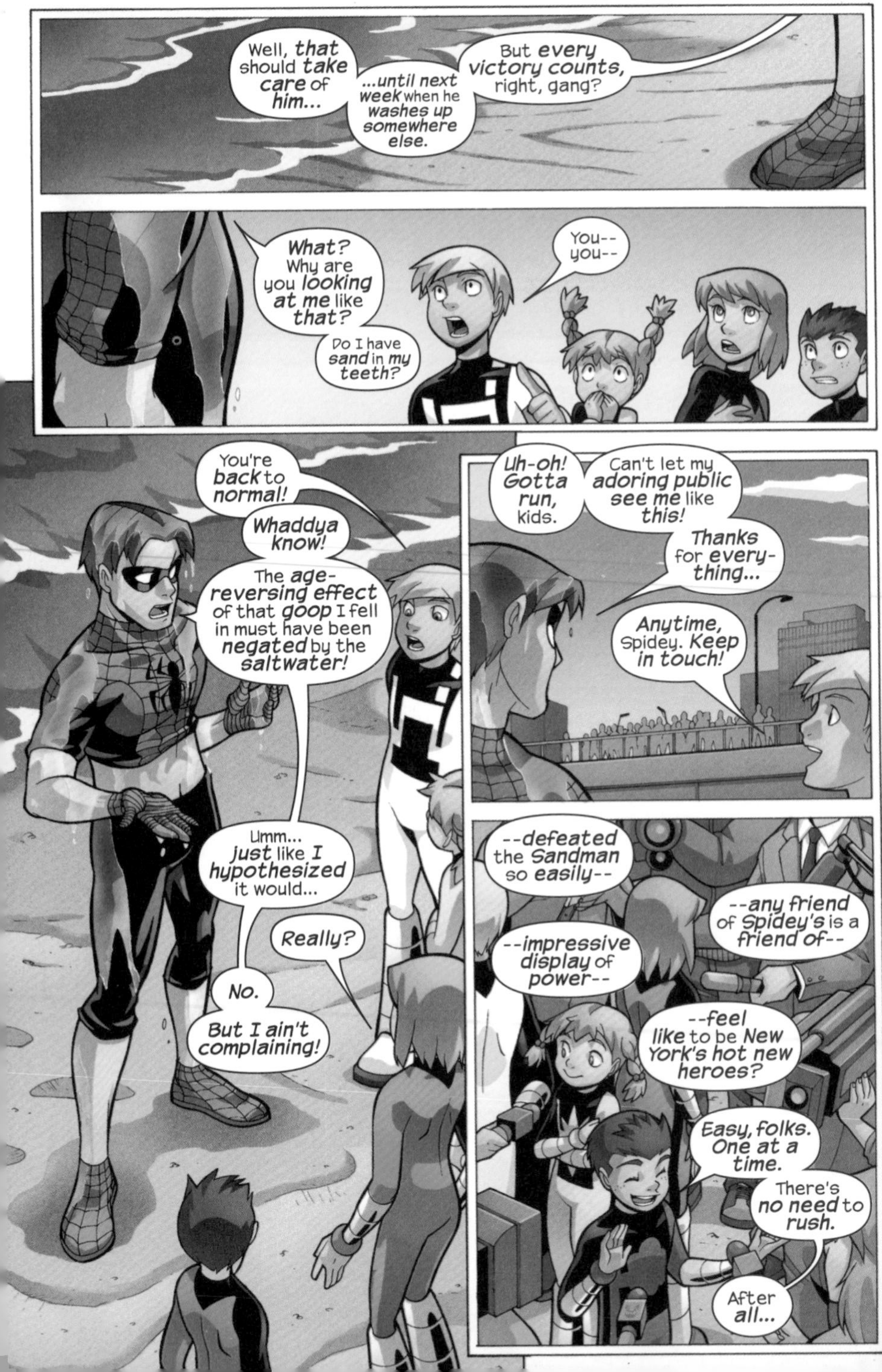
Well, that should take care of him...
...until next week when he washes up somewhere else.
But every victory counts, right, gang?
What? Why are you looking at me like that?
Do I have sand in my teeth?
You-- you--
You're back to normal!
Whaddya know!
The age-reversing effect of that goop I fell in must have been negated by the saltwater!
Umm... just like I hypothesized it would...
Really?
No.
But I ain't complaining!
Uh-oh! Gotta run, kids.
Can't let my adoring public see me like this!
Thanks for every-thing...
Anytime, Spidey. Keep in touch!
--defeated the Sandman so easily--
--impressive display of power--
--any friend of Spidey's is a friend of--
--feel like to be New York's hot new heroes?
Easy, folks. One at a time.
There's no need to rush.
After all...

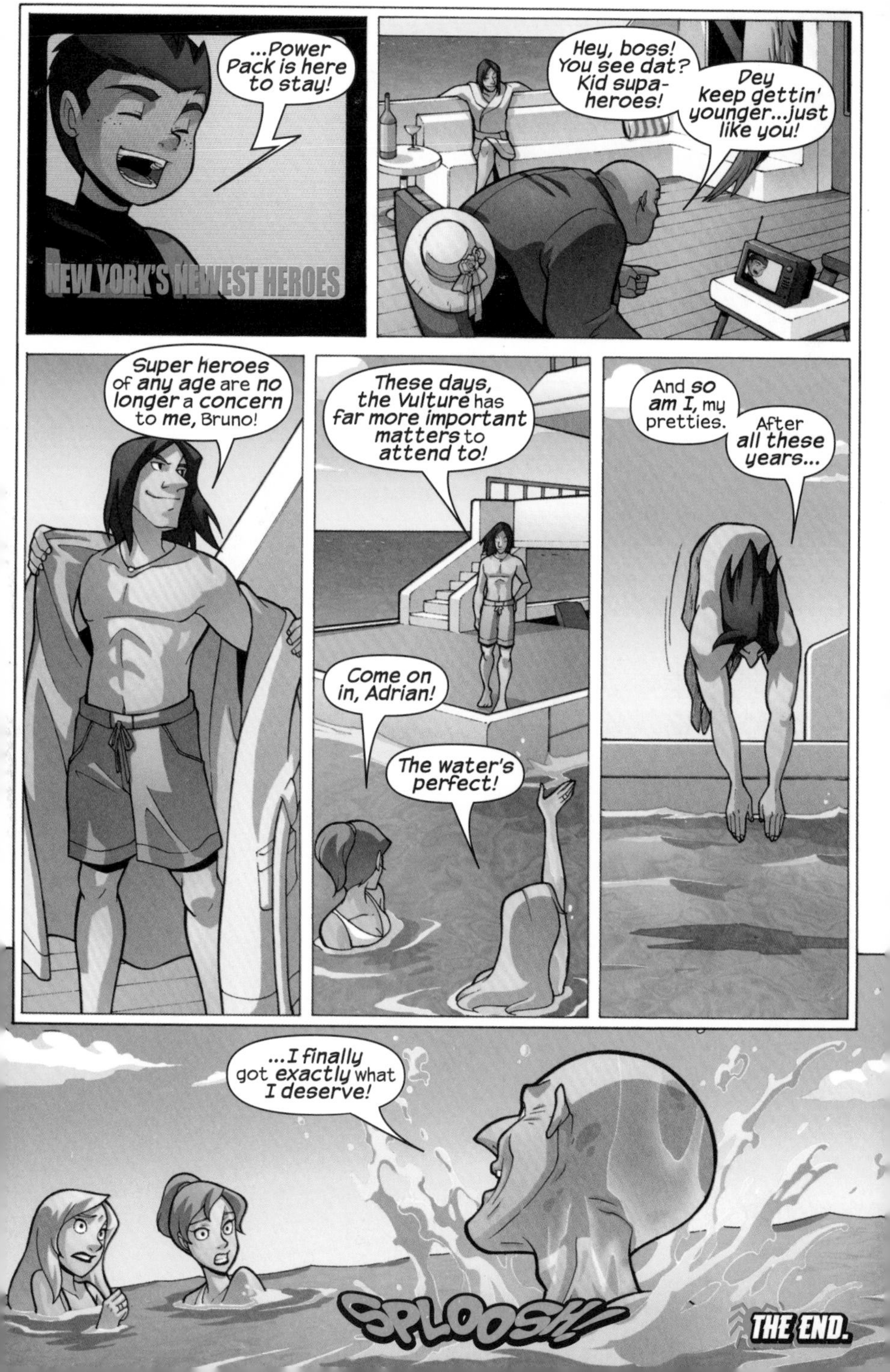
...Power Pack is here to stay!
NEW YORK'S NEWEST HEROES
Hey, boss! You see dat? Kid supa-heroes!
Dey keep gettin' younger...just like you!
Super heroes of any age are no longer a concern to me, Bruno!
These days, the Vulture has far more important matters to attend to!
Come on in, Adrian!
The water's perfect!
And so am I, my pretties.
After all these years...
...I finally got exactly what I deserve!
SPLOOSH!
THE END.

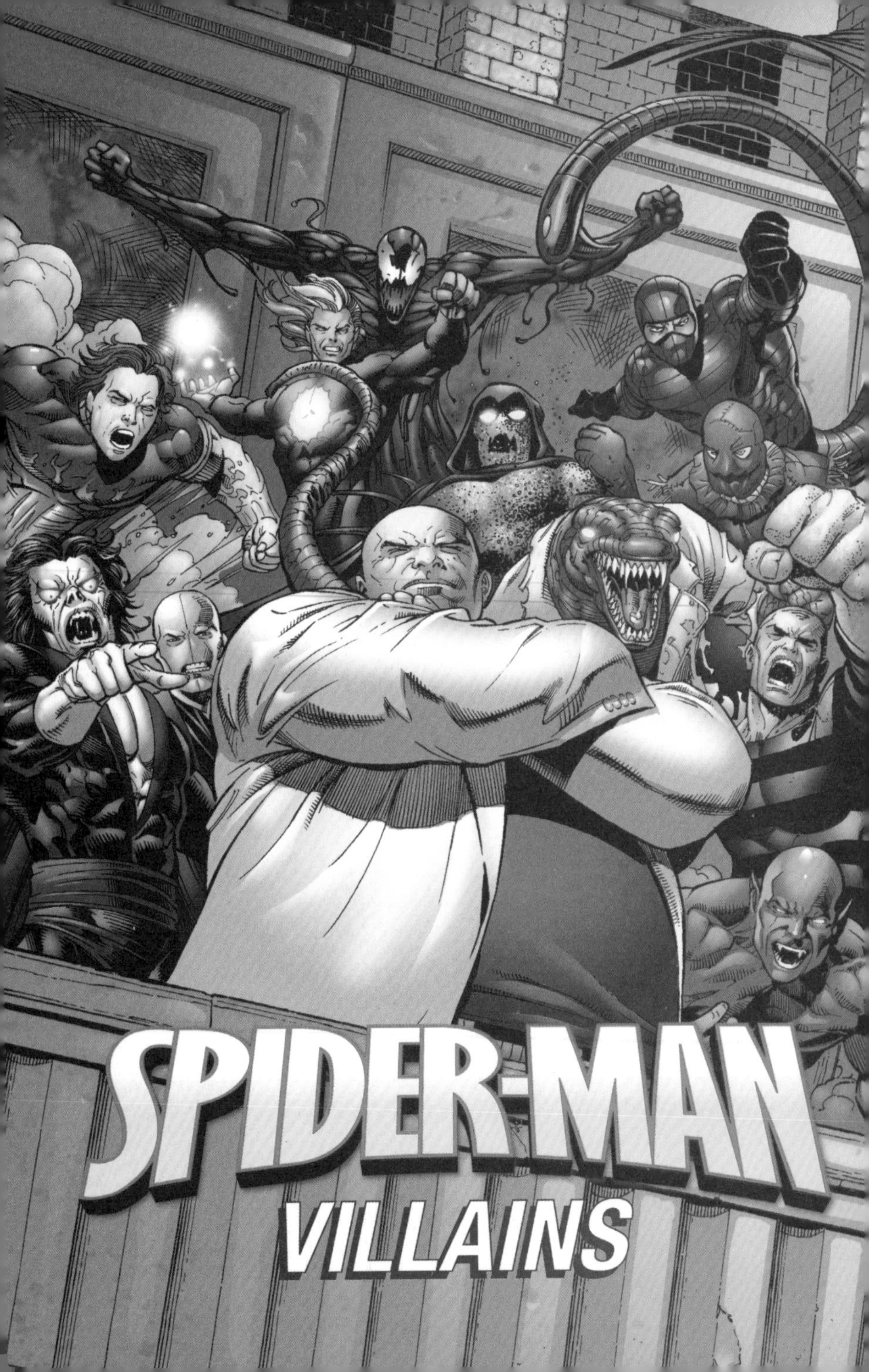
SPIDER-MAN
VILLAINS

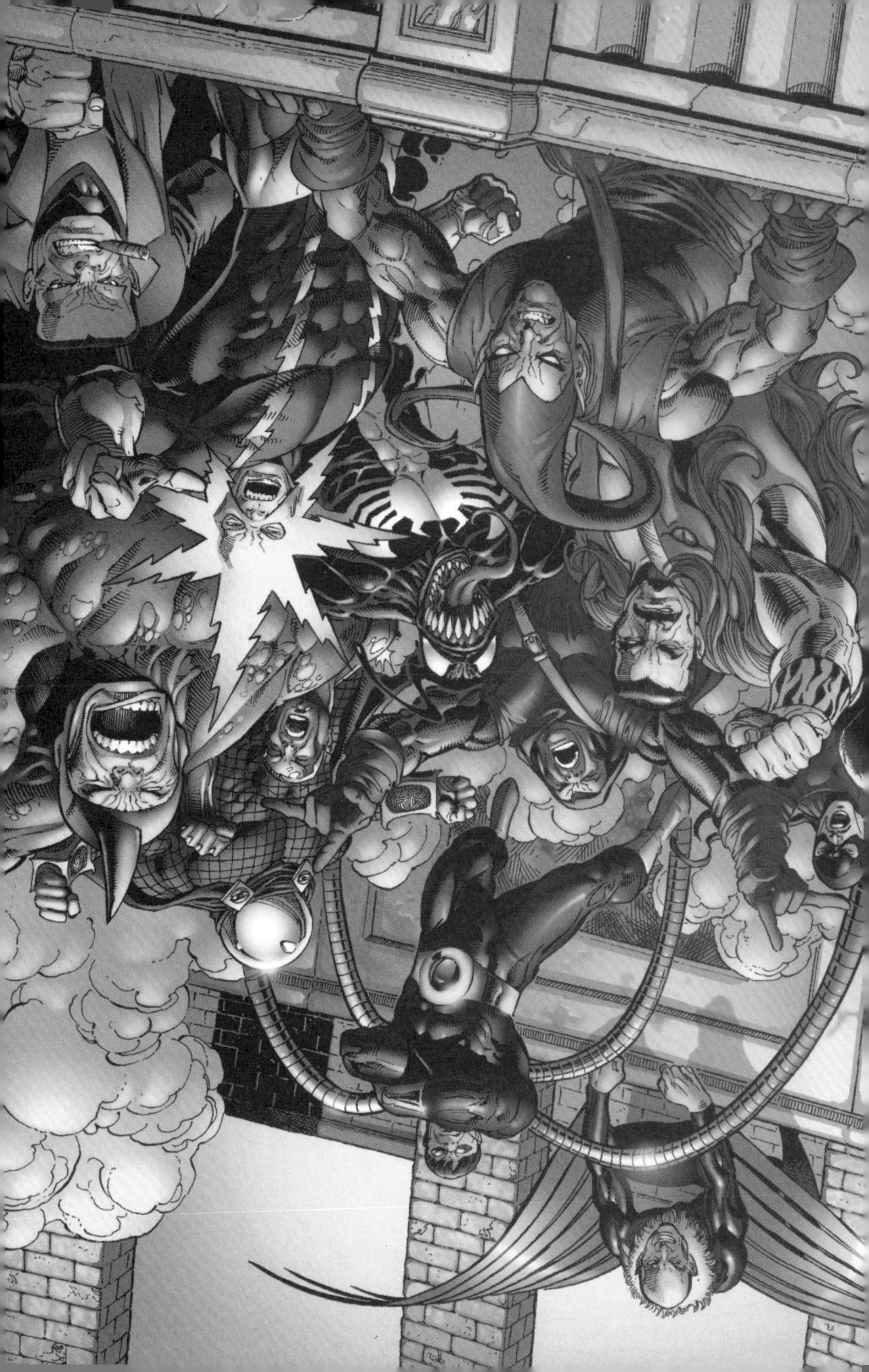

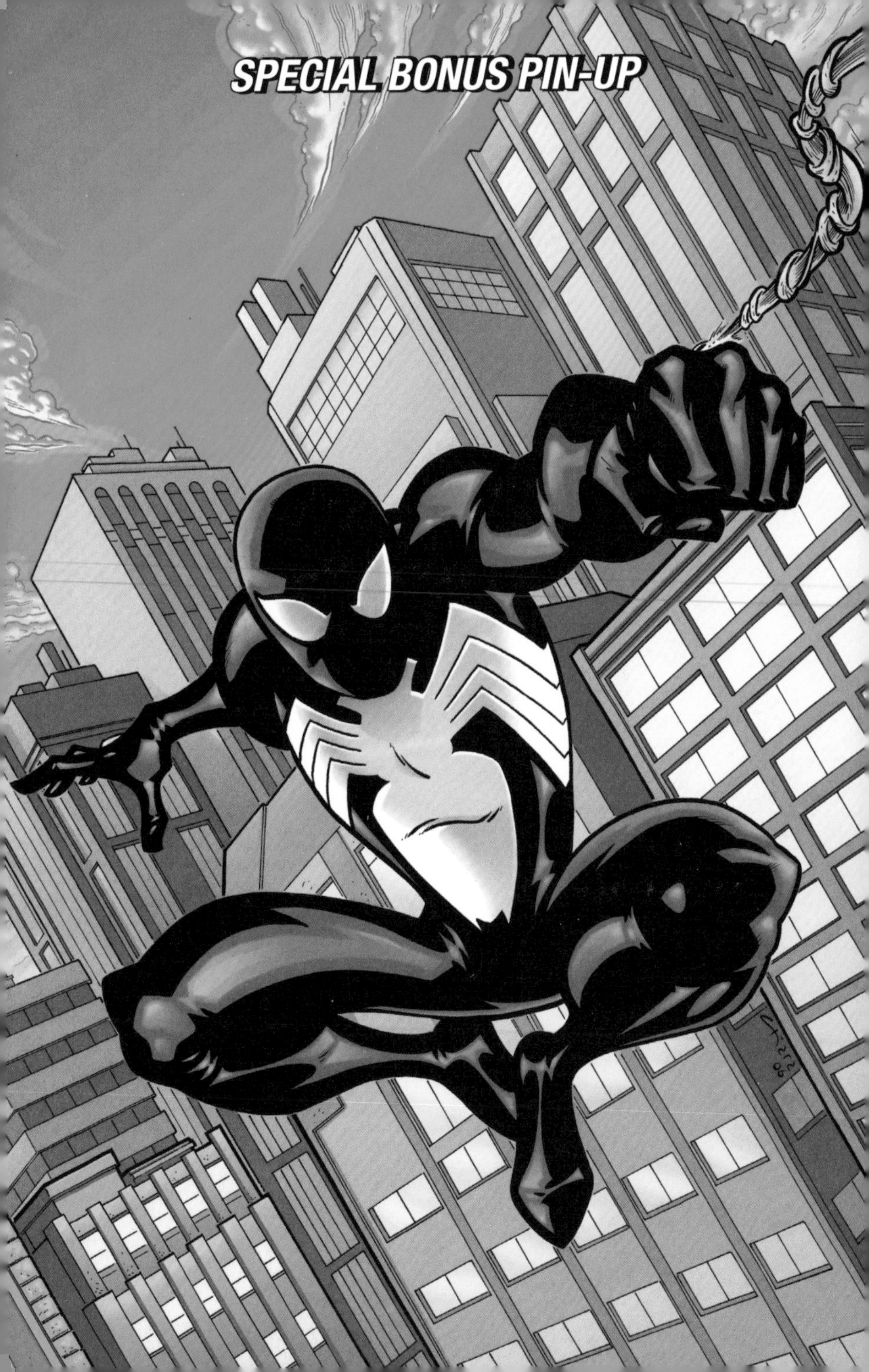
SPECIAL BONUS PIN-UP